Advances in Japanese Business and Economics

Volume 38

Advances in Japanese Business and Economics (AJBE) showcases the work of Japanese and non-Japanese scholars researching the Japanese economy and Japanese businesses. Published in English, the series highlights for a global readership the unique perspectives of Japan's most distinguished and emerging scholars of business and economics. It covers research of either theoretical or empirical nature, in both authored and edited volumes, regardless of the sub-discipline or geographical coverage, including, but not limited to, such topics as macroeconomics, microeconomics, industrial relations, innovation, regional development, entrepreneurship, international trade, globalization, financial markets, technology management, and business strategy. At the same time, as a series of volumes written by Japanese and non-Japanese scholars studying Japan, it includes research on the issues of the Japanese economy, industry, management practice, and policy, such as the economic policies and business innovations before and after the Japanese "bubble" burst in the 1990s.

AJBE endeavors to overcome a historical deficit in the dissemination of Japanese economic theory, research methodology, and analysis. The volumes in the series contribute not only to a deeper understanding of Japanese business and economics but to revealing underlying universal principles.

Overseen by a panel of renowned scholars led by Editor-in-Chief Professor Ryuzo Sato, AJBE employs a single-blind review process in which the Editor-in-Chief, together with the Managing Editors and specialized scholars designated by the Editor-in-Chief or Managing Editors, rigorously reviews each proposal and manuscript to ensure that every submission is a valuable contribution to the global scholarly readership.

All books and chapters in AJBE are indexed in Scopus.

Takayuki Yamashita · Tamaki Morita
Editors

On the Structural Transformation of the Japanese Economy 1985–2023

Springer

Editors
Takayuki Yamashita
School of Global Studies and Collaboration
Aoyama Gakuin University
Sagamihara, Kanagawa, Japan

Tamaki Morita
Faculty of Aviation Management
J. F. Oberlin University
Tama, Tokyo, Japan

ISSN 2197-8859 ISSN 2197-8867 (electronic)
Advances in Japanese Business and Economics
ISBN 978-981-95-7229-8 ISBN 978-981-95-7230-4 (eBook)
https://doi.org/10.1007/978-981-95-7230-4

This Springer imprint is published by the registered company Springer Nature Singapore Pte Ltd.
The registered company address is: 152 Beach Road, #21-01/04 Gateway East, Singapore 189721, Singapore

Preface

Since the collapse of the bubble economy, Japan has experienced over 30 years of prolonged economic stagnation, often referred to as the "Lost Three Decades." Economists have attempted to explain the reasons behind this long-lasting stagnation, suggesting various theories. However, there remains no consensus on the cause. We assert that this stagnation stems from changes in the economic structure during this period. Therefore, this book examines the structural transformation of the Japanese economy from 1985 to 2024.

The bubble economy of the late 1980s inflated real estate prices. This price surge gave rise to the "land myth"—the belief that land prices would always rise. Banks consistently expanded lending using land as collateral. The "land myth" not only fostered a false sense of security about the future but also changed our society. The harder people worked, the more their salaries increased, and they were able to enjoy everyday consumption fully.

When the bubble economy collapsed, the sharp fall in land and stock prices cast a shadow of uncertainty over society. Banks were left with massive amounts of non-performing loans. Consumer spending decreased, and a deep sense of stagnation spread through a society once full of vitality. To weather the wave of bankruptcies and restructurings, both companies and individuals were thrust into fierce competition where "efficiency" and "capability" became the new standards of value.

These shifts in mindset and lifestyle led to structural changes on both the demand and supply sides of the Japanese economy. In adapting to these changes, the Japanese economy faced challenges such as the rise of non-regular employment—forms of employment that lack guaranteed job security or benefits—and deflation, where wages and prices failed to increase.

As members of the generation that entered the workforce during the bubble era, only to be soon buffeted by its collapse, we wish to unravel the truth of the "Lost Three Decades" that have profoundly shaped our lives.

We owe a particular intellectual debt to Professor Ryuzo Sato. Our collaboration began when we joined the "Sato Workshop," which was originally held as the International Workshop of Japan in 1983 when Professor Paul Samuelson visited Japan. The first workshop meeting was held at the Nihon Keizai Shimbun where Professor

Sato was asked to chair the session. It was then transferred to New York University's Modern Economics Workshop held in Japan. After he retired from New York University, it was changed to a private workshop known as Sato Workshop. Most of the time meetings have been held at the Komaba Campus of the University of Tokyo.

The Workshop aims to foster engaging interdisciplinary discussions on critical economic issues of the time and has been held several times a year. We are privileged to attend the workshops, where we have gained valuable insights that enhance our research endeavor. Our discussions with Professor Sato have led to a closer collaboration, and we are grateful for his contributions to the chapters of this book. Additionally, Professor Sato has provided ongoing advice and critique throughout the writing process, helping to shape both the arguments and the overall structure of this volume.

We want to acknowledge the valuable comments from many participants of the Sato Workshop. We thank the following for their constructive comments: Professors Rama Ramachandran (formerly of New York University), Hajime Hori (Tohoku University), Kazuo Mino (Kyoto University), Hiroshi Yoshikawa (University of Tokyo), Toshihiro Ihori (University of Tokyo), Yoshio Sasajima (Meiji Gakuin University). Professors Megumi Suto (Waseda University), Kimiko Terai (Keio University), Tetsuji Okazaki (University of Tokyo), and Mariko Fujii (University of Tokyo). Thanks is also given to Professors Takahiro Masuda (Jikei University), Akiko Kamesaka (Aoyama Gakuin University), Aiko Ikeo (Waseda University), Mariko Tanigaki (University of Tokyo), and Monsieurs Hideaki Haoka (formerly Hokuriku Bank) and Hideki Yoshii (Institute for Future Engineering) who helped improve both the presentation and the contents of this text. Special mention is given to Hiroki Nikaido (Tohoku Electric Company) who gave us particular advice regarding Chapter 4 by Morita. We are also grateful to the late Professors Masahiro Matsushita and Michihiro Oyama.

In Chapter 4, Determinants of Subjective Well-being of the Japanese Consumers, Morita benefited greatly from comments from Professors Shunsuke Managi (Kyushu University), Sunbin Yoo (Kyushu University), Junya Kumagai (Fukuoka University), Tetsuya Tsurumi (Nanzan University), Keisaku Higashida (Kwansei Gakuin University), Kenta Tanaka (Musashi University) and Keeley Alexander (Kyushu University) at the RIETI workshop held in September 2023, January 2024, and November 2024.

Last but not least, we are grateful to Ms. Juno Kawakami and the editorial staff at Springer Japan for their guidance and professionalism throughout the publication process.

Any remaining errors and omissions remain solely our responsibility.

Sagamihara, Japan Takayuki Yamashita
Tama, Japan Tamaki Morita

Contents

Editors and Contributor

About the Editors

Takayuki Yamashita is a Professor of Economics at Aoyama Gakuin University. He is the author of articles on Industrial Organization and Regional Economics. In several articles, he analyzes the impact of exchange rate changes on competition among domestic retailers and manufacturers. He serves as vice president and editorial board chair of the Japan Chapter of the System Dynamics Society and previously served on the board of directors of the Japan Economic Policy Association.

Tamaki Morita is a Professor of Economics in the Faculty of Aviation Management at J. F. Oberlin University. She is an interdisciplinary applied economist whose research bridges macroeconomic growth theory and micro-level analysis, investigating subjective well-being, resource allocation, education, and the evolving role of artificial intelligence (AI). Her work contributes to empirically grounded approaches to economic policy that enhance social welfare.

About the Contributor

Ryuzo Sato is C. V. Starr Professor Emeritus of Economics at the Stern School of Business, New York University. He was director of the Center for Japan-U.S. Business and Economic Studies at the Stern School. Prior to becoming a Stern faculty member, he was a professor of economics at Brown University. Professor Sato also taught at Harvard University, the University of Tokyo, Kyoto University, and Bonn University. He was the founding chief editor of *Japan and the World Economy*, an international theory and policy journal. He holds his B.A. in economics and his Dr. of Economics from Hitotsubashi University in Tokyo, and his Ph.D. in economics from Johns Hopkins University. His work includes *Biased Technical Change and Economic Conservation Laws* (Springer, 2006), *Symmetry and Economic Invariance*

(Springer, 1998/2004), *Growth Theory and Technical Change*, The Selected Essays of Ryuzo Sato Volume One, Economists of the Twentieth Century series (Elgar, 1996), *Production, Stability and Dynamic Symmetry*, The Selected Essays of Ryuzo Sato Volume Two, Economists of the Twentieth Century series (Elgar, 1999), and *Theory of Technical Change and Economic Invariance: Application of Lie Groups* (Academic Press, 1981, reprinted and published by Elgar, 1999).

Chapter 1
Introduction

Takayuki Yamashita and Tamaki Morita

Abstract Japan's asset bubble economy (1986–1991) not only triggered financial problems but also brought transformative changes to both the demand and supply sides of the Japanese economy. Changes in employment and labor productivity emerged around the time of the bubble economy. We examine Japan's economic growth by focusing on the interaction between manufacturing and service industries.

Keywords Bubble economy · Lost three decades · Employment · Labor productivity · Manufacturing industry · Service industry

This chapter opens with the story of Yamashita.

As an undergraduate, an American professor asked me in his international economics lecture: "Why do Japanese students want to work at banks or securities firms?"

> According to him, Japanese banks and securities firms did not have an international comparative advantage, while Japanese manufacturing companies had an excellent comparative advantage. So why do they choose a weak sector? His question arose the year before the asset bubble economy.
>
> Time has passed, and I am now teaching economics at universities. However, I do not yet have a clear answer to his question. The bubble economy burst 30 years ago. The service sector of the Japanese economy continued to grow, and fewer students chose to work in the manufacturing industries. Japan's economic growth has slowed down.

The story resonates with Morita, and she believes we should find a persuasive answer to the question.

T. Yamashita (✉)
School of Global Studies and Collaboration, Aoyama Gakuin University, Sagamihara City, Kanagawa, Japan
e-mail: yamashita.takayuki@gsc.aoyama.ac.jp

T. Morita
Faculty of Aviation Management, J. F. Oberlin University, Tama City, Tokyo, Japan
e-mail: morita_t01@obirin.ac.jp

T. Yamashita and T. Morita (eds.), *On the Structural Transformation of the Japanese Economy 1985-2023*, Advances in Japanese Business and Economics 38,
https://doi.org/10.1007/978-981-95-7230-4_1

This monograph explores the factors contributing to Japan's "Lost Three Decades," with a focus on the relationship between the manufacturing and service sectors in the context of economic growth.

1.1 From Bubble Economy to the "Lost Three Decades"

Japan has achieved economic growth by specializing in high-value-added manufacturing. With few natural resources, Japan has developed its economy by importing most of its raw materials from overseas, processing them domestically, and exporting the finished products. Japan has become a world leader in the production of automobiles and electrical machinery.

Following the post-war reconstruction, the Japanese economy experienced robust growth known as the "rapid economic growth" from the mid-1950s to the early 1970s. An ample supply of cheap, high-quality labor, a high savings rate, and a substantial investment by corporations drove this rapid growth. In 1968, Japan's GNP ranked second in the world.

In reality, the Japanese economy is not as dependent on exports as those of other countries, but manufacturing is still susceptible to exchange rate fluctuations. The rapid growth of Japan came to an end with the 1971 Nixon Shock, a series of economic measures undertaken by the United States, and the sharp rise in the yen exchange rate following the transition to a floating exchange rate system in 1973.

Amidst various periods of yen appreciation, the Plaza Accord of 1985, aimed at correcting the U.S. trade deficit, had a significant impact on the Japanese economy. Japan faced international pressure to increase domestic demand to reduce its trade surplus with the United States. The Bank of Japan cut its discount rate five times by February 1987. As a result of the Plaza Accord, the yen appreciated rapidly. Exchange losses on dollar-denominated assets occurred, and funds seeking to avoid foreign exchange risk also flowed back into Japan. This domestic demand expansion triggered a boom in domestic investment in real estate and stocks, creating an asset bubble. Stock prices quadrupled, and land prices soared sixfold. The surge in real estate prices gave rise to the "land myth"—the belief that land prices would inevitably keep rising. Banks consistently expanded lending using land as collateral. This myth led companies to divert profits from their core businesses into real estate, further inflating land prices.

The asset bubble did not merely cause financial problems; it also brought transformations to both the demand and supply sides of the Japanese economy. Owning luxury cars and brand-name goods became a symbol of "success," leading to an abnormal expansion of consumption. The wealthy considered land as collateral to obtain loans from banks, and then used those funds to purchase more land, thereby increasing their assets. As more people took up golf and skiing, the leisure industry expanded.

These shifts in consumer behavior also impacted employment. Figure 1.1 illustrates the percentage of the workforce by industry. Despite the challenges faced by the

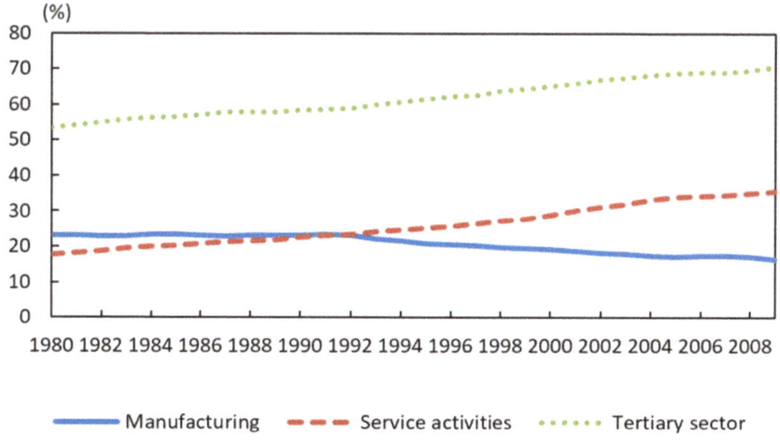

Fig. 1.1 Share of employment by sector. *Note* Service activities in 1993SNA consist of community and social service activities, business activities, and personal service activities. *Source* Compiled by the author with data from the Cabinet Office, Annual Report on National Accounts

manufacturing sector in exports, it remained relatively stable. In contrast, the service industry demonstrated remarkable growth. When the bubble economy burst in 1992, the number of employees in the service industry had reached a level comparable to that in manufacturing. Post-bubble, the proportion of manufacturing declined, but the service industry's share continued to rise.

The Japanese government imposed restrictions on real estate loans in 1990 to stop the overheated bubble economy. However, this triggered a significant stock and real estate price crash, pushing the bubble economy over the edge. The Nikkei Stock Average crashed to half its October 1990 level, and real estate prices began to fall after peaking in 1992. The real economy also began to decline in 1991, and the Heisei recession (1991–2002) was underway.

There were bank failures burdened with non-performing loans, securities company collapses, banks becoming reluctant to lend, restructuring, and pay cuts. The decline in consumption led to increased demand for cheaper goods and services. Distribution systems were simplified, and retail competition, known as "price destruction," was in fashion, but this gradually transformed into prolonged deflation. Figure 1.2 shows labor productivity. The number of people employed in the service activity continued to increase, but their labor productivity decreased. The shift in employment toward labor-intensive sectors where technological innovation was difficult became a factor in Japan's prolonged economic stagnation.

Japan became the only advanced nation to experience deflation after World War II. The Japanese economy fell into the vicious cycle of the so-called deflationary spiral, leading to stagnation in corporate profits, capital investment, employment, wages, and consumption.

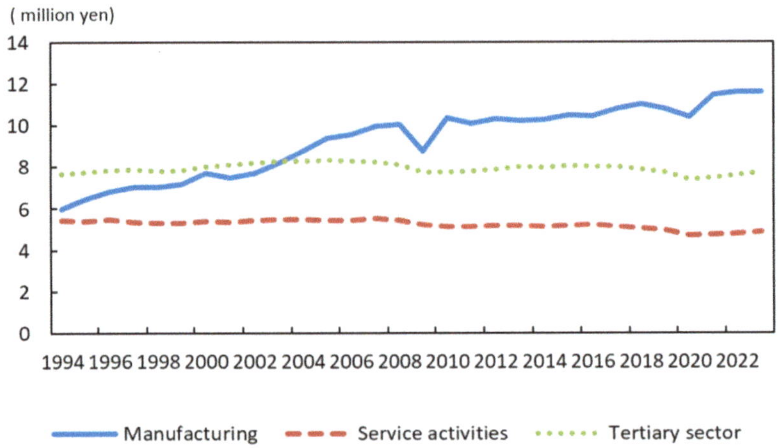

Fig. 1.2 Labor productivity by sector. *Note* Services include market services (Trade; Transportation; Accommodation and food; and Business and administrative services) and non-market services (Public administration; Community, social and other services and activities) in accordance with International Standard Industrial Classification. *Source* Compiled by the author with data from the Cabinet Office, Annual Report on National Accounts

1.2 Objective of This Study

After World War II, Japan rebuilt itself from the ashes, but from the mid-1950s, it experienced rapid economic growth, becoming an economic powerhouse and boasting the world's second-largest GDP by 1968. However, thirty years later, it became the only advanced nation suffering from deflation. What went wrong? Can Japan's experience serve as a lesson for other countries?

The national economy consists of several industrial sectors. This chapter examines the growth of the national economy by focusing on the interactions and coordination between these sectors. It was François Quesnay (1694–1774) who first pointed out that economic systems expanded through the interaction between productive and unproductive industries. Quesnay (1758) regarded agriculture as productive, while commerce and manufacturing were unproductive in his "Tableau économique." Believing that wealth arises from production, Quesnay explained that it flows from person to person, like blood circulating within the body, reaching every corner of the country. Therefore, enhancing the productivity of the high-productive sector is crucial for driving national economic growth.

Currently, the center of production activity has shifted to manufacturing, but the differences in productivity among economic sectors have not disappeared. In the United States, the most productive sector is shifting from manufacturing to services, yet the fundamental pattern remains unchanged: high-productivity sectors drive national income growth and raise wages. When Professor Sato and I presented these findings at a workshop, we received diverse opinions. The process of seeking answers to these questions broadened our research scope, shaping the chapters of this monograph.

In the United States, consumer spending on services continues to rise, and economic activity in the service sector remains robust, yet productivity growth rates remain low. However, wages in the service sector continue to rise. William Baumol (1922–2017) termed this shift in spending toward services the "cost disease" (Baumol et al., 1989).

In Japan, too, economic activity in the service sector is expanding, and there are high expectations for its outcomes. However, at present, the underperformance of the service sector is determining the overall performance of the Japanese economy. In the long term, it is hoped that the most rapid technological progress in the goods-producing sector will spread to the service-producing sector and transform its performance.

This monograph sheds new light on the dynamics of economic growth through a unique perspective focused on the productivity gap between manufacturing and services. This viewpoint is particularly important for the Japanese economy after the bubble burst, where expectations that a shift to a service economy would bring success were disappointed.

How do differences in technological progress across economic sectors affect economic growth? The literature on developing countries emphasizes the interrelationships between economic sectors. However, research focusing on sectoral differences in advanced economies is scarce. This book aims to uniquely analyze the causes of Japan's economic stagnation from the perspective of sectoral growth, filling this research gap and providing a deeper understanding of the issue.

1.3 Outline of the Monograph

Japan's high economic growth after World War II is often cited as an example of success through free trade. Until the mid-1980s, Japan achieved economic growth through an export-led economy. Japanese low-priced, high-quality products have made big inroads into foreign markets, particularly the United States. However, as Japan's exports and economic power expanded, interdependence with its trading partners deepened.

Chapter 2 explores the impact of exchange rates and Japan's deindustrialization, a topic that discussions on deflation and prolonged economic stagnation have often overshadowed. The less-explored but significant progression of industrial hollowing-out is a key focus.[1] The direct trigger for the decline in manufacturing employment was the bubble economy of the late 1980s; however, prior to the bubble lay the yen's appreciation. This chapter examines the impact of several rounds of yen appreciation on the domestic economy and explores scenarios for manufacturing revival.

[1] "Hollowing out" was first used to describe the implications of offshoring by U.S. manufacturers in 1970s. In Japan, the term "hollowing out" is more widely used than "negative deindustrialization."

Exchange rates influence the economy through multiple channels. The most representative channels are exports and imports. However, a crucial strategy that emerged was the increased foreign direct investment aimed at mitigating losses from yen appreciation. The expansion of overseas production bases and the globalization of supply chains led to irreversible and significant changes in the domestic industrial and employment structures surrounding manufacturing. Understanding these changes is also crucial for identifying the causes of long-term economic stagnation.

Economic growth requires efficient allocation or reallocation of resources to enhance the performance of each industry. Given that economic activities are spread across the country, it becomes vital to accurately assess how economic activities and employment in a specific region contribute to demand both within and outside the region. Understanding the dynamics of economic growth at a regional level is crucial. Chapters 3–5 address this issue.

Shift-share analysis, an analytical method for measuring such contributions, is the focus of Chap. 3, which delves into Japan's economic growth from a regional economic perspective. Shift-share analysis is a technique for separating a region's economic growth into components that can be explained by its industrial structure and those that cannot. Differences in industrial structure between regions are often cited as a cause of income disparities. Regions with growing industries naturally enjoy steady economic growth. On the other hand, regions with declining industries experience stagnant economic growth. However, even when there are no differences in industrial structure, specific regional circumstances can lead to differences in growth rates. Beginning with an analysis of Shizuoka Prefecture, known as a manufacturing hub, and exploring the national shifts underlying its growth and stagnation, we will clarify the impact of the Lost Three Decades on regional economies.

Chapter 4 discusses Japanese consumers' subjective well-being. Since the 1980s, subjective well-being (SWB) measures have been adopted as one of the key policy goals by countries and international organizations, alongside traditional macroeconomic indicators like Gross Domestic Product (GDP). SWB primarily measures individual cardinal utility, which is generally gathered from surveys, compensating for the limitations of ordinal utility that have dominated academics in recent years. This study, using three years of survey data collected by the Japanese government—specifically, "Well-being Survey and Quality of Life" data—employed an ordinary least square method for each year, a panel fixed model, and a linear mixed-effects model to identify the determinants of SWB in Japan. The findings include the following: individuals without community ties experience lower SWB when feeling lonely; women feel higher SWB than men overall, and men in their 30s and 40s report lower SWB levels than others; and regionally, SWB is higher in the Kinki and Kyushu/Okinawa regions compared to Hokkaido (used as a baseline for comparison). These results suggest that policies aimed at reducing social isolation within communities are essential in Japan. Furthermore, these policies should be designed with simultaneous consideration for gender, age groups, and regions.

The SWB measure used in Chap. 4 is, as a dependent variable, included in the analysis of Chap. 5. Chapter 5 examines the overconcentration in a metropolis from the relationship between current economic growth and internal migration. Maintaining population has become a critical challenge for regional economies in Japan, which face population decline due to low birth rates. This chapter first raises the issues in internal migration—the concentration of population and industry in the Tokyo Metropolitan area on the grounds of the development of a service economy. Then, it focuses on women's behavior and reveals the factors that push and pull women to migrate. Migration among young women has intensified, and gender imbalances in rural areas are affecting economic activity and marriage rates. Analysis of migration data from the 2020 Census, using a modified gravity model, revealed that the expansion of the service industry is driving population movement and that females tend to migrate based on their subjective well-being.

Long-term economic stagnation and declining birth rates raise doubts about the efficiency of capital and labor in the Japanese economy. Chapter 6 examines the divergent technological change in the Japanese and US economies, demonstrating that improving factor productivity efficiency is essential for Japan. To ensure methodological consistency with the authors' prior research on the period from 1960 to 2004, the authors first re-estimate growth rates for this period using a new dataset. The primary focus of this study is the period from 1980 to 2020, marked by significant structural changes, including globalization, technological advancements, and demographic shifts. By providing updated insights into long-term growth dynamics based on the latest measurement standards and presenting a consistent analytical framework that bridges historical and contemporary growth analysis, this study contributes to a deeper understanding of recent economic trends. The findings highlight Japan's immediate need to improve both capital and labor efficiency, especially in consideration of its declining population. The burden of overinvestment has recently decreased, and promoting new, efficient investments may stimulate economic growth. However, Japan's labor efficiency remains lower than expected, indicating a need for policies that better develop human resources. Additionally, the study emphasizes the robust stability of the U.S. economy while addressing the belatedness in Japan's stability.

Why has Japan's economy faced serious problems, and why has the U.S. economy maintained a relatively healthy state for three decades? French economist Francois Quesnay is known as an economist of the physiocratic school and a physician. However, it is not widely known that he was the first economist to emphasize growth based on differences in productivity. As a physician, Quesnay believed that the human body and the economy were similar. Like the organs of the body, the various sectors of the economy interact with each other. Like the blood circulation in the human body, all economic sectors are linked through the cyclical flow of products and income. Individual sectors are healthy only when other sectors are healthy. If one sector is unhealthy, how will it affect other sectors? Chapter 7 assumes an economy consisting of two sectors with different productivity levels and analyzes theoretically and empirically how this disparity affects production and prices.

Finally, Chap. 8 deals with the log-run macroeconomic equilibrium, adjustment time, and economic conservation laws. The original version of this chapter was a lecture (in Japanese) entitled "Dynamic analysis and the role of subjective time" by Sato on June 28, 2014. It was presented at the Sato Workshop, held at the Komaba Campus of the University of Tokyo. The current version is based on the works expanded by Sato, Yamashita, and Morita. The primary purpose is to provide a reasonable justification for analyzing the trend of the Japanese bubble economy. The concept of "subjective time and subjective discount rate" is a useful device for explaining the time horizon during the period.

The concepts of long run and short run in modern economics stem from the Marshallian equilibrium idea. In the short run, supply and demand adjust with fixed production factors, while in the long run, all factors can be changed. Economists like Wilhelm Georg Friedrich Roscher proposed the roundabout methods of production, highlighting the benefits of investing in production tools. Bohm Bawerk and Wicksell discussed optimal production periods, noting that technological progress requires time after investment. Economists must consider adjustment time.

Inspired by the conservation laws in physics, similar principles exist in economics, suggesting specific quantities remain invariant across time frames. Concepts from group theory, like Noether's theorem, help formulate economic conservation laws. Ramsey discovered an "economic conservation law" through his model, identifying the bliss point as a constant. Weitzman and Sato later found a conservation law of the ratio of GDP and National Wealth being equal to the time-invariant discount rate.

Although the discount rate varies in some economies, when subjective time is a Lie group function of objective time, applying the concept of subjective time and using it will enable us to justify the variable (declining) discount rate. It is also possible that the discount rate may not remain constant throughout the entire period. We will explore factual cases that involve variable discount rates that decline over time. If we apply the concepts of subjective and objective time, we can explain the following: Under the time expansion, subjective time is perceived as moving slowly, and impatience falls. Time expansion reduces the discounting effect of subjective time, resulting in higher present values and making earlier investment more optimal. The subjective time and variable discounting model was applied to the Japanese bubble period to explain the trend of declining discount rate.

References

Baumol, W. J., Blackman, S. A. B., & Wolff, E. N. (1989). *Productivity and American leadership: The long view*. The MIT Press.

Quesnay, F. (1758). *The Oeconomical Table, an attempt towards ascertaining and exhibiting the source, progress, and employment of riches, with explanations, by the friend of mankind, the celebrated Marquis de Mirabeau*. W. Owen.

Chapter 2
Exchange Rates and Deindustrialization

Takayuki Yamashita

Abstract This chapter examines the impact of exchange rates on the Japanese economy. Exchange rates influence the economy through several channels. The most representative channels are exports and imports. However, the expansion of overseas production bases and the globalization of supply chains, driven by increased foreign direct investment aimed at mitigating losses from yen appreciation, have led to changes in the industrial and employment structures surrounding the manufacturing industry. Additionally, the experience of the bubble economy, a period of rapid economic expansion followed by a severe economic downturn, has also contributed to these structural changes. Understanding these changes is not just important but crucial for identifying the causes of Japan's long-term economic stagnation.

Keywords Bubble economy · Deindustrialization · Hollowing out · Yen appreciation · Foreign direct investment · Reshoring

2.1 Introduction

After the prosperity of the late 1980s bubble economy, Japan has been mired in a prolonged stagnation, often referred to as the "lost decade," the "lost two decades," or the "lost three decades." As pointed out by Hamada and Okada (2009, p. 201), "most studies of the 'lost decade of Japan' broadly focused on real and domestic aspects, such as TFP growth decline, non-performing loans, and governance." However, international conditions also affect business and employment in a variety of ways, particularly as a strong yen has repeatedly caused distress among Japanese manufactures.

Prior to the bubble economy, Japan had enjoyed the rapid economic growth under a fixed exchange rate of 1 U.S. dollar = 360 Japanese yen. The cancellation of

T. Yamashita (✉)
School of Global Studies and Collaboration, Aoyama Gakuin University, Sagamihara City, Kanagawa, Japan
e-mail: yamashita.takayuki@gsc.aoyama.ac.jp

T. Yamashita and T. Morita (eds.), *On the Structural Transformation of the Japanese Economy 1985-2023*, Advances in Japanese Business and Economics 38,
https://doi.org/10.1007/978-981-95-7230-4_2

the international convertibility of the U.S. dollar to gold in 1971, in response to increasing inflation in the U.S., taken by U.S. President Richard Nixon, forced the yen exchange rate up. This cancellation was the end of the Bretton Woods System, which maintained fixed exchange rates. Furthermore, the Yom Kippur War in 1973 brought the first oil crisis and raised the price of oil. These external shocks brought an end to Japan's rapid growth.

A further appreciation of the yen after the Plaza Accord of 1985 created a recession in which exporting firms went bankrupt, and the reduction of the official discount rate, which was implemented to overcome this high recession, led to the bubble economy. Figure 2.1 shows the GDP growth rate and USD-JPY exchange rate. Economic growth decreases in phases when the yen moves to a higher level.

The strong yen had various effects on the Japanese economy. The most important effects were structural changes in the late 1980s. One noticeable change was a rapid increase of outward foreign direct investment (FDI). With the rise in export prices due to the strong yen and the escalation of trade friction, manufacturers have embarked on local production overseas. To avoid the voluntary export restraints proposed by the U.S. government, Japan's automobile manufacturers started a full-scale outward FDI in the U.S. A strong request from the United Auto Workers was a key factor behind manufacturers' decision to engage in local production (Urata, 2020).

Figure 2.2 shows the history of the yen's exchange rate and the volume of outward FDI. Matsushita et al. (2011) argued that every yen appreciation phase

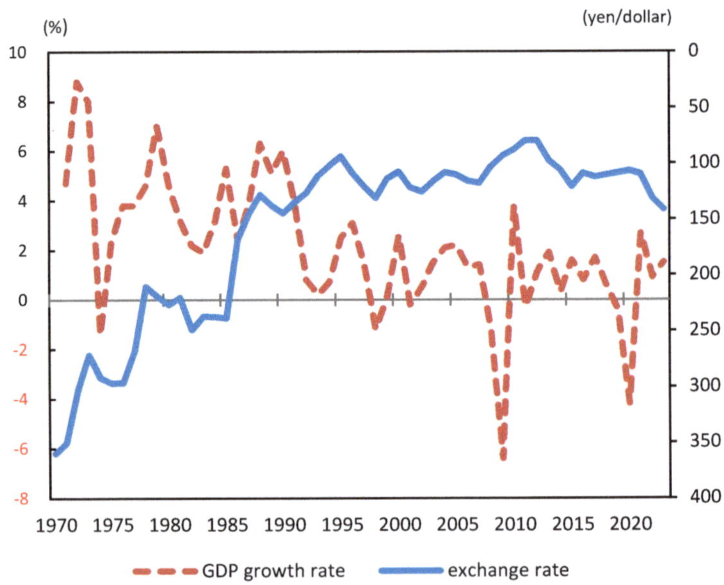

Fig. 2.1 GDP growth rate and exchange rate. *Source* Compiled by the author with data from OECD, *Economic Outlook*, and Bank of Japan, Time-Series Data Search

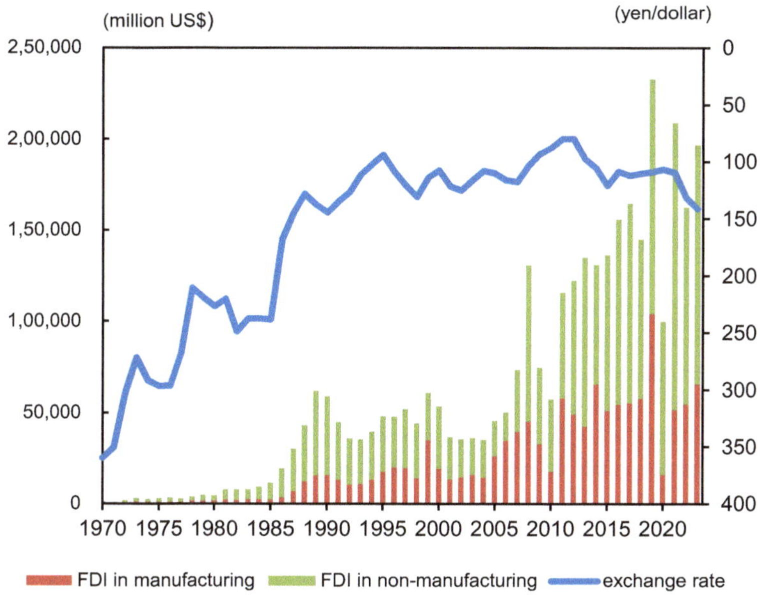

Fig. 2.2 Exchange rate and foreign direct investment. *Source* Compiled by the author with data from OECD, Economic Outlook, JETRO, Japanese Trade and Investment Statistics, and Bank of Japan, Time-Series Data Search

led to the outward FDI. In the 1980s, the correlation coefficient between the yen-dollar exchange rate and outward FDI was as high as −0.8731 in the manufacturing industry and −0.9046 in the automobile industry. There is no doubt that the strong yen promoted outward FDI.

2.2 From Bubble Economy to Lost Decade

The Plaza Accord of 1985 marked a significant turning point for the Japanese economy. It aimed at correcting the U.S. trade deficit caused by the strong dollar. At the Plaza meeting, the leaders of the G5 countries agreed to coordinate their interventions in foreign exchange markets to weaken the dollar. This decision, with its far-reaching implications, led to a sharp rise in the dollar-yen exchange rate. The yen's appreciation resulted in foreign-exchange losses on dollar-denominated assets, such as U.S. Treasury bonds, prompting a return of capital to Japan, a country perceived as having no foreign-exchange risk. The Plaza Accord's significance in economic history is undeniable.

In order to counter the recession brought about by the rapid appreciation of the yen, the Bank of Japan eased the monetary policy, lowering the official discount rate five times from 5.0% to 2.5% between January 1986 and February 1987 to help the competitiveness of domestic exporters and manufacturers (Okina et al., 2001). Subsequently, large amounts of capital flowed into the real estate and stock markets, triggering an investment boom. Between 1986 and 1991, commercial real estate prices and stock prices rose more than fourfold. Banks expanded their loans by accepting land as collateral. The rise in asset values and resulting unrealized profits only encouraged individuals and corporations to invest more. This rapid acceleration of asset prices overheated economic activity, and an uncontrolled money supply and credit expansion triggered an asset price bubble in Japan. In 1989, the Bank of Japan adopted a tight-money policy, and in 1990, it raised the official discount rate to 6%. This increase caused the Japanese bubble economy to collapse in 1991.

The burst of the bubble economy and the subsequent prolonged stagnation have generally been discussed as distortions in financial markets and failures of monetary policy. However, significant changes also occurred in the real economy. Labor rapidly shifted from manufacturing to the service sector. The index statistics in Fig. 2.3 clearly show that employment in the service sector surged during the bubble economy, whereas employment in manufacturing has continued to decline since the bubble's collapse. This contrast highlights the speed and magnitude of the economic structural transformation.

Wages are an important motivating factor in employment. Figure 2.4 shows average wages from 1980 to 2022. Wages in the service sector exceeded those in manufacturing until 1992. However, after the collapse of the bubble economy, wages in the service sector fell below those in manufacturing, despite an increase in the service sector's share.

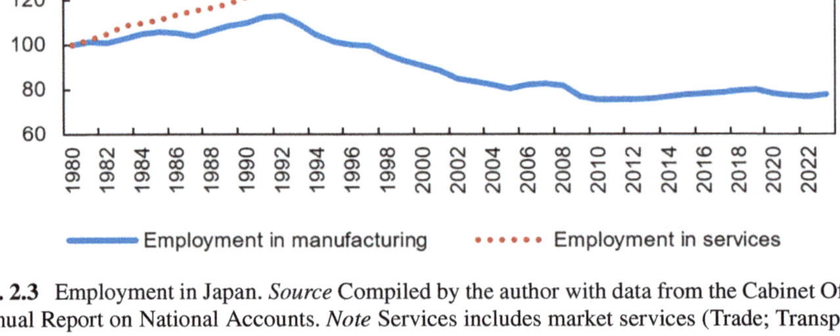

Fig. 2.3 Employment in Japan. *Source* Compiled by the author with data from the Cabinet Office, Annual Report on National Accounts. *Note* Services includes market services (Trade; Transportation; Accommodation and food; and Business and administrative services) and non-market services (Public administration; Community, social and other services and activities) in accordance with International Standard Industrial Classification

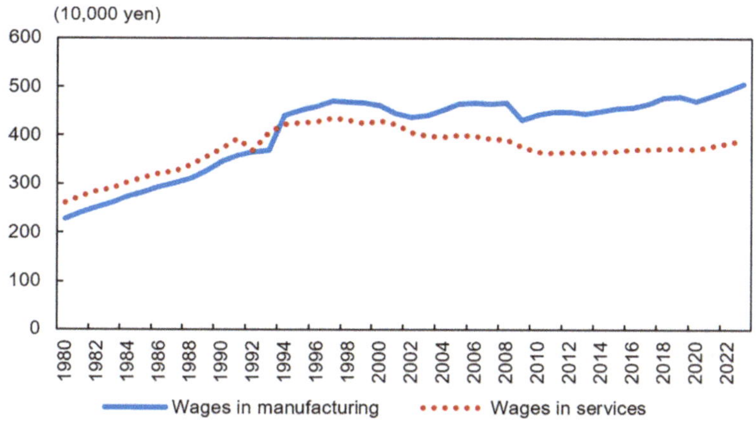

Fig. 2.4 Wages in Japan. *Source* Compiled by the author with data from the Cabinet Office, Annual Report on National Accounts

Wages reflect labor productivity. Labor productivity in the service sector improved during the bubble economy but has since declined and remained sluggish. This low productivity in the service sector is the fundamental cause of Japan's long-term economic stagnation (Fig. 2.5).

The theoretical model can also confirm the changes brought about by the bubble economy (Appendix 1).

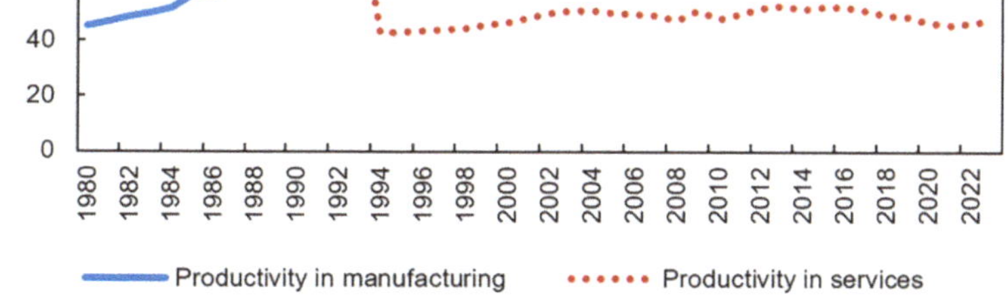

Fig. 2.5 Labor productivity in Japan. *Source* Compiled by the author with data from the Cabinet Office, Annual Report on National Accounts

2.3 Deindustrialization

The fact that labor reallocation progressed during the bubble economy, yet did not lead to economic growth, raises the issue of deindustrialization, or the hollowing out of industry. Deindustrialization, a long-term decline in the share of manufacturing in national employment or output, is a prevalent and crucial phenomenon widely observed in mature advanced economies. This phenomenon has a profound impact on various aspects of our lives, including GDP growth rates, balance of payments, exchange rates, inflation rates, and interest rates.

In 1992, Japan's manufacturing employment reached a peak of 15.7 million (OECD data). However, between 1992 and 2022, it decreased by 5 million. During the same period, employment in the service sector increased by 10.7 million while economic growth stagnated. The issue of deindustrialization demands immediate and thorough consideration.[1]

Rowthorn and Wells (1987) distinguish between explanations that view deindustrialization as a positive process associated with economic maturity and those that link it to negative factors such as economic failure. The dual nature of deindustrialization—both a result of a poor economic performance and a cause of it—underscores its profound complexity and presents an intriguing intellectual challenge that requires a comprehensive approach.

Figure 2.6 illustrates the process of deindustrialization from 1970 to 2022. The timing and experience of deindustrialization varies among individual advanced economies. The United States experienced a decline in manufacturing share, involving the stagnation of real income in the 1970s. Factories were forced to close as manufacturers began offshoring production, resulting in a "hollowing out" of the local economy and the communities surrounding the plant (Bluestone & Harrison, 1982). However, a shift in employment from manufacturing to the service sector later proceeded smoothly, and real income increased. The United Kingdom experienced a sharp drop in manufacturing share in the early 1980s. Rowthorn and Wells described this as a "negative" deindustrialization because real income hardly rose, and unemployment rose high. Low productivity in the service sector became a problem. In Japan, this process began later. Concerns about "industrial hollowing out" arose around 1985, when foreign direct investment began, but the bubble economy dispelled these concerns. A "negative" deindustrialization phenomenon emerged in the late 1990s.

Deindustrialization is a positive one if the increase in jobs created by the service sector absorbs the labor shed by the manufacturing sector. However, Fig. 2.7 indicates that the service sector in Japan could not absorb the loss of jobs in the manufacturing sector in the 1990s.

The literature on deindustrialization has less focused on external factors than on internal factors such as consumption, technological progress, and productivity. According to Rowthorn and Ramaswamy (1997), the most important domestic factors

[1] The deindustrialization phenomenon was first discussed at the end of the 1980s, next in the middle of the 1990s, and then in 2011 during Japan's rapid yen appreciation phases.

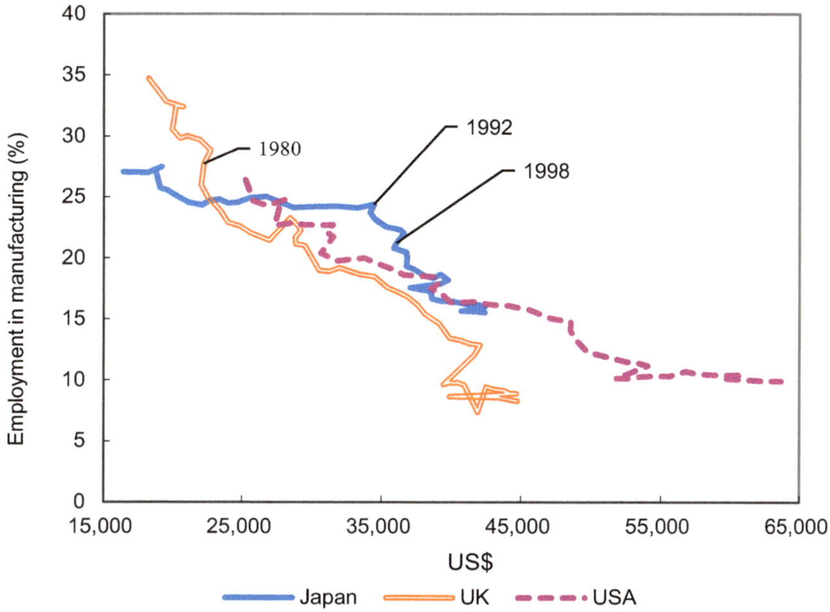

Fig. 2.6 Comparison of deindustrialization process (1970–2022). *Source* Compiled by the author with data from ILO, Labour Statistics. OECD, Economic Outlook

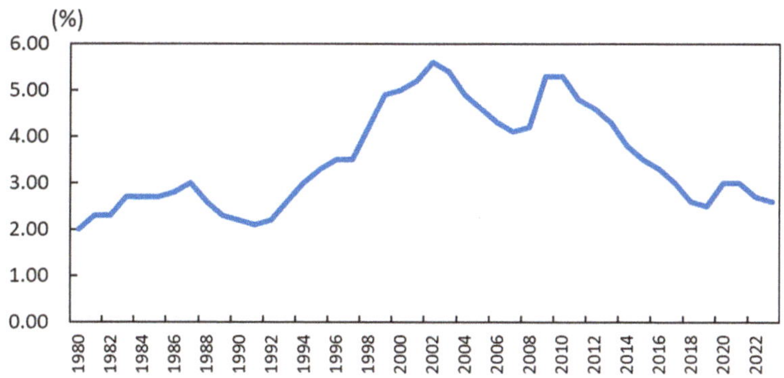

Fig. 2.7 Unemployment rate in Japan. *Source* OECD, Economic Outlook

contributing to deindustrialization are productivity growth in the manufacturing sector and the shift in domestic expenditure away from manufacturing to services.

However, the appreciation of the exchange rate repeatedly hurt the Japanese economy during the "lost three decades." Obstfeld (2011) pointed out that Japan's real economic growth rate has been strongly negatively correlated with the yen's real effective exchange rate. Although the yen's appreciation drives manufacturers to relocate production bases overseas, few studies have examined the potentially deindustrializing effect of a strong yen. According to Belke and Voltz (2020, p. 375), "only few studies can be found [that] systematically try to verify the hypothesis that the strong yen has contributed to de-industrialization and outsourcing of industry in Japan, including Dekle (1996), Dekle et al. (2011) and Yamashita (2013, 2015)." Dekle (1996) and Dekle et al. (2011) find that the yen appreciation in 1985 and 1995 hurt Japanese international competitiveness, raising the relative production costs of Japanese industries. Yamashita (2013) provides a simulation analysis of deindustrialization under the yen appreciation in 2011.

2.4 Structure of the Model

The macroeconomic model examined in this chapter is based on two sectors (manufacturing and non-manufacturing sectors). The combinations of explained and explanatory variables in each equation reflect the causal relationships identified by the regression analysis. However, the most important explanatory variables are exchange rates and foreign direct investment.

External factors can affect the internal structure of an economy in various ways. Overseas production led by FDI has four effects: reverse import effect, export inducement effect, export substitution effect, and import diverting effect. The reverse import effect refers to increased imports from the invested country to the investing country. The export inducement effect refers to increased exports from the investing country to the invested country because capital and intermediate goods are provided in the early stages of production. The export substitution effect refers to decreased exports from the investing country because finished products are substituted by those produced in the invested country. The import-diverting effect refers to reduced imports of materials when production operates outside the home economy. These effects are reflected in equations.

2.4.1 *Foreign Direct Investment*

Based on the consideration of the previous sections, outward FDI in the manufacturing sector is assumed to be dependent on the exchange rate.

$$FDIM_t = FDIM\,(EXR_t) \tag{2.1}$$

A subscript means time t. An estimation with the Bai-Perron equation test of (2.1) suggests a breakpoint in 2005 (see Appendix 2). From 1980 to 2005, $FDIM_t$ is negatively correlated with the exchange rate. A strong yen made outward FDI. Total outward FDI is linked to *FDIM*.

$$FDI_t = FDI(FDIM_t) \tag{2.2}$$

2.4.2 Macroeconomic Sector

The standard Keynesian aggregate demand model can be applied to the national economy. Gross domestic expenditure (GDE_t) consists of private final consumption expenditure (CP_t), private capital formation (IP_t), government capital formation (IG_t), government expenditure (GC_t), exports (EX_t), and imports (IM_t) at time t.

$$GDE_t = CP_t + IP_t + IG_t + GC_t + EX_t - IM_t \tag{2.3}$$

Private Final Consumption Expenditure

Private final consumption expenditure is a large and stable component of GDE. Private final consumption expenditure function is assumed as a Keynesian-type function in which the level of consumption depends on the previous gross domestic product (GDE_{t-1}), the current population (POP_t), and the exchange rate. A weak yen raises import prices and reduces consumption.

$$CP_t = CP\left(\frac{GDE_{t-1}}{POP_t}, EXR_t\right) \tag{2.4}$$

POP_t is a population. From 2022 onward, we will use population projections based on the National Institute of Population and Social Security Research's medium fertility scenario.

Gross Private Fixed Capital Formation

Gross private fixed capital formation or investment leads to changes in the amount of capital. Capital is a stock that accumulates a flow of net fixed capital formation. We will consider capital formation (IP_t) separately for manufacturing and non-manufacturing sectors of the national economy:

$$KM_t = KM\,(IPM_t, KM_{t-1}) \tag{2.5a}$$

$$KN_t = KN(IPN_t, KN_{t-1}) \tag{2.5b}$$

where KM_t is capital stock and IPM_t is fixed capital formation in the manufacturing sector. N denotes the non-manufacturing sector.

Regarding investment, it is assumed that a certain portion of production is invested:

$$IPM_t = IPM\,(YM_t, EXR_t) \tag{2.6a}$$

$$IPN_t = IPN(YN_t) \tag{2.6b}$$

Equation (2.6a) has breakpoints in 1988 and 2001.

We assume the Cobb–Douglas production function for each sector:

$$YM_t = A_0 KM_t^{\alpha} LM_t^{1-\alpha} \tag{2.7a}$$

$$YN_t = B_0 KN_t^{\beta} LN_t^{1-\beta} \tag{2.7b}$$

where A_0 and B_0 are total factor productivities, $0 < \alpha, \beta < 1$, and LM_t and LN_t are labor stocks.

Government Capital Formation

Government capital formation changes in step with the gross private fixed capital formation. From 1992 to 2004, which corresponds to the "lost decade" following the collapse of the bubble economy, there was a trend toward supplementing private fixed capital formation.

$$IG_t = IG(IP_t) \tag{2.8}$$

Government Expenditure

The government expenditure grows with the population.

$$GC_t = GC(POP65_t) \tag{2.9}$$

$POP65_t$ is a population over 65 years of age. Government expenditure is treated as an exogenous variable in many macroeconomic studies. However, it shows a positive correlation with the elderly population because social security services are an indispensable part of government expenditure.

Exports

Manufactured goods, which account for a substantial 80% of Japan's exports, are primarily driven by the electrical machinery and transportation equipment industries. These two industries, with their starkly contrasting employment trends, were the second- and first-largest employers, respectively, during the 1980s. The number of people employed in electrical machinery decreases as outward FDI increases, while the number employed in transport equipment increases. Total exports are intricately linked to the performance of these two industries. Japan's exports (EX_t) are dependent on exports in the electrical machinery industry (EXE_t) and exports of the transport equipment industry (EXT_t).

$$EX_t = EX(EXE_t, EXT_t) \tag{2.10}$$

Outward FDI in manufacturing ($FDIM_t$) and exchange rate (EXR_t) affect EXE_t and EXT_t differently. Outward FDI harms the electrical machinery industry and benefits the transport equipment industry. In the electrical machinery industry, we observe an export-substitution effect, whereas in the transportation machinery industry, we observe an apprarent export-inducing effect.

$$EXE_t = EXE(FDIM_t, EXR_t) \tag{2.11}$$

$$EXT_t = EXT(FDIM_t) \tag{2.12}$$

Equation (2.11) has breakpoints in 1986 and 1996. Until the mid-1980s, Japan achieved economic growth through an export-led economy. The electrical machinery industry would have had to change its exports to overcome a strong yen and avoid trade friction.

Imports

Imports are assumed to rise with income and depend on the GDE and exchange rate.

$$IM_t = IM(GDE_{t-1}, EXR_t) \tag{2.13}$$

2.4.3 Employment Sector

According to Petty-Clark's Law,[2] labor moves from a depressed sector to a growing sector. Employment in this study is classified into two types of economic sectors, the manufacturing sector and the non-manufacturing sector, because we would like to model deindustrialization.

The manufacturing sector consists of several sub-industries. Total employment in manufacturing (LM_t) depends on the production of electrical machinery and transport equipment for export.

$$LM_t = LM(EXE_t, EXT_t) \tag{2.14}$$

Equation (2.14) has a breakpoint in 1990. This finding suggests that structural changes occurred during the bubble economy.

The non-manufacturing sector depends on previous employment and the elderly population.

[2] Clark (1940) examined the significance of this tendency and called it "Petty's Law" after Sir William Petty who first found this type of tendency in *Political Arithmetic* (1690). This theory is now referred to as "Petty-Clark's Law."

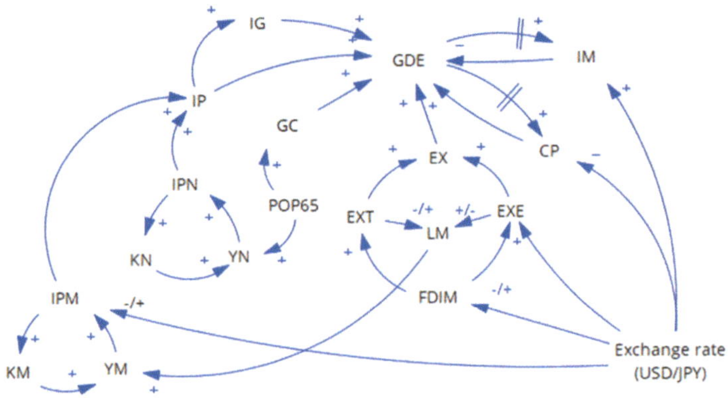

Fig. 2.8 Causal loop diagram of the model

$$LN_t = LN(LN_{t-1}, POP65_t) \tag{2.15}$$

In this way, the exchange rate affects an economy's internal structure in several ways. The effects are summarized in the following causal loop diagram (Fig. 2.8).

2.5 Simulation

Let us examine how the model works before analyzing several scenarios. The author's model was designed as a system dynamic model, including time lags, accumulations (stocks), and feedback loops, to enhance the macroeconomic model. Using differential equations, we can capture economic behavior that linear equations often overlook. Time delays in feedback channels respond differently in the short and long terms (Sterman, 2000, p. 22). Furthermore, modeling by system dynamics enables us to account for structural bifurcations.

By building on Solow-type economic growth and recreating the cyclical structure of employment in manufacturing and non-manufacturing (primarily service industries) due to yen appreciation and overseas production shifts, we can link "manufacturing hollowing out" to "low productivity in the service sector." Fig. 2.9 shows the forecast for GDP. The Root Mean Squared Percentage Error (RMSPE) between predicted and actual values is 5.14%.

Figure 2.10 indicates the share of manufacturing in total employment and the GDP per capita (thousand yen). The model in this chapter reproduces the movement of the Japanese economy, as shown in Fig. 2.6.

As discussed, the Japanese economy changed its industrial structure in response to exchange rate fluctuations. Let us examine the impact of future exchange rate changes. Based on the data from 1980 to 2022, we examine two scenarios

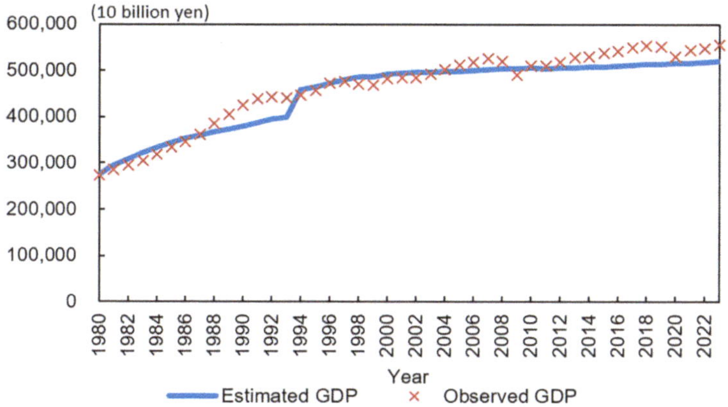

Fig. 2.9 Forecast for GDP

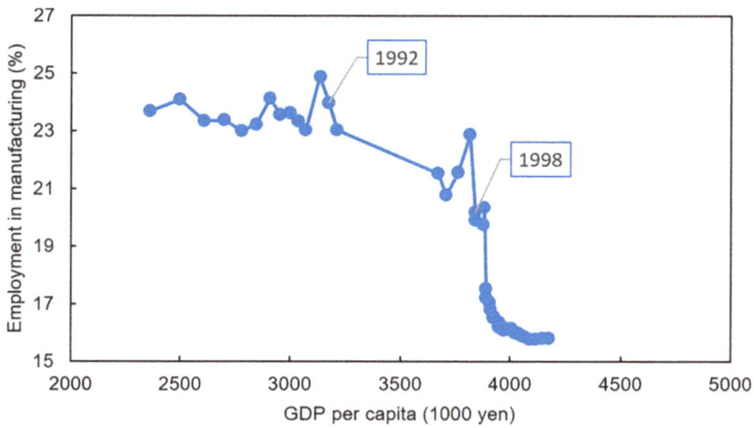

Fig. 2.10 Deindustrialization in the model

from 2023 to 2040: yen depreciation[3] and yen appreciation.[4] If the yen depreciation continues, employment in manufacturing, a crucial sector for the Japanese economy, will not decline, although economic growth is low. On the other hand, if the yen turns to appreciation, employment in manufacturing will decline, although economic growth will improve (Fig. 2.11). This result explains an important implication for the exchange rate policy.

[3] The yen soared to the 160-yen level, triggered by the Bank of Japan Governor's comments on April 26, 2024, that could be interpreted as "acceptance of a weaker yen." The Ministry of Finance is intervening in the currency market to ensure the exchange rate does not exceed 160 yen per dollar. Therefore, we assume 165 yen for appreciation.

[4] The yen appreciation scenario adopts 91 yen per dollar. Based on consumer prices, the International Monetary Fund estimates PPP (Purchasing Power Parity) at 91 yen to the dollar in 2022.

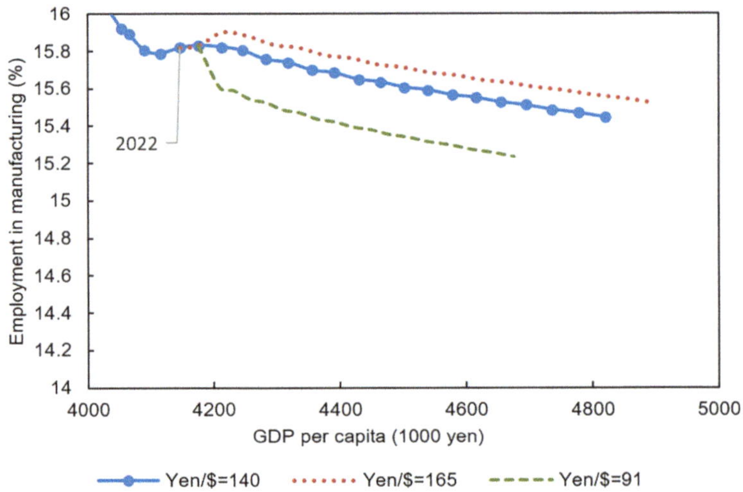

Fig. 2.11 Deindustrialization under different exchange rates

Following traditional thinking, a weaker yen is desirable for export industries. However, this is not always the case in a global supply chain built by FDI, as evidenced by Teikoku Databank's reports of "weak yen-related bankruptcies" from 2008 to 2015. Bankruptcies increased rather than decreased under the yen depreciation phase (Fig. 2.12).

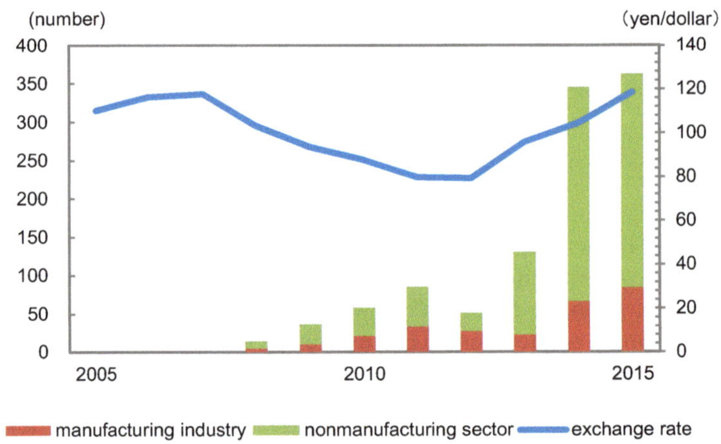

Fig. 2.12 Exchange-related bankruptcies. *Source* Compiled by the author with data from Teikoku Databank

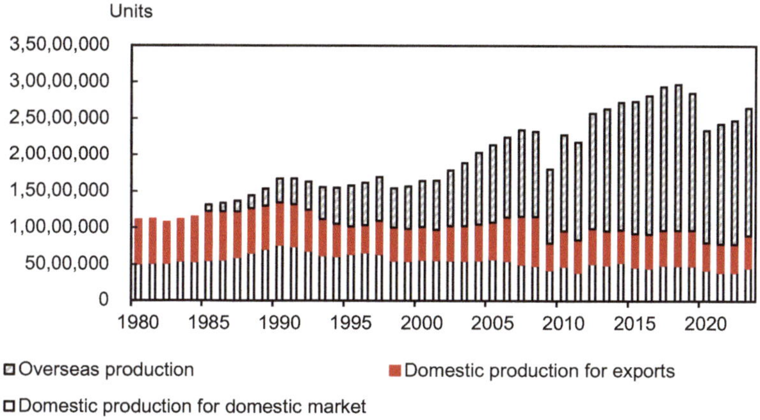

Fig. 2.13 Japan's automobile production: Domestic and overseas. *Source* Compiled by the author with data from Japan Automobile Manufacturers Association, "Statistics Monthly," and the Active-Matrix Database System

2.6 Reshoring

The super-strong yen in 2011 prompted a strategic shift in the Japanese automobile industry. Faced with the potential exchange loss in exports, many firms accelerated their overseas production, effectively countering the "hollowing out of industry" concerns. The subsequent yen depreciation in late 2014 further showcased the industry's strategic adaptability. The weak yen is now prompting some Japanese firms to consider bringing overseas production back home, a decision that is not only raising expectations of a "reshoring" phenomenon similar to what was observed in the United States in previous years[5] but also heralding a potential positive shift in the industry's dynamics.

The trend of overseas or offshore production in the Japanese automobile industry is noteworthy. In terms of volume, overseas production surpassed exports in 1994 and outpaced domestic production in 2007 (Fig. 2.13), indicating the industry's significant global expansion.

Such an increase in outward FDI reduced domestic investment and employment. As a result, employment in the manufacturing sector declined after peaking in 1992. What would have happened if the manufacturing sector returned its offshore production base to its home country? The author uses data for the "transportation manufacturing industry" as a proxy for the "automobile industry". Figure 2.14 shows the actual domestic employment and simulated overseas employment.

[5] American television personality Lou Dobbs (2004) argued that offshoring to overseas countries harmed American workers, viewing this as both an economic and a social issue. His opinion, though extreme, is crucial to understand as it sheds light on the problems of offshoring from the perspective of the national economy. At the very time of writing this article, US President Donald Trump is aggressively promoting the revival of US manufacturing.

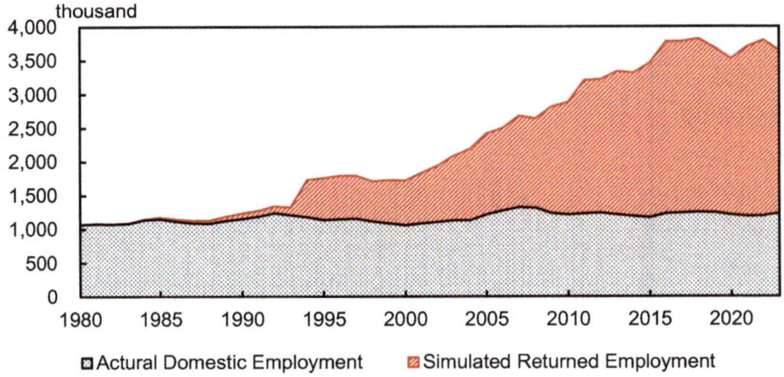

Fig. 2.14 Employment in the Japanese transportation manufacturing industry. *Source* Original data is taken from the Japan Automobile Manufacturers Association, "Statistics Monthly," Cabinet Office, Annual Report on National Accounts. *Note* Simulated returned employment = overseas production × domestic labor / domestic production

The simulation assumes that 5% of overseas employment will return to Japan after 2023. Domestic manufacturing employment could recover to the level of the 2010s when the yen was strong (Fig. 2.15).

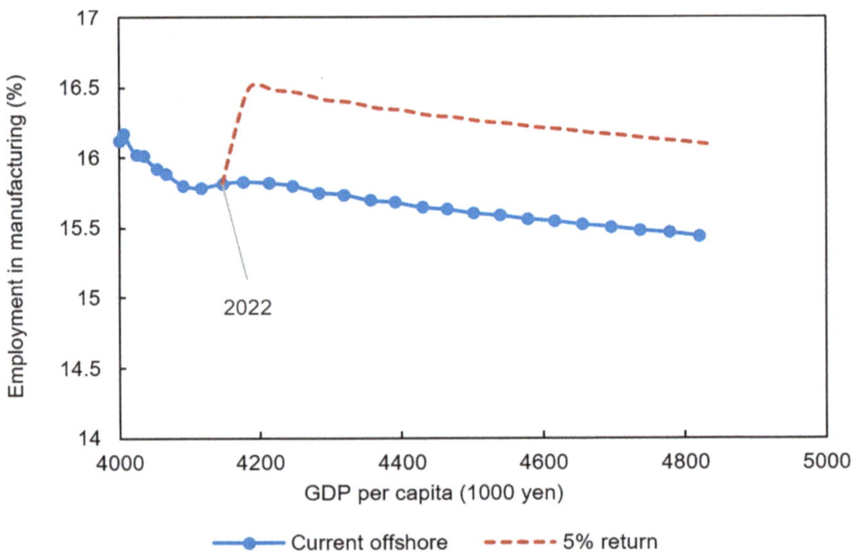

Fig. 2.15 Employment in reshoring

2.7 Conclusion

The deindustrialization process led by FDI is examined in this chapter. The findings are summarized as follows:

(1) Currency appreciation often brings negative deindustrialization.
(2) FDI has a significant effect on the home country. Offshoring in FDI enhanced the pace of deindustrialization.
(3) Reshoring is adequate to escape from the negative deindustrialization.
(4) Currency intervention designed to strengthen the currency is ineffective in recovering manufacturing employment.

Offshoring within FDI is a complex issue that significantly impacts international trade. As Blinder (2006) proposed, offshoring can lead to a large-scale redistribution of labor within the home country, potentially disrupting the nation's welfare.

A simulation analysis of a yen depreciation scenario underscores the complexity of reshoring. Bringing back manufacturing is not a straightforward task, as it is deeply entrenched in the highly developed global supply chain that manufacturers benefit from.

Appendix 1

The following model explains how asset bubbles affect the distribution of wealth among workers. Consider an economic model consisting of two sectors: a high-productivity sector (H) and a low-productivity sector (L). In each sector, we assume a Cobb–Douglas production function:

$$Y_t^H = AK_t^{H\alpha} L_t^{H(1-\alpha)} \tag{2.16a}$$

$$Y_t^L = BK_t^{L\beta} L_t^{L(1-\beta)} \tag{2.16b}$$

where Y^H is total output, K^H is capital stock and L^H is labor force for a high productivity sector. Y^L is total output, K^L is capital stock, and L^L is labor force for a low productivity sector. A and $B$are total factor productivities and α and β are the output elasticities of capital in each sector. In a competitive market, the marginal product of labor is equal to the real wage.

$$w^H = MP_L^H = \frac{\partial Y^H}{\partial L^H} = \frac{(1-\alpha)Y^H}{L^H} \tag{2.17a}$$

$$w^L = MP_L^L = \frac{\partial Y^L}{\partial L^L} = \frac{(1-\beta)Y^L}{L^L} \tag{2.17b}$$

Change in capital stock equals investment minus depreciation with the depreciation rate δ_i $(i = h,\ l)$.

$$\frac{dK^H}{dt} = I_t^H - \delta_h K_{t-1}^H \tag{2.18a}$$

$$\frac{dK^L}{dt} = I_t^L - \delta_l K_{t-1}^L \tag{2.18b}$$

$$I_t^H = s_h Y_t^H \tag{2.19a}$$

$$I_t^L = s_l Y_t^L \tag{2.19b}$$

where s_h and s_l are saving rates.

Allocation of labor force changes in accordance with economic growth. Labor can migrate between sectors based on wage differentials.

$$\frac{dL^H}{dt} = L_t^{LH} - L_t^{HL} \tag{2.20a}$$

$$\frac{dL^L}{dt} = L_t^{HL} - L_t^{LH} \tag{2.20b}$$

$$L^{LH} = m_i \times \left(w^H - w^L\right) \times L^L \tag{2.21a}$$

$$L^{HL} = m_h \times \left(w^L - w^H\right) \times L^H \tag{2.21b}$$

where m_l and m_h are migration rates.

For simplicity, we set $K_0^H = K_0^L = 50$, $L_0^H = L_0^L = 50$, $\alpha = \beta = 0.3$, $A = 1.2$, $B = 1$, $\delta_h = \delta_l = 0.5$, $s_h = s_l = 0.25$, $m_h = m_l = 1$. Simulation reveals that wage differentials will be eliminated by the migration of labor.

Labor moves from the low productivity sector to the high productivity sector and the gap in wages is reduced (Fig. 2.16).

Next, let us introduce the concept of a bubble economy. The system dynamics model, a powerful tool, adeptly handles nonlinearities and feedback effects, such as booms and bursts. In a bubble boom, the prices of non-productive assets, such as stocks and land, rise, and funds, flow into labor-intensive industries that are not productive (such as real estate). In the model, we assume that heated money flows into industry L. Let p be the asset price, p^e be the fundamental price of the asset, and σ be the price increase rate. When $\frac{p(1+\sigma)}{p^e} > 1$, a bubble begins from the fifth to the tenth year. We assume s_l increases to $\frac{p(1+\sigma)}{p^e} \times s_l$ during the bubble period. Setting $p_0 = p^e = 100$ and $\sigma = 0.18$ yields the following results (Fig. 2.17).

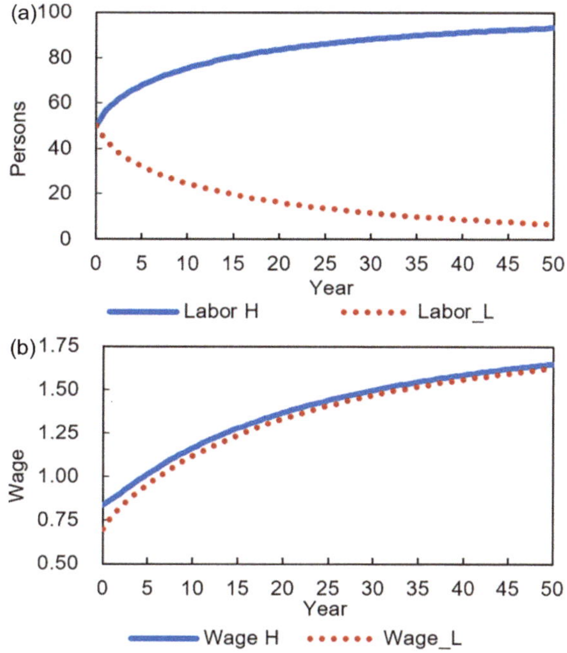

Fig. 2.16 Inter-sectoral migration. **a** labor allocation**b** wage movements

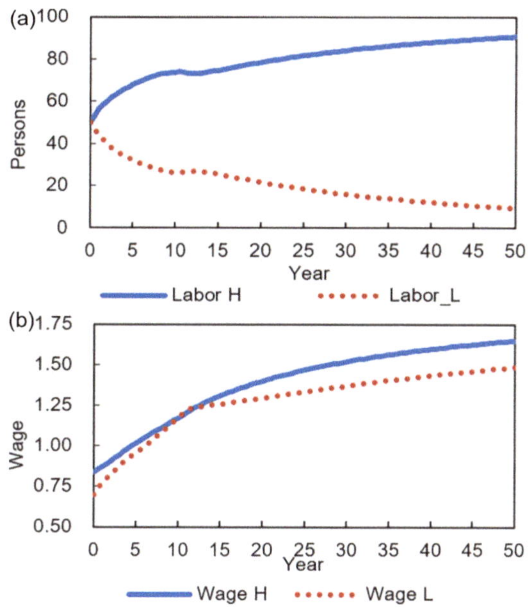

Fig. 2.17 Inter-sectoral migration with bubble. **a** labor allocation **b** wage movements

Figure 2.18 shows the trend in total production. An economy experiencing a bubble undergoes a temporary expansion in total production; however, when the bubble bursts, performance declines due to the temporary misallocation of resources.

As in the case of the Japanese economy, the return of employment to the high-productivity sector after the bubble bursts is crucial for recovery. If this does not happen, the decline will be even greater, highlighting the significant role of the high-productivity sector in economic recovery (Fig. 2.19).

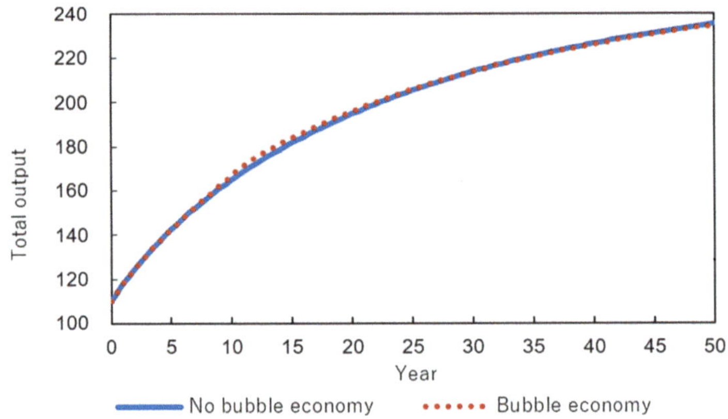

Fig. 2.18 Comparison of total output

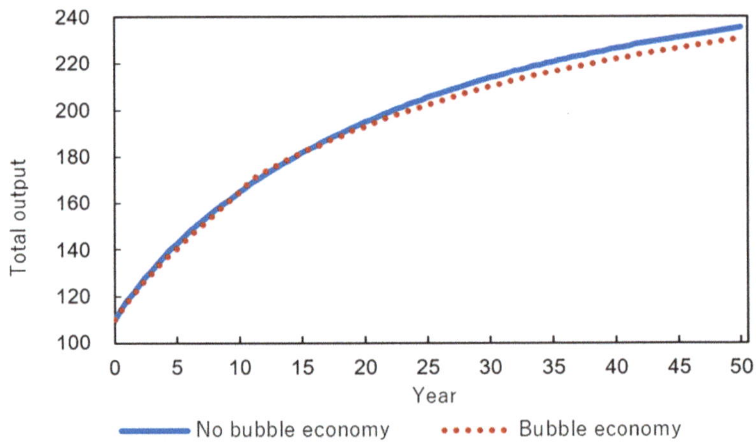

Fig. 2.19 Comparison of total output without migration

Appendix 2: Estimation of Equations

A data set was assembled for the years from 1980 to 2022. A value in parentheses under the coefficient is t-distribution, R^2 is a coefficient of determination, and $\overline{R}^2$ is a coefficient of determination adjusted for degrees of freedom.

$$\log(FDIM_t) = \begin{cases} \underset{(18.953)}{23.38823} - \underset{(-11.573)}{2.882489}\log(EXR_t) \\ +u_t, \quad t \le 2005, \\ \underset{(2.568)}{7.857973} + \underset{(0.931)}{0.613887}\log(EXR_t) \\ +u_t, \quad 2006 \le t \le 2022, \end{cases} R^2 = 0.8839.$$

$$\log(FDI_t) = \underset{(6.952)}{2.568009} + \underset{(22.498)}{0.846877}\log(FDIM_t), \quad R^2 = 0.9250.$$

$$\log(CP_t) = \underset{(65.328)}{11.74473} + \underset{(21.673)}{0.893719}\log\left(\frac{GDE_{t-1}}{POP}\right) - \underset{(-3.501)}{0.96073}EXR_t, \quad \bar{R}^2 = 0.9833.$$

$$KM_t = \underset{(16.055)}{0.515802}IPM_t + \underset{(151.079)}{0.916634}KM_{t-1}, \quad \overline{R}^2 = 0.9983.$$

$$KN_t = \underset{(2.276)}{144182.6} + \underset{(0.967)}{0.869144}IPN_t + \underset{(10.426)}{0.806563}KN_{t-1}, \quad \overline{R}^2 = 0.8593.$$

$$IPM_t = \begin{cases} \underset{(16.638)}{0.463024}YM_t - \underset{(-1.252)}{15.22236}EXR_t + u_t, t \le 1988, \\ \underset{(3.378)}{0.340014}YM_t + \underset{(1.841)}{146.6706}EXR_t + u_t, 1989 \le t \le 2001, \\ \underset{(7.560)}{0.255982}YM_t + \underset{(4.619)}{156.4366}EXR_t + u_t, 2002 \le t \le 2022, \overline{R}^2 = 0.8520. \end{cases}$$

$$\log(IPN_t) = \underset{(2.510)}{2.204018} + \underset{(10.471)}{0.718097}\log(YN_t), \quad R^2 = 0.7278.$$

$$\log\left(\frac{YM_t}{LM_t}\right) = \underset{(0.953)}{0.189281} + \underset{(21.036)}{0.794135}\left(\frac{KM_t}{LM_t}\right), R^2 = 0.9152.$$

$$\log\left(\frac{YN_t}{LN_t}\right) = \begin{cases} -\underset{(-4.310)}{0.745339} + \underset{(27.955)}{0.914080}\log\left(\frac{KN_t}{LN_t}\right) + u_t, \quad t \le 1993, \\ \underset{(4.882)}{1.585205} + \underset{(8.378)}{0.508819}\log\left(\frac{KN_t}{LN_t}\right) + u_t, \quad 1994 \le t \le 2022, R^2 = 0.9837. \end{cases}$$

$$\log(IG_t) = \begin{cases} \underset{(4.094)}{3.777947} + \underset{(7.150)}{0.566570}\log(IP_t) + u_t, t \le 1991, \\ -\underset{(-3.571)}{14.32324} + \underset{(6.231)}{2.103479}\log(IP_t) + u_t, 1992 \le t \le 2004, \\ \underset{(2.208)}{5.571465} + \underset{(1.842)}{0.394243}\log(IP_t) + u_t, 2005 \le t \le 2022, R^2 = 0.9481. \end{cases}$$

$$\log(GC_t) = \underset{(17.061)}{25901.70} + \underset{(39.961)}{2.457832}\log(POP65_t), \qquad R^2 = 0.9749.$$

$$\log(EX_t) = \underset{(0.849)}{0.200997} + \underset{(2.046)}{0.120395}\log(EXE_t) + \underset{(17.296)}{1.08467}\log(EXT_t), \bar{R}^2 = 0.9811.$$

$$\log(EXE_t) = \begin{cases} \underset{(-2.524)}{-11.73354} + \underset{(5.968)}{1.583501}\log(FDIM_t) + \underset{(2.502)}{1.458110}\log(EXR_t) \\ +u_t, \ t \le 1986, \\ \underset{(4.556)}{-12.08789} + \underset{(1.491)}{0.210126}\log(FDIM_t) - \underset{(-2.846)}{1.034376}\log(EXR_t) \\ +u_t, \ 1987 \le t \le 1996, \\ \underset{(8.065)}{-8.240948} + \underset{(2.224)}{0.087659}\log(FDIM_t) + \underset{(0.542)}{0.09767}\log(EXR_t) \\ +u_t, \ 1997 \le t \le 2022, \\ \bar{R}^2 = 0.9825. \end{cases} \quad ..$$

$$\log(EXT_t) = \begin{cases} \underset{(26.076)}{6.966332} + \underset{(7.467)}{0.220091}\log(FDIM_t) \\ +u_t, \quad t \le 2001, \\ \underset{(14.097)}{7.384785} + \underset{(4.592)}{0.228236}\log(FDIM_t) \\ +u_t, \quad 2002 \le t \le 2022, \end{cases} \qquad R^2 = 0.9336.$$

$$\begin{aligned} \log(IM_t) = & \underset{(-7.124)}{-22.9782} + \underset{(12.865)}{2.455027}\log(GDE_{t-1}) \\ & + \underset{(1.644)}{0.233922}\log(EXR_t), \\ & \bar{R}^2 = 0.9310 \end{aligned}$$

$$\log(LM_t) = \begin{cases} \underset{(10.773)}{6.655452} + \underset{(1.327)}{0.090483}\log(EXE_t) + \underset{(-0.154)}{-0.020687}\log(EXT_t) \\ +u_t, \ t \le 1990, \\ \underset{(9.007)}{10.01485} \underset{(-6.996)}{-0.530233}\log(EXE_t) + \underset{(1.963)}{0.237926}\log(EXT_t) \\ +u_t \ 1991 \le t \le 1997, \\ \underset{(19.365)}{10.41726} + \underset{(0.120)}{0.012040}\log(EXE_t) - \underset{(-4.791)}{0.367837}\log(EXT_t) \\ +u_t \ 1998 \le t \le 2005, \\ \underset{(8.745)}{4.611657} + \underset{(3.885)}{0.258290}\log(EXE_t) + \underset{(-0.321)}{-0.014340}\log(EXT_t) \\ +u_t \ 2006 \le t \le 2022, \\ \bar{R}^2 = 0.9825. \end{cases}$$

$$\bar{R}^2 = 0.9825.$$

$$\log(LN_t) = \begin{cases} \underset{(1.635)}{1.557310} + \underset{(4.160)}{0.709424}\log(LN_{t-1}) \\ + \underset{(1.831)}{0.096157}\log(POP65_t) + u_t, \ t \le 1997, \\ \underset{(1.675)}{1.035152} + \underset{(10.250)}{0.841999}\log(LN_{t-1}) \\ + \underset{(2.875)}{0.031967}\log(POP65_t) + u_t, \ 1998 \le t \le 2022, \end{cases}$$

$$\overline{R}^2 = 0.9938.$$

References

Belke, A., & Voltz, U. (2020). The yen exchange rate and the hollowing out of the Japanese industry. *Open Economic Review, 31*, 371–406.

Blinder, A. (2006). Offshoring: The next industrial revolution? *Foreign Affairs, 85*(2), 113–128.

Bluestone, B., & Harrison, B. (1982). *The deindustrialization of America*. Basic Books.

Clark, C. (1940). *The conditions of economic progress*. Macmillan.

Dekle, R. (1996). *Endaka and Japanese employment adjustment* (Center on Japanese economy and business working paper No. 113), Columbia Business School.

Dekle, R., Fukao, K., & Ungor M. (2011). The Japan-US exchange rate, productivity, and the competitiveness of Japanese industries. In K. Hamada, A. K. Kashyap, & D. E. Weinstein (Eds.), *Japan's bubble, deflation, and long-term stagnation* (pp. 105–128). MIT Press.

Dobbs, L. (2004). *Exporting America: Why corporate greed is shipping American jobs to overseas*. Warner Business Books.

Hamada, K., & Okada, Y. (2009). Monetary and international factors behind Japan's lost decade. *Journal of the Japanese and International Economies, 23*, 200–219.

Matsushita, M., Goto, F., & Yamashita, T. (2011). Kawase hendō, taigai chokusetsu tōshi, oyobi sangyō no kūdōka-saikin 10 nen no ugoki wo mite [Exchange rates, foreign direct investments, and hollowing out phenomena: Last decade's movement]. *Aoyama Keizai Ronshū [Aoyama Economic Review], 63*(3), 5–43.

Obstfeld, M. (2011). Time of troubles: the yen and Japan's economy, 1985–2008. In K. Hamada, A. K. Kashyap, & D. E. Weinstein (Eds.), *Japan's bubble, deflation, and long-term stagnation* (pp. 51–103). MIT Press.

Okina, K., Shirakawa, M., & Shiratsuka, S. (2001). The asset price bubble and monetary policy: Japan's experience in the late 1980s and the lessons. *Monetary and Economic Studies, 19*(S-1), 395–450.

Rowthorn, R., & Ramaswamy, R. (1997). *Deindustrialization: Causes and implications* (International Monetary Fund Working Paper No. 97/42).

Rowthorn, R., & Wells, J. (1987). *De-industrialization and foreign trade*. Cambridge University Press.

Sterman, J. (2000). *Business dynamics: Systems thinking and modeling for a complex world*. Irwin/McGraw-Hill.

Urata, S. (2020). US–Japan trade frictions: The past, the present, and implications for the US–China Trade War. *Asian Economic Policy Review, 15*, 141–159.

Yamashita, T. (2013). *Exchange rates and reindustrialization: Japanese experiences*. Proceedings of the 31st international conference of the system dynamics society, pp. 1–14.

Yamashita, T. (2015). *Exchange rates and reshoring*. Proceedings of the 33rd international conference of the system dynamics society, pp. 1–20.

Additional Bibliography

Alderson, A. (1991). Explaining deindustrialization: Globalization, failure, or success? *American Sociological Review, 64*(5), 701–721.

Basu, D., & Miroshnik, V. (2000). *Japanese foreign investments, 1970–1998: Perspectives and analyses.* M.E. Sharpe.

Bazen, S., & Thirlwall, T. (1997). *Deindustrialization* (3rd ed.). Heinemann Educational Publishers.

Brunnermeier, M., & Reis, R. (2023). *A crash course on crises: Macroeconomic concepts for run-ups, collapses, and recoveries.* Princeton University Press.

Collie, D. R. (2011). Multilateral trade liberalisation, foreign direct investment and the volume of world trade. *Economic Letters, 113*, 47–49.

de Groot, H. L. F. (2000). *Growth, unemployment and deindustrialization.* Edward Elgar Publishing.

Grossman, G., & Rossi-Hansberg, E. (2008). Trading tasks: A simple theory of offshoring. *American Economic Review, 98*(5), 1978–1997.

Kollmeyer, C. (2009). Explaining deindustrialization: How affluence, productivity growth, and globalization diminish manufacturing employment. *American Journal of Sociology, 114*(4), 1644–1674.

Low, G. (1980). The multiplier-accelerator model of business cycles interpreted from system dynamics perspectives. In J. Randers (Ed.), *Elements of the system dynamics method* (pp. 76–94). Pegasus Communications.

Milberg, W., & Winkler, D. (2013), *Outsourcing economics: Global value chains in capitalist development.* Cambridge University Press.

Tanaka, A. (2012). *The effects of FDI on domestic employment and workforce composition* (RIETI Discussion Paper Series, No. 12-E-069).

Weber, L. (2009). *Demographic changes and economic growth: Simulations on growth models.* Physica-Verlag.

Wren, A. (Ed.). (2013). *The political economy of the service transition.* Oxford University Press.

Yoshikawa, H. (2002). *Japan's lost decade.* I-House Press.

Chapter 3
Regional Economies and Biased Labor Productivity

Takayuki Yamashita

Abstract Differences in industrial structure between regions are often cited as a cause of income disparities. Regions with growing industries naturally enjoy steady economic growth. On the other hand, regions with declining industries experience stagnant economic growth. However, even when there are no differences in industrial structure, specific regional circumstances can lead to differences in growth rates. Shift-share analysis, which examines the factors behind economic growth, provides insight into the details of Japan's postwar economic growth.

Keyword Shift-share analysis · Core-periphery · Location quotient · High economic growth · Labor productivity · Technical progress

3.1 Economic Growth and the Regional Economy

Economic growth does not proceed uniformly across the country. Factors specific to each region will influence and determine its actual economic growth rate. Some regions experience high growth rates; others do not.

Furthermore, economic development does not appear everywhere at the same time. The dynamics of a firm or an industry generate development. While a propulsive industry emerges, some existing industries become obsolete or decline. There are differences in the production or industrial structures of each region, and these differences affect regional economic development.

Figure 3.1 shows the compound annual growth rate of gross prefectural domestic product from 1980 to 2020, calculated from the Annual Report on Prefectural

T. Yamashita (✉)
School of Global Studies and Collaboration, Aoyama Gakuin University, Sagamihara, Japan
e-mail: yamashita.takayuki@gsc.aoyama.ac.jp

T. Yamashita and T. Morita (eds.), *On the Structural Transformation of the Japanese Economy 1985-2023*, Advances in Japanese Business and Economics 38,
https://doi.org/10.1007/978-981-95-7230-4_3

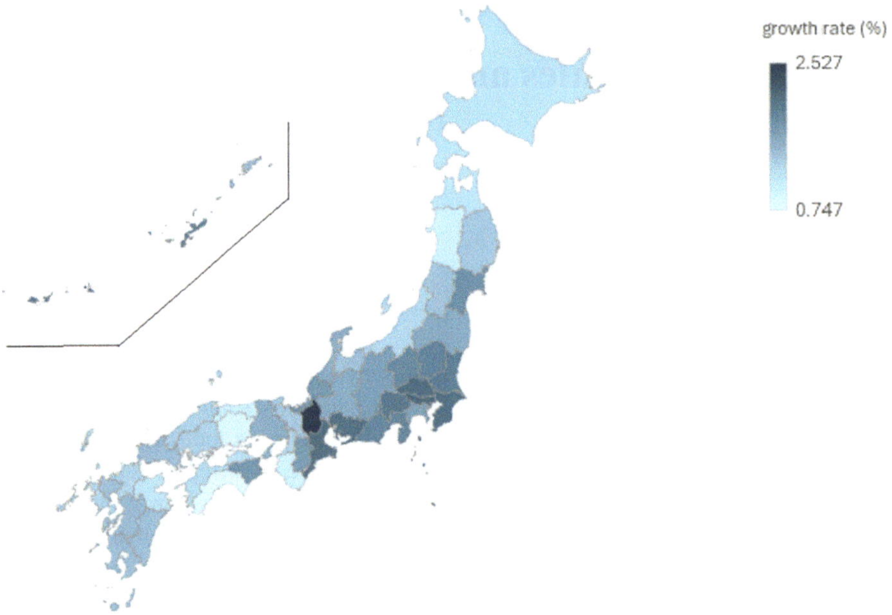

Fig. 3.1 CAGR of gross prefectural domestic product

Accounts.[1] Although the national average is 1.655%, growth rates vary from 0.747% to 2.527%, depending on the prefecture.

As a result, there are income disparities in each region. Labor moves to industries offering the highest wages. Labor's inter-industry transition is also accompanied by geographic migration. Examining labor migrants in terms of regional economies traces shifts in the driving force of economic growth.

3.2 Shift-Share Analysis

Shift-share analysis offers a retrospective view of the factors contributing to economic growth. It is a technique for separating a region's economic growth into components that can be explained by its industrial structure and those that cannot. Daniel Creamer (1942) developed this idea in the early 1940s, and Edgar S. Dunn formalized it in 1960. The richness of the implications obtained from the analysis results has led to its use in numerous empirical studies, mainly in Europe and the United States.

The shift-share analysis breaks down the factors that cause regional economic growth to diverge from national economic growth into two parts: one that can be

[1] The prefectures of Japan are the nation's 47 sub-national jurisdictions: one "metropolis," Tokyo; one "circuit," Hokkaidō; two urban prefectures, Osaka and Kyoto; and 43 other prefectures.

attributed to the region's industrial mix and one that cannot (i.e., regional factors). It then analyzes the impact of each of these two indicators on regional economic growth.

The divergence between the growth of the regional economies and that of the national economy is referred to as a shift. The analysis examines changes in an economic variable between the two years. By focusing on regional employment or output by industry sector, this analytical tool has been used to assess a region's performance relative to other regions and to assess the relative importance of an industry sector. Let us use employment as an indicator of the regional economic growth. The analysis decomposes employment changes within an economy over a specific period into three contributing factors. Let the number of workers in the industrial sector i in the region be e_i, the number of workers in the nation as a whole E_i. The total number of workers at the national level is E. The subscripts in the upper right-hand corner denote the base year (0) and comparison year (t), respectively. The change in regional employment is

$$\sum_{i=1}^{n} e_i^t - \sum_{i=1}^{n} e_i^0 \tag{3.1}$$

The increase in employment in a region differs from the increase in employment if the region had the same growth rate as the nation. The region's share of total employment would remain the same. Equation (3.1) is equivalent to

$$\begin{aligned}\sum_{i=1}^{n} e_i^t - \sum_{i=1}^{n} e_i^0 &= \left(\frac{E^t}{E^0}\sum_{i=1}^{n} e_i^0 - \sum_{i=1}^{n} e_i^0\right) + \left(\sum_{i=1}^{n} e_i^t - \frac{E^t}{E^0}\sum_{i=1}^{n} e_i^0\right)\\ &= \sum_{i=1}^{n} e_i^0\left(\frac{E^t}{E^0} - 1\right) + \sum_{i=1}^{n}\left(e_i^t - \frac{E_i^t}{E_i^0}e_i^0\right) + \sum_{i=1}^{n}\left(\frac{E_i^t}{E_i^0} - \frac{E^t}{E^0}\right)e_i^0\end{aligned} \tag{3.2}$$

Three factors explain the growth of the regional economy: the national growth factor, the differential shift (a regional-specific factor), and the proportional shift (an industry structure factor). The first term on the right side of Eq. (3.2) implies regional growth when the industrial structure is the same as that of the national economy. Growth is attributable to the growth of the national economy. The second term refers to the effect of changes in each industry sector in the region and is called the differential shift or region-specific factor. Growth is attributable to the competitive nature of the local industries. The third term refers to the effect of changes in specific industry sectors nationwide and is called the proportional shift or industry mix. Growth is attributed to the mix of faster-or slower-than-average-growing industries. Adding differential and proportional shifts yields the actual shift. If the actual shift is positive, regional employment will grow faster than national employment.

This technique reveals the regional development of a national economy by examining the possible combinations of differential and proportionality shifts. Dividing

Table 3.1 Combinations of differential and proportional shifts

Type	Relative differential shift (RS_d)	Relative proportional shift (RS_p)		Shift
1	+	+	$\lvert RS_d\rvert < \lvert RS_p\rvert$	+
2	+	+	$\lvert RS_d\rvert > \lvert RS_p\rvert$	+
3	+	−	$\lvert RS_d\rvert > \lvert RS_p\rvert$	+
4	−	+	$\lvert RS_d\rvert < \lvert RS_p\rvert$	+
5	−	+	$\lvert RS_d\rvert > \lvert RS_p\rvert$	−
6	+	−	$\lvert RS_d\rvert < \lvert RS_p\rvert$	−
7	−	−	$\lvert RS_d\rvert > \lvert RS_p\rvert$	−
8	−	−	$\lvert RS_d\rvert < \lvert RS_p\rvert$	−

both sides by the $\sum_{i=1}^{n} e_i^0$ obtains the growth rate of the region. The relative components of the shift-share analysis enable an interregional comparison of their contributions to competitiveness.

$$\frac{\sum_{i=1}^{n} e_i^t - \sum_{i=1}^{n} e_i^0}{\sum_{i=1}^{n} e_i^0} = \left(\frac{E^t}{E^0} - 1\right) + \frac{\sum_{i=1}^{n}\left(e_i^t - \frac{E_i^t}{E_i^0} e_i^0\right)}{\sum_{i=1}^{n} e_i^0} + \frac{\sum_{i=1}^{n}\left(\frac{E_i^t}{E_i^0} - \frac{E^t}{E^0}\right) e_i^0}{\sum_{i=1}^{n} e_i^0} \tag{3.3}$$

Heijman and Schipper (2010) referred to two shifts as the relative differential shift and the relative proportional shift, respectively. Dunn (1960) classified regions into six categories using the combinations of differential and proportional shifts from Eq. (3.2). Boudevill (1966) further classified them into eight categories, focusing on combinations of absolute differential and proportional shift values because the differential shift may relate to the growth core. This chapter follows Boudevill's classification using Eq. (3.3) because his classification is particularly effective in indicating the core-periphery structure in the regional analysis (Table 3.1).[2]

The Boudeville classification is a powerful tool that helps us identify the type of economic problems occurring in different regions. Regions 1–4 are growing at a faster rate than average, while regions 5–8 are growing at a slower rate than average. However, while the slow growth in a Type 5 region is due to its relatively unfavorable specific regional circumstances, the slow growth in a Type 6 region results from an unfavorable industrial mix.

By applying this classification to the core-periphery distinction, valuable insights are obtained that are directly relevant to regional economic analysis. Core areas are characterized by positive proportional shifts (Types 1, 2, 4, and 5); spillover areas are characterized by negative proportional shifts and positive differential shifts (Types 3 and 6). Finally, peripheral regions are characterized by two negative shifts (Types 7 and 8). Economic growth does not occur uniformly across the country. When

[2] Dunn (1960) did not distinguish between types 1 and 2 or 7 and 8.

analyzing the spatial structure of regional economic activity, the shift-share analysis offers valuable insights into the development process.

3.3 Case Study: Shizuoka Prefecture

Shift-share analysis, a less commonly used method in the study of regional economies in Japan, has been previously employed by Ohta (1982) and Kobayashi (2004). Their analyses were limited to prefectures or large cities in Japan and covered a limited time span. In contrast, this chapter takes a comprehensive approach, conducting a shift-share analysis of all regional municipalities in Japan, demonstrating the thoroughness of our research. Japan is composed of 47 prefectures.

The analysis commences in Shizuoka Prefecture, a pivotal manufacturing hub situated midway between Tokyo and Aichi Prefecture (Fig. 3.2). The economic trajectory of Shizuoka Prefecture mirrors broader shifts in the Japanese economy, making it a significant area of study in regional economics (Yamashita, 2016).

Fig. 3.2 Prefectures in Japan

Fig. 3.3 Cities and towns in Shizuoka Prefecture

Shizuoka City (former Sumpu (駿府)), the prefectural capital, was the home base of Tokugawa Ieyasu, who founded the Tokugawa Shogunate (1603–1868). Along with the capital, Edo (now Tokyo), Sumpu prospered as a supplemental central castle town for politics and diplomacy (Fig. 3.3).

Hamamatsu City in the western part of the Prefecture is an industrial city where musical instrument manufacturers are located, represented by piano manufacturing with a 100% market share in Japan, and is also home to the world-famous motorcycle manufacturers Honda Motor, Suzuki, and Yamaha Motor, which hold an annual event called "Hamamatsu, Hometown of Motorcycles." The most significant contribution to the prefectural gross domestic product comes from those exports.

Numazu City, a central city in the eastern part of the Prefecture, has an industrial cluster that cooperates with major machine tool and electrical machinery manufacturers. The Izu Peninsula is located in the southeast part of the Prefecture. It is a popular tourist destination for visitors from the Kanto region,[3] and is mainly known as a hot spring resort area, with Atami and Ito Cities.[4]

Table 3.2 summarizes the classification of cities and towns in Shizuoka Prefecture based on the shift-share analysis of employed persons (15 years old and over) in the Population Census.[5]

The following are some of the distinctive changes that have occurred in the process of economic growth. Figure 3.4 shows the distribution of each region in the 1960s. During the period of nationwide high economic growth (1955–1973), cities with manufacturing industries were the driving force in the economic growth of Shizuoka

[3] The Kanto region is one of the regional divisions of Japan. It generally refers to the seven prefectures of Ibaraki, Tochigi, Gunma, Saitama, Chiba, Tokyo, and Kanagawa Prefecture. There are eight regions in Japan: Hokkaido, Tohoku, Kanto, Chubu, Kansai, Chugoku, Shikoku, and Kyushu.

[4] "Shi" is a Japanese term that can refer to a city. "Cho" refers to a town.

[5] The population census in Japan has been conducted every five years since 1920.

Table 3.2 Type of cities in Shizuoka Prefecture

City, Town	1960–65	1965–70	1970–75	1975–80	1980–85	1985–90	1990–95	1995–00	2000–05	2005–10	2010–15	2015–20
Atami	5	5	5	5	5	5	5	5	5	5	7	5
Ito	4	5	4	5	5	4	5	5	5	7	7	5
Shimoda	5	2	5	5	5	5	5	5	7	8	7	5
Izu	7	8	7	5	5	7	5	5	8	7	5	5
Izunokuni	5	2	5	2	2	2	3	7	6	8	5	5
Higashi Izu	5	6	5	5	5	5	5	5	7	7	7	5
Kawazu	7	8	8	7	8	8	5	7	7	8	7	5
Minami Izu	7	8	8	5	7	7	5	5	7	8	5	5
Matsuzaki	7	6	7	7	7	7	5	5	7	7	7	5
Nishi Izu	6	6	8	7	7	7	7	7	7	7	7	5
Numazu	2	1	5	4	2	5	7	7	8	6	7	7
Mishima	2	1	1	2	2	2	3	3	7	3	4	5
Fuji	2	2	3	3	2	2	3	3	3	3	7	3
Fujinomiya	4	3	3	3	2	3	3	3	3	3	5	3
Gotenba	6	2	2	2	2	3	8	3	3	3	5	5
Susono	5	3	3	2	2	2	3	3	8	6	5	7
Oyama	5	5	5	5	5	5	7	7	7	6	5	7
Nagaizumi	5	2	2	3	2	1	3	3	3	3	2	3
Shimizu	5	2	2	1	2	2	3	3	3	3	2	3
Kannami	5	3	3	3	3	2	3	3	3	6	5	4
Shizuoka	2	4	5	5	5	5	5	7	8	6	7	3
Yaizu	5	3	3	3	3	3	3	3	3	6	7	3

(continued)

Table 3.2 (continued)

City, Town	1960–65	1965–70	1970–75	1975–80	1980–85	1985–90	1990–95	1995–00	2000–05	2005–10	2010–15	2015–20
Fujieda	6	3	3	3	3	3	3	3	3	6	3	4
Shimada	1	3	6	6	8	6	6	6	3	6	7	7
Makinohara	7	3	6	3	6	6	6	3	3	6	7	7
Yoshida	5	3	3	3	3	3	3	3	3	3	3	3
Kawanehoncho	8	6	8	8	8	8	7	7	7	8	7	7
Iwata	5	3	3	3	3	3	3	3	3	8	3	3
Kakegawa	7	3	6	3	3	3	3	3	3	6	3	6
Fukuroi	3	3	3	3	3	3	3	3	3	3	3	3
Omaezaki	7	6	6	3	3	6	6	3	6	6	7	7
Kikukawa	7	3	6	6	6	3	3	3	3	6	3	3
Mori	5	6	6	8	7	6	6	6	6	6	7	7
Hamamatsu	4	2	8	3	3	7	3	3	3	8	2	3
Kosai	5	2	6	3	3	3	6	6	6	6	8	6

Source Compiled by the author with data from National Population Census

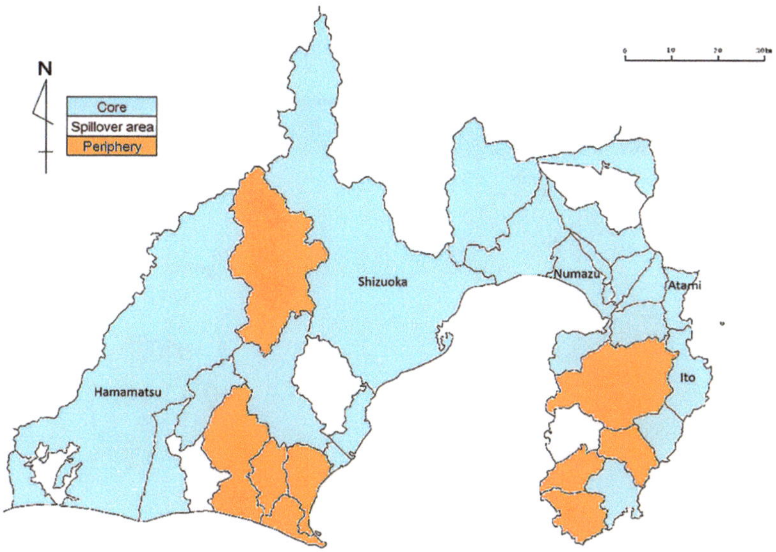

Fig. 3.4 Classification of cities and towns in Shizuoka Prefecture (1960–1965)

Prefecture. Shizuoka Prefecture is the center of Japan's green tea production and tuna fishing, but areas whose primary industries are agriculture or fisheries have shifted to the periphery.

Figure 3.5 illustrates Shizuoka Prefecture during the bubble economy period (1985–1991). The manufacturing industry in Hamamatsu City struggled with a slump in exports due to the rapid appreciation of the yen. However, the holiday resorts on the eastern side of the Izu Peninsula were busy. Ample funds in the bubble economy flowed into land and stocks but were also invested in golf course development, creating a golf boom. Not only people who take a hot spring cure, but also golfers from Tokyo, visited the Izu Peninsula.

Figure 3.6 shows the distribution in the 1990s. Against the backdrop of the manufacturing slump during the bubble economy, the negative value of the proportional shift began to exceed the positive value of the differential shift, and the core areas of economic growth were shrinking. Due to a severe shortage of unskilled labor in the manufacturing industry, Hamamatsu City led the nationwide in hiring foreign workers (initially Japanese-Brazilians).

During the bubble economy, manufacturing industries considered relocation. This nationwide trend led to population decline in Numazu City, the first case driven by the relocation and closure of factories in the Prefecture. However, the southern areas of the Izu Peninsula were experiencing a different trend—a significant boom in tourism development which, in turn, further developed the service sector.

Shizuoka City regulated the establishment of large retail stores through the "Shizuoka Method" of the Large-Scale Store Law, which effectively regulated the establishment of large stores, and the "City Store Establishment Guidelines," which

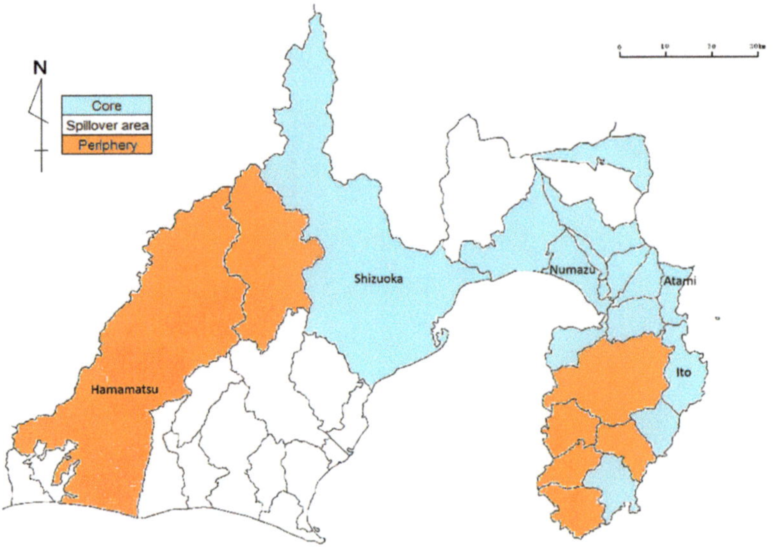

Fig. 3.5 Classification of cities and towns in Shizuoka Prefecture (1985–1990)

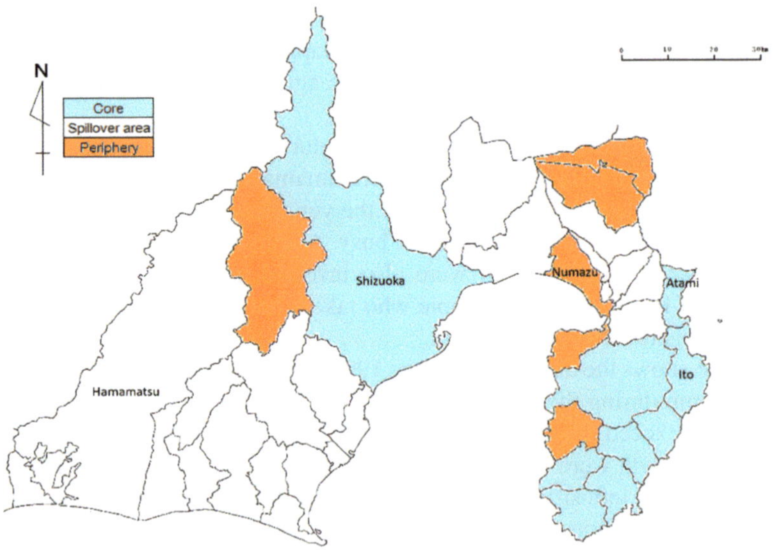

Fig. 3.6 Classification of cities and towns in Shizuoka Prefecture (1990–1995)

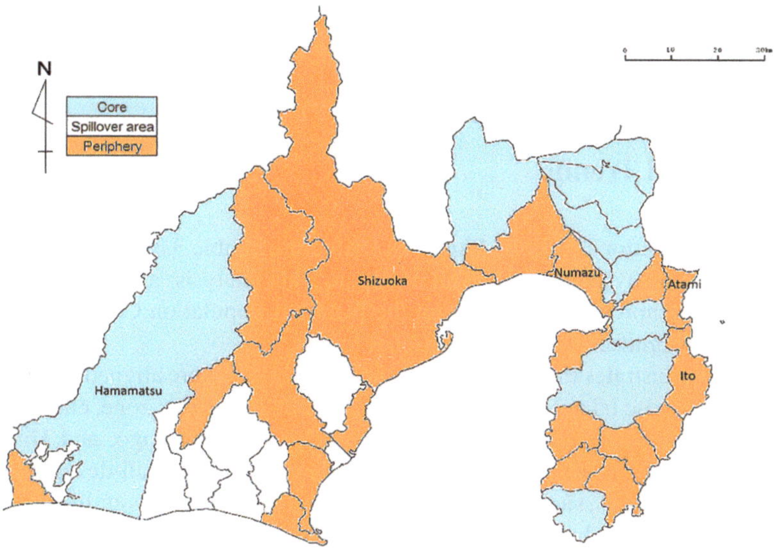

Fig. 3.7 Classification of cities and towns in Shizuoka Prefecture (2010–2015)

regulated the establishment of national chains, including convenience stores, until the mid-1990s. The impact of these regulations was evident. Shizuoka City was characterized by its many small and medium-sized retail stores and micro-retail stores and was famous for its high consumer prices (Yamashita et al., 2000).

There was a significant change from 2010 to 2015 (Fig. 3.7). The population leaving Shizuoka Prefecture started to exceed the population moving in. Shizuoka City, the capital of the Prefecture, is no exception, and in 2016, the number of people moving out of the city exceeded the number of people moving in.

Hamamatsu City, a manufacturing center, has returned to its core position. However, there were factory move-outs, such as Honda Motor Co.'s withdrawal from motorcycle production (2008) and Yamaha Corporation's relocation of its grand piano factory from Hamamatsu City to Kakegawa City (2009).

In Atami City, one of Japan's three major hot spring resorts, the local economy is declining due to a decrease in tourists. Several years later, COVID-19 caused further losses to tourist destinations in the Izu Peninsula, but the decline in tourist numbers had already begun before it. Despite the Japanese government's policy of promoting tourism, traditional hot spring tourism may not be attracting inbound demand. The slump in tourism revenue is facing residents to leave the area, creating a vicious cycle of labor shortages in the tourism industry.[6]

[6] The author has identified a concerning trend in the Izu Peninsula of Shizuoka Prefecture. A downward trajectory in tourism revenues, attributed to an ongoing labor shortage, could have significant long-term consequences for the region's economy and development (see Appendix). The neighboring hot spring resorts of Yugawara and Hakone in Kanagawa Prefecture are also experiencing a similar trend.

In this way, a regional economy has developed through the exchange of products and the movement of labor between regions (and sometimes overseas).

3.4 National Trends

Is the above transition unique to Shizuoka Prefecture? Table 3.3 shows the results of the shift-share analysis applied to all of Japan. This analysis, a robust method that relies on the comprehensive data from the National Population Census, provides a reliable and insightful overview of national trends.

Figure 3.8 illustrates that in the 1960s, the core regions were aligned on the Pacific side of the Japanese Islands, forming the Pacific Belt Zone. This zone, encompassing Tokyo Metropolitan, Kanagawa, Shizuoka, Aichi, Osaka, Hyogo, and Hiroshima prefectures, was a key driver of Japan's economic growth. The well-developed transportation and facilities, such as railroads, roads, and ports, led to a significant concentration of approximately 60% of the population and 70% of industrial shipments in the zone, underscoring its economic importance. By concentrating heavy chemical industries in these areas, the zone made a significant contribution to Japan's high economic growth.

The industrial composition of a regional economy is better understood using the "location quotient." A regional location quotient is given as

$$LQ_i = \frac{e_i/\sum e_i}{E_i/E}$$

Tokyo Metropolitan, Kanagawa, Shizuoka, Aichi, Osaka, Hyogo, and Hiroshima prefectures have LQs greater than 1 for the manufacturing industry. An LQ greater than 1 implies a greater than national average concentration of employment. Kanagawa, Shizuoka, Aichi, and Hiroshima Prefectures are automobile manufacturing bases: Nissan Motor Corporation in Kanagawa Prefecture, Toyota Motor Corporation in Aichi Prefecture, Suzuki Motor Corporation in Shizuoka Prefecture, and Mazda Motor Corporation in Hiroshima Prefecture.

However, during the bubble economy, the manufacturing industry suffered from sluggish exports due to the strong yen. Shizuoka Prefecture and Hiroshima Prefecture lost their power as drivers of economic growth (Fig. 3.9). In their place, Saitama Prefecture and Chiba Prefecture, which promoted urban planning as suburbs of Tokyo, joined the core by attracting companies and workers, forming the "Greater Tokyo Area" with an LQ of over 1.24 in the real estate industry. A significant outcome of this was the concentration of approximately 21% of the population in the Greater Tokyo Area, underscoring the demographic impact of the economic changes.

The bubble economy came to an end in 1991. The bubble period, characterized by asset price inflation, had led to pronounced asset income inequality and wage

Table 3.3 National trends

Prefecture	1960–65	1965–70	1970–75	1975–80	1980–85	1985–90	1990–95	1995–2000	2000–05	2005–10	2010–15	2015–20
Hokkaido	6	8	4	4	7	7	4	5	5	5	7	7
Aomori	6	6	6	6	8	8	8	7	7	8	7	7
Iwate	8	6	6	6	8	8	8	7	7	8	2	5
Miyagi	6	3	3	3	3	3	3	7	7	6	3	1
Akita	8	6	6	6	8	8	7	7	7	8	5	5
Yamagata	8	6	6	6	8	8	8	7	8	8	2	5
Fukushima	8	6	6	6	8	8	8	7	8	8	5	7
Ibaraki	6	6	3	3	3	3	3	3	6	3	6	7
Tochigi	6	3	3	3	3	3	6	3	3	6	6	7
Gunma	6	6	6	3	6	3	6	3	3	6	2	2
Saitama	3	2	2	2	2	2	2	2	2	1	3	8
Chiba	3	3	3	3	2	2	2	1	2	4	3	2
Tokyo	4	5	5	5	4	5	5	5	5	4	7	3
Kanagawa	2	2	1	1	2	2	1	4	2	5	2	2
Niigata	8	6	6	8	7	7	8	8	6	6	5	5
Toyama	7	8	8	7	7	7	6	6	6	6	5	5
Ishikawa	7	7	7	2	5	5	3	7	8	3	5	5
Fukui	7	7	8	8	7	7	7	6	6	6	4	1
Yamanashi	7	6	6	6	3	6	3	3	6	8	5	5
Nagano	8	6	6	6	6	8	6	3	6	6	5	7
Gifu	7	8	8	3	7	7	6	3	3	6	2	5
Shizuoka	4	2	3	3	3	3	6	3	3	6	5	5

(continued)

Table 3.3 (continued)

Prefecture	1960–65	1965–70	1970–75	1975–80	1980–85	1985–90	1990–95	1995–2000	2000–05	2005–10	2010–15	2015–20
Aichi	1	4	2	1	1	2	3	3	3	3	3	3
Mie	8	8	8	8	3	6	3	8	3	3	7	7
Shiga	8	6	6	3	3	3	3	3	3	3	4	4
Kyoto	4	5	5	5	5	5	5	5	4	4	5	5
Osaka	1	4	5	5	4	5	5	5	5	5	4	5
Hyogo	1	4	5	5	5	4	5	2	1	4	5	5
Nara	5	3	2	2	2	2	2	4	5	5	4	5
Wakayama	7	7	7	7	7	7	6	7	7	7	5	5
Tottori	8	6	6	6	7	7	8	6	7	8	7	5
Shimane	8	8	8	6	7	7	7	8	7	6	5	5
Okayama	8	6	8	7	7	7	6	8	3	6	5	7
Hiroshima	5	2	5	5	5	7	3	7	2	8	2	1
Yamaguchi	7	7	7	7	7	7	7	7	7	8	2	5
Tokushima	7	6	8	6	7	7	7	7	5	7	5	5
Kagawa	7	6	8	8	7	7	6	8	7	8	5	4
Ehime	8	8	8	6	7	7	8	8	7	6	5	5
Kochi	8	8	8	6	7	7	7	7	7	7	5	5
Fukuoka	5	5	4	4	5	5	1	1	1	2	2	2
Saga	8	6	8	3	7	8	6	6	3	6	2	5
Nagasaki	7	8	7	8	7	7	5	7	5	6	4	5
Kumamoto	8	8	6	3	8	8	8	3	2	6	2	4
Oita	8	8	6	6	7	7	7	8	3	6	4	7

(continued)

Table 3.3 (continued)

Prefecture	1960–65	1965–70	1970–75	1975–80	1980–85	1985–90	1990–95	1995–2000	2000–05	2005–10	2010–15	2015–20
Miyazaki	8	6	6	3	8	8	6	6	7	6	5	5
Kagoshima	8	8	6	3	8	7	8	3	4	6	5	4
Okinawa	—	—	2	2	3	2	4	2	2	3	2	1

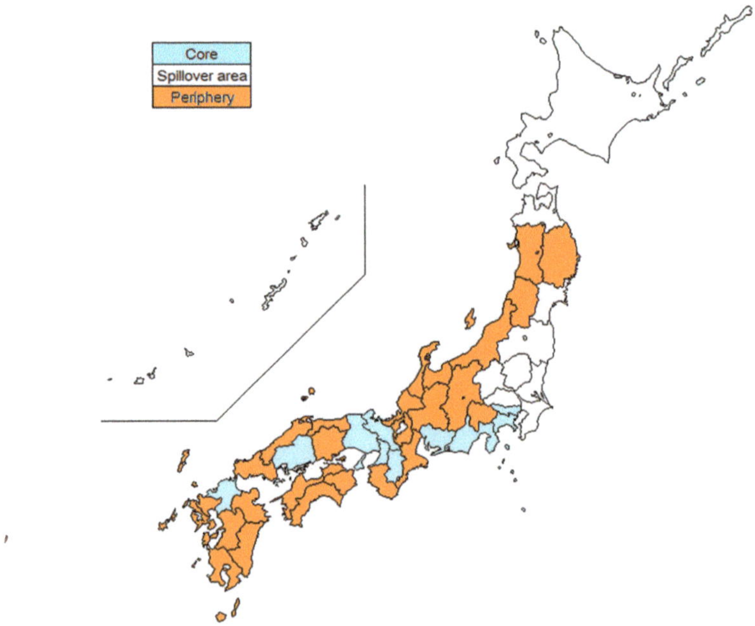

Fig. 3.8 Classification of prefectures (1960–65)

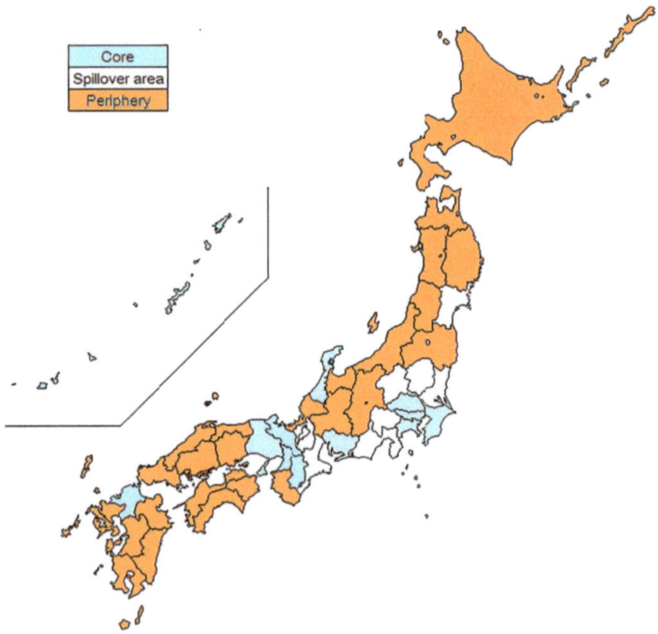

Fig. 3.9 Classification of Prefectures (1985–90)

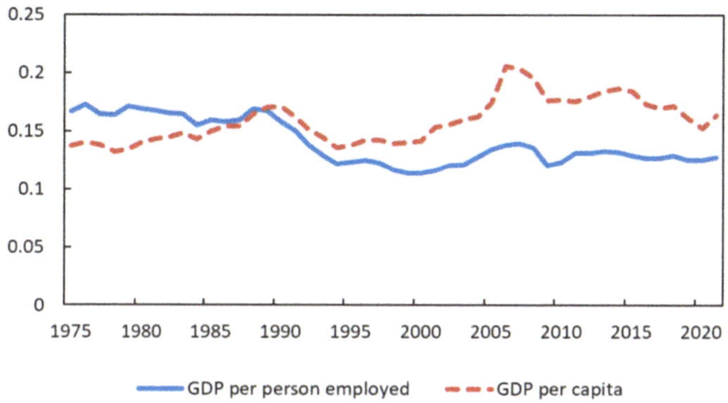

Fig. 3.10 Coefficient of variation in income. *Source* Compiled by the author with data from Economic and Social Research Institute, *Prefectural Accounts*

disparities between the financial and manufacturing sectors. This economic situation sparked concerns about the widening income gap. Figure 3.10 presents the coefficient of variation in prefectural GDP per capita from fiscal year1975 to fiscal year 2021.[7] This measure of income inequality reveals a troubling trend. Since the 1980s, income inequality, gauged by per capita GDP, has stubbornly persisted, remaining unresolved.

In contrast, per capita income inequality, measured by prefectural GDP per person employed, exhibited a narrowing trend, with large and small waves of expansion and contraction. It declined from 0.158 to 0.123 between 1990 and 1995. One reason is that the recession's impact in metropolitan areas was greater than in rural areas, and the income gap between farming families and city dwellers decreased.

Additionally, changes in the industrial structure of rural areas played a role. In the 1990s, an increasing number of agricultural prefectures began to transition away from their peripheral regions (Fig. 3.11). Aichi Prefecture, home to Toyota Motor Corporation, one of Japan's largest corporations, fell out of the core. This shifting coincides with a period when outward foreign direct investment to ASEAN and the People's Republic of China increased, and signs of domestic manufacturing hollowing out became apparent.[8]

Figure 3.12 shows the current situation.[9] The national economy has been improving. However, many core prefectures are Type 5, experiencing low growth due to regional factors.

A notable trend is the decline of the "Greater Tokyo Area". Employment in the wholesale and retail trade decreased significantly. While Kanagawa Prefecture

---

[7] Prefectural accounts are based on fiscal-year data. Japan's fiscal year begins on April 1 and ends on March 31 of the following year.

[8] Since 1972, the relaxation of Japan's FDI regulations has contributed to the rapid growth of Japanese corporate FDI into ASEAN and China (Ikeo, 2017, p. 202).

[9] The period from 2010 to 2015 is examined because from 2015 to 2020 includes the impact of COVID-19 pandemic.

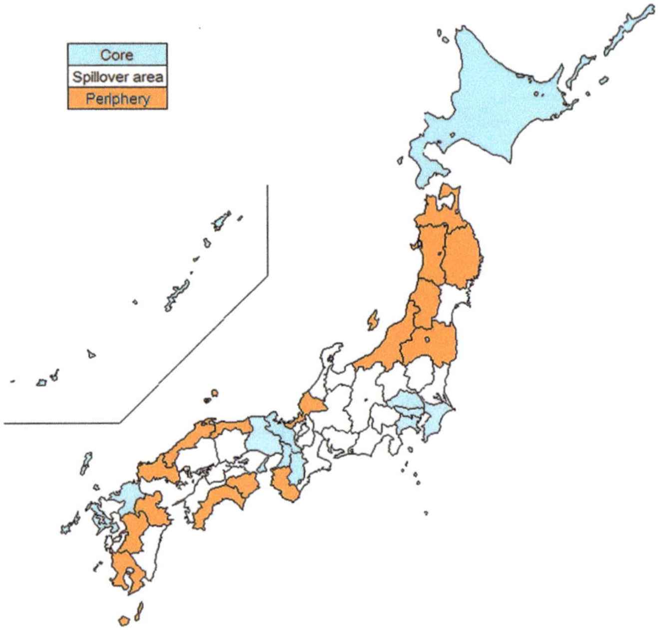

Fig. 3.11 Classification of prefectures (1990–1995)

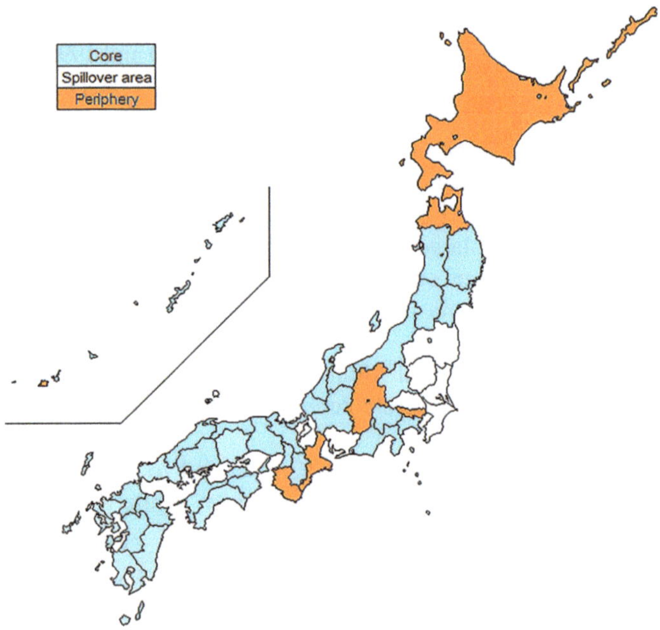

Fig. 3.12 Classification of prefectures (2010–15)

remains a core area, parts of the prefecture are showing signs of stagnation, including the closure of automobile factories and an economic downturn in the Hakone region, one of Japan's leading hot spring resorts.

3.5 Productivity

In the shift-share analysis presented in the previous section, the trend in Japan's economic growth is examined by analyzing changes in the number of employees in across regions. The distribution of employees across industries corresponds to changes in demand. However, whether it is possible to supply products that meet the demand depends on the level of technology that effectively utilizes labor and capital. In this section, production activities are analyzed from the perspective of supply capacity.

Assuming the Cobb-Douglas production function, the author performs regression analysis under a time-series framework. The production factors are capital (K) and labor (L). The production function is augmented with a trend term $e^{\gamma t}$, setting γ as the rate of technical progress ($t = 0, 1, 2, \ldots$). This time series framework is crucial for our comprehensive understanding of the economic growth trend.

$$Y = T_0 e^{\gamma t} K^{\alpha} L^{1-\alpha} \tag{3.4}$$

where T_0 is the initial total factor productivity and α is the share of capital. Eq. (3.4) can be divided by L.

$$\frac{Y}{L} = T_0 e^{\gamma t} \left(\frac{K}{L}\right)^{\alpha}$$

Therefore, regional disparities in labor productivity growth per labor can be attributed to differences in the rate of technical progress and in the growth of the capital-labor ratio. When expressed in logarithmic form, this is written as follows.

$$\log\left(\frac{Y}{L}\right) = \log T_0 + \gamma t + \alpha \log\left(\frac{K}{L}\right) \tag{3.5}$$

The estimation results using data from 1980 to 2020 are shown in Table 3.4.[10] The results of the ordinary least squares method are all significant. These results, obtained using ordinary least squares, are not just significant but crucial to our understanding of regional labor productivity disparities.

---

[10] The capital stock used in the estimation is the Private-sector Capital Stock by Prefecture (in the 2000 calendar year prices, based on the National Accounts, as of March 2011) converted to the 2015 calendar year prices and extended to 2020 using the benchmark year method.

Table 3.4 Estimations of the Cobb–Douglas production function (1980–2020)

Prefecture	$\log T_0$	γ	Prefecture	$\log T_0$	γ
Hokkaido	1.361055	0.015217	Shiga	1.510675	0.014224
Aomori	1.095554	0.016752	Kyoto	1.355813	0.007196
Iwate	1.082724	0.017435	Osaka	1.480012	0.011167
Miyagi	1.344678	0.013448	Hyogo	1.424782	0.014767
Akita	1.098411	0.016499	Nara	1.373749	0.011174
Yamagata	1.216675	0.015938	Wakayama	1.212070	0.019014
Fukushima	1.194166	0.015595	Tottori	1.061650	0.013257
Ibaraki	1.407029	0.017791	Shimane	0.942308	0.019909
Tochigi	1.461133	0.015327	Okayama	1.473657	0.011755
Gunma	1.352178	0.016906	Hiroshima	1.367939	0.014535
Saitama	1.437381	0.012190	Yamaguchi	1.287017	0.019973
Chiba	1.291326	0.014949	Tokushima	1.109641	0.024554
Tokyo	1.601350	0.017517	Kagawa	1.188952	0.016662
Kanagawa	1.509693	0.011606	Ehime	1.050168	0.018157
Niigata	1.173624	0.015896	Kochi	1.056130	0.017475
Toyama	1.320189	0.015892	Fukuoka	1.361329	0.012854
Ishikawa	1.213994	0.015024	Saga	1.170654	0.014793
Fukui	1.197563	0.017846	Nagasaki	1.151592	0.015267
Yamanashi	1.254434	0.017058	Kumamoto	1.200103	0.014995
Nagano	1.215179	0.015983	Oita	1.215752	0.016469
Gifu	1.292417	0.013940	Miyazaki	0.982121	0.018758
Shizuoka	1.365694	0.017313	Kagoshima	1.037403	0.018143
Aichi	1.509921	0.015892	Okinawa	1.254971	0.010182
Mie	1.352897	0.019003	All pref.	1.393029	0.015289

Source Economic and Social Research Institute, *Prefectural Accounts*. *Note* All coefficients are significant at the 99% level.

If other things are equal, employees prefer to be employed in an industry with higher wages. Real wages will increase in tandem with labor productivity. If the labor distribution is kept constant, technical progress increases labor productivity. The following five prefectures show increases in both the rate of technical progress and the number of employed persons that were higher than the national average from 1980 to 2020 (Fig. 3.13).

Technical progress typically leads to labor-saving production. During the observation period, a negative correlation coefficient of −0.48 was observed between the growth rate of the number of employed persons and the rate of technical progress. Only four prefectures—Tochigi, Ibaraki, Aichi, and Mie—had growth rates for both the number of employed persons and the rate of technical progress that exceeded the national average. The basic industries (industries with the highest LQ) in Aichi

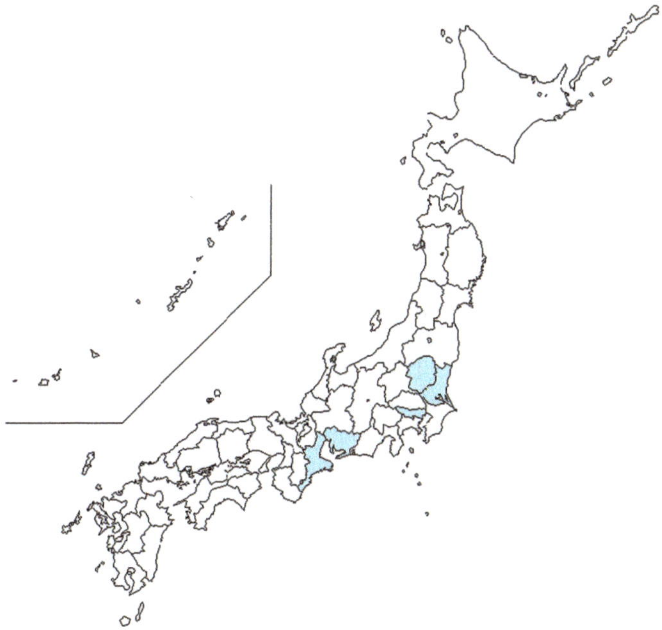

Fig. 3.13 Prefectures with labor growth and technical progress

and Mie Prefectures are manufacturing, and improvements in technical progress support non-basic industries that supply intermediate goods and services to primary industries or provide for the livelihoods of residents within the region.[11] However, the most striking transitions were in Tochigi and Ibaraki Prefectures, which were once agricultural regions that successfully transitioned to manufacturing during the high-growth era and the bubble economy.

3.6 Conclusion

Shift share analysis reveals the growth and decline of industries at both the prefectural and national levels. During the period of high economic growth, manufacturing led the Japanese economy. However, the bubble economy altered domestic demand, and as the supply side responded to these changes, the country's industrial structure transformed. Shizuoka Prefecture played a significant role during Japan's period of high economic growth and is a microcosm of the Japanese economy.

[11] The classification into basic industries and non-basic industries was first introduced by Haig (1927).

Since the collapse of the bubble economy, Japan's economy has demonstrated its adaptability. Attention has shifted to creating new industries to replace manufacturing. However, backed by steady technical progress, manufacturing continues to contribute to Japan's economic growth.

Appendix

In recent years, the importance of promoting tourism has grown due to the recognition of the mutual relationship between tourism and economic growth. It is known as the tourism-led growth hypothesis. This hypothesis demonstrated that tourism has a positive impact on national and regional growth, using the conditional convergence hypothesis. Using variables related to tourism as conditioning factors, the following equation is employed to assess the impact of tourism on regional growth and the rate of convergence (Barro & Sala-I-Martin, 2003).

$$\Delta \ln y_{i,t} = \alpha_i + \beta \ln y_{i,t-1} + \gamma \ln X_{i,t} + u_{i,t}$$

Here, y is the per capita gross regional domestic product, X is a variable that explains the differences in the steady states of each region, and u is a random error. The subscript i refers to individual regional economies and t refers to time. α is the steady state, β is the convergence coefficient, and absolute convergence holds when $\beta < 0$ and $\gamma = 0$. As a variable indicating differences in steady states, X is the number of hotel rooms on the supply side of tourism. This variable indicates the capacity to accommodate a larger number of tourists. Soukiazis and Proença (2008) reported that it took on positive values in Portugal.

Following previous studies, let us examine the situation in Japan. The data used is the number of hotel rooms from the "Ryokan and Hotel Operations" section of the Ministry of Health, Labour and Welfare's Health Administration Report. The author adjusted the values related to total production to chained 2015 yen. The category "Food and Accommodation Services" first appeared in the "Prefectural Gross Domestic Product" section of the report starting from the 2006 edition. Therefore, the author created a panel dataset covering the 14 years from 2006 to 2020 for all 47 prefectures. Table A.1 shows the results of the fixed-effects model selected by the Hausman test. The values in parentheses are the t-statistics.

Table A.1 presents intriguing findings. The coefficient γ, which represents the number of hotel rooms, a key indicator of the tourism sector's supply capacity, is negatively signed. A negative sign suggests that an oversupply of hotel rooms may be detrimental to the per capita regional gross domestic product in Japan. This finding not only contributes to the academic discourse on regional development and tourism studies but also has practical implications for policymakers and industry stakeholders. For the background behind the oversupply of guest rooms in the Izu Peninsula, please refer to Yamashita (2023).

Table A.1 Estimates from the fixed effects model (47 prefectures)

	Absolute convergence	Conditional convergence
α_i	1.1680 (51.24)	1.2100 (40.41)
$\ln(y_{i,\,t-1})$	−0.0203 (−7.349)	−0.0196 (−7.08)
$\ln(X_{i,\,t})$	–	−0.0046 (−2.15)
R^2	0.1043	0.1110
F-statistic	1.51	1.58
Prob(F-statistic)	0.017631	0.008653

Note The number in parentheses is the t-value.

References

Barro, R. J., & Sala-I-Martin, X. I. (2003). *Economic growth* (second ed.). The MIT Press.

Boudeville, J. R. (1966). *Problems of regional economic planning*. Edinburgh University Press.

Creamer, D. (1942). Shifts of manufacturing industries. In *Industrial location and national resources* (pp. 85–104). National Resources Planning Board, United States Government Printing Office.

Dunn, E.S. (1960). A statistical and analytical technique for regional analysis. In *Papers and proceedings of the regional Science Association*, Vol. 6 (pp. 97–112).

Haig, R. M. (1927). Major economic factors in the metropolitan growth and arrangement; A study of trends and tendencies in the economic activities within the region of New York and its environs. *Regional survey of New York City and Its Environs, 1.*

Heijman, W. J. M., & Schipper, R. A. (2010). *Space and economics: An introduction to regional economics*. Wageningen Academic Publishers.

Ikeo, A. (2017). *Globalization ga wakaru (Globalization reconsidered).* Soseisha.

Kobayashi, N. (2004). Industrial structure and manufacturing growth during Japan's bubble and post-bubble economies. *Regional Studies, 38*(4), 429–444.

Ohta, M. (1982). Shift-share bunseki to sono tekiyō (Shift-share analysis and its application). *Kagawa Daigaku Keizai Ronsō (Kagawa University Economic Review), 55*, 127–139.

Soukiazis, E., & Proença, S. (2008). Tourism as an alternative source of regional growth in Portugal: A panel data analysis at NUTS II and III levels. *Portuguese Economic Journal, 7*, 43–61.

Yamashita, T., ed. (2016). *Chiiki keizai bunseki handbook* (Handbook of regional economic analysis). Koyo Shobo.

Yamashita, T., Nogata, H., & Doi, E. (2000). Why is the price level so high in Shizuoka City? A comparative study on the effect of regulations. *Shizuoka Daigaku Keizai Kenkyū (Economic Review, Shizuoka University), 4*(3), 41–52. https://doi.org/10.14945/00001844

Chapter 4
Determinants of Subjective Well-Being of Japanese Consumers

Tamaki Morita

Abstract This chapter examines the subjective well-being of Japanese consumers. Since around the 1980s, subjective well-being (SWB) measures have been adopted as one of the key policy goals by countries and international organizations, alongside traditional macroeconomic indicators like Gross Domestic Product (GDP). SWB is primarily a measure of individual cardinal utility, compensating for the limitations of ordinal utility that have dominated academics in recent years. This study uses three years of survey data collected by the Japanese government and employs a linear mixed-effects model to identify the determinants of SWB in Japan. The findings reveal the following points: individuals lacking community connections tend to experience lower levels of happiness when they feel lonely; men in their 30s and 40s report lower happiness levels; and regionally, happiness is higher in the Kinki and Kyushu/Okinawa regions compared to Hokkaido (used as a baseline for comparison). These results suggest that policies aimed at reducing social isolation within communities are essential in Japan, and further investigation into the regional environment is needed. The SWB measure used in this chapter, as a dependent variable, is included in the analysis of Chap. 5.

Keywords Cardinal utility · Loneliness · Multilevel modeling · Panel data · Social connections · Subjective well-being (SWB)

T. Morita (✉)
Faculty of Aviation Management, J. F. Oberlin University, Tama City, Tokyo, Japan
e-mail: morita_t01@obirin.ac.jp

T. Yamashita and T. Morita (eds.), *On the Structural Transformation of the Japanese Economy 1985-2023*, Advances in Japanese Business and Economics 38,
https://doi.org/10.1007/978-981-95-7230-4_4

4.1 Introduction

4.1.1 Background

Well-being or happiness has been studied by psychologists since the 1930s but has become a significant concern for academics in various fields and politicians in the twenty-first century. As developed countries reach near their steady-state growth rates, people have come to think that countries should be evaluated not only by economic growth rates, which can be measured by Gross Domestic Product (GDP) and other monetary units, but also by each individual's spiritual affluence. Consumers can express their spiritual affluence by responding to questions such as their life satisfaction, i.e., avowed Subjective Well-being (SWB)—the higher the SWB, the higher the consumers' utility. SWB can even be a metric of Utilitarian "greatest happiness principle."[1] In 2012, the University of Oxford's Well-being Research Centre, in partnership with Gallup and the UN Sustainable Development Solutions Network, presented the first World Happiness Report, which has been published annually since then.

According to the recent *World Happiness Report* (Helliwell et al., 2024), Japan's happiness ranking for the 2021–2023 average was 51st among the world's 143 countries and scored 6.06[2] (Fig. 4.1). Finland was first (7.74), the UK was 19th (6.75), and the US was 24th, scoring 6.72.

Among the above four countries excerpted from the rankings, Japan has a relatively high contribution to healthy life expectancy, a relatively low contribution to social support compared to the top country, Finland, and almost equal to the US and UK, but much lower generosity than the other two countries.

4.1.2 A Brief History of Utility and SWB in Economics

Before the marginal revolution of the 1870s, classical economists treated utility in qualitative and ethical terms. Adam Smith (1776) distinguished "value in use" from "value in exchange" (that is, price), but he did not formalize utility. Jeremy Bentham (1789) introduced the utilitarian principle, defining utility as the balance of pleasure

---

[1] The expression of "greatest happiness principle" originates in Bentham (1776).

[2] The World Happiness Report is a partnership of Gallup, the Oxford Well-being Research Centre, the UN Sustainable Development Solutions Network, and the WHR's Editorial Board. The following question's responses are averaged to the score: "The English wording of the question is "Please imagine a ladder, with steps numbered from 0 at the bottom to 10 at the top. The top of the ladder represents the best possible life for you, and the bottom represents the worst possible life for you. On which step of the ladder would you say you personally feel you stand at this time?" This measure is also referred to as Cantril life ladder, or just life ladder in our analysis" (Helliwell et al. 2024, Appendix 1). Then the Cantril life ladder score is explained by six factors—GDP per person, healthy life expectancy, social support, perceived freedom to make life choices, generosity, and perception of corruption.

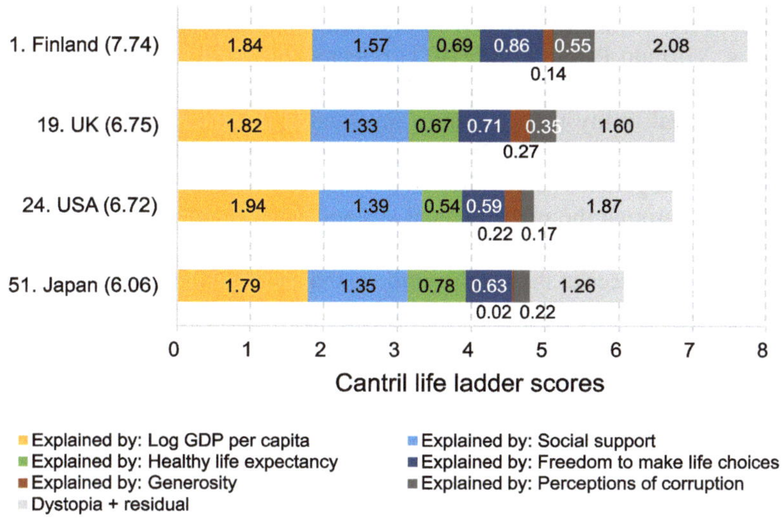

Fig. 4.1 Happiness of Finland, the UK, the US, and Japan. *Source* Excerpted from Helliwell et al. (2024, Fig. 2.1)

over pain, which John Stuart Mill (1863) later refined. Bentham, with consideration that "promoting good" and "preventing bad" are equivalent, defines utility as:

> By utility is meant that property in any object, whereby it tends to produce benefit, advantage, pleasure, good, or happiness, (all this in the present case comes to the same thing) or (what comes again to the same thing) to prevent the happening of mischief, pain, evil, or unhappiness to the party whose interest is considered: if that party be the community in general, then the happiness of the community: if a particular individual, then the happiness of that individual. (Bentham, 1789, Chapter I, Section 3)

Neither Bentham nor Mill treated these concepts as a mathematical model of individual choice, in any case.

In the late nineteenth century, the marginal revolution, led by William Stanley Jevons, Léon Walras, and Carl Menger in the 1870s–1880s, which Alfred Marshall (1890) synthesized, introduced marginal utility as a foundational concept in demand theory, where they treated utility as cardinal, considering that actual measurement was difficult. Armed by the development of "psychophysics" in psychology, Francis Ysidro Edgeworth (1881) proposed a cardinal measurement of utility based on a person's capacity for pleasure (called "hedonimeter"), which would make interpersonal comparison conceptually possible.[3]

When we assumed cardinal utility, some problems arose. Utility was not observable, and the measurement of utility in units was not empirically valid at the time. Interpersonal comparisons had also been philosophically controversial in welfare economics.

[3] See Colander (2007) about Edgeworth's hedonimeter.

Alternatively, in the twentieth century, ordinal utility became mainstream in economics. Vilfredo Pareto (1906/1971) rejected the need for cardinal utility and instead advocated ordinal preferences. The concepts of "indifference" are associated with ordinal utility theory. Pareto invalidated the interpersonal comparisons of utility.[4] Lionel Robbins (1932) argued against using utility for interpersonal or social welfare judgments.[5] John Hicks and R.G.D. Allen (1934) further formalized ordinal utility through the mathematical system of indifference curves, reinforcing Pareto's idea. Marginal Rate of Substitution (MRS) equals the ratio of Marginal Utilities (MU) or prices at the equilibrium, so that demand theory works using only preference order, not utility levels. Utility functions embody preference rankings, not quantities of satisfaction. Thereafter, Paul Samuelson (1938, 1948) introduced the revealed preference approach. It allowed economists to derive preferences from observed behavior, abandoning the use of introspective utility. Samuelson asserted that economic theory could avoid metaphysical concepts of utility entirely. Building on this, Kenneth Arrow (1951) offered a formal axiomatization of rational choice conditioned by asymmetry and negative transitivity.

However, from the 1980s onward, behavioral economics began to challenge the assumptions underlying rational choice. Behavioral economists such as Daniel Kahneman showed that actual choices often violate consistency, due to framing, adaptation, and other cognitive biases (Kahneman & Krueger, 2006; Kahneman & Sugden, 2005; Kahneman et al., 1997). These observations prompted economists to revisit introspective measures of utility.

SWB, i.e., measures of life satisfaction and affective states, emerged as a valuable empirical alternative. Pioneers such as Richard Layard, Kahneman, and others argued that SWB can complement or even replace ordinal utility in some policy applications. Though SWB is treated as cardinal, its empirical robustness and ability to reflect actual welfare result in its increasing use in economics. We discuss the history of SWB in Sect. 4.4.

4.1.3 Structure of the Study

Using the national survey data, we measure the SWB of Japanese consumers and investigate the determinants of their SWB. Past literature suggests that multiple variables contribute to SWB; however, we will focus on how human relationships serve as determinants of SWB and examine the differences among regions, ages, and genders. To reveal this importance, we will use the Cabinet Office (CAO)'s "Well-being Survey and Quality of Life" data from 2022 to 2024.

---

[4] A.C. Pigou (1920) stood in contrast by maintaining cardinal and interpersonally comparable utility. He used this framework to analyze taxation, externalities, and policy evaluation. His approach extended Marshallian economics into welfare theory, giving prominence to cardinal utility's role in applied economics.

[5] Robbins (1932, Chapter VI) explains why there is no way of comparing satisfaction of different people.

Section 4.2 provides an overview of the history and literature of SWB. Section 4.3 explains the data used. Section 4.4 shows the results of three types of estimation methods: annual and pooled ordinary least squares (OLS) analysis (Sect. 4.4.1), panel fixed analysis (Sect. 4.4.2), and linear mixed effects analysis (Sect. 4.4.3).

4.2 Overview of the Literature

Happiness or SWB should be a major objective for a national economic and social policy. The history of eliciting people's SWB is long, and although not empirical in a modern sense, the positive analysis of well-being started in the 1930s (Watson, 1930). The methodology had been developed and tried in small samples in the 1950s (Goldings, 1954), and international comparisons have been conducted on childhood happiness (Barschak, 1951).

The survey-based empirical investigation of nationwide happiness originates in Gurin et al. (1960), who conducted structured interviews concerning happiness with 2460 American adults in 1957. Measurement tools are further developed by Bradburn and Caplovitz (1965) and Cantril (1965). Cantril proposed a self-anchoring scale for life satisfaction by asking, "Please imagine a ladder with steps numbered from 0 at the bottom to 10 at the top. The top of the ladder represents the best possible life for you, and the bottom of the ladder represents the worst possible life for you. On which step of the ladder would you say you personally feel you stand at this time?" This setting is called "Cantril's ladder"[6] and it is to date extensively used worldwide (Gallup World Poll, GWP, and United Nations Sustainable Development Solutions Network, SDSN). Bradburn and Noll (1969) elaborated on Bradburn and Caplovitz (1965) to form the Affect Balance Scale, i.e.:

> The Affect Balance Scale is a multidimensional construct for measuring certain components of quality of life in national and international contexts. It is a 10-item rating Subjective Well-Being Scale including five statements reflecting positive feelings and five statements reflecting negative feelings. The answers to the questions are offered without differentiation in a "yes" or "no" format, and there is no possibility of grading the feelings. (Glatzer & Gulyas, 2014, "Affect Balance Scale")

Wilson (1967) provided a literature survey at the time on self-reported, or avowed, happiness.

Andrews and Withey (1974, 1976) gave empirical bases for measuring perceived quality of life and evaluated multiple indicators. As relationships between income and happiness, hinted by Abramovitz (1959)'s insights that "we must be highly skeptical of the view that long-term changes in the rate of growth of welfare can be gauged

---

[6] Nilsson et al. (2024) revealed that although the Cantril Ladder has been widely used, the interpretation should be cautious because the respondents unconsciously evaluate the ladder with biases. They state that "The Cantril Ladder is arguably the most prominent measure of well-being, but the results suggest caution in its interpretation—the Cantril Ladder's structure appears to influence participants to attend to a more power- and wealth-oriented view of well-being" (p. 14: 2642).

even roughly from changes in the rate of growth of output" (p. 21), Easterlin (1974) raised the Easterlin Paradox. It states that at a point in time, happiness varies directly with income, both among and within nations, but over time, happiness does not trend upward in correspondence with income growth (Easterlin & O'Connor, 2020).

The concept of SWB is noticeably mentioned in the literature by Campbell (1976) and formalized later by Diener. Diener (1984) defined SWB as composed of (1) life satisfaction, (2) positive affect (frequent positive feelings), and (3) negative affect (infrequent negative feelings). Diener also developed and tested a multi-item scale, "Satisfaction With Life Scale (SWLS)[7]" in Diener et al. (1985).

SWB has been added to a measure of the abundance of nations, other than economic indicators. In the same year as Andrews and Withey (1976), the OECD published a progress report on the development of social well-being measurement (OECD, 1976).

At the end of the 1980s, Ryff (1989a) defined six criteria of well-being as: self-acceptance, positive relations with others, autonomy, environmental mastery, purpose in life, and personal growth. Ryff (1989b) noted that research on SWB had previously lacked these important psychological factors and proposed to include these six qualities as key components of well-being. Her inclusion of psychological[8] dimensions has been influential.

SWB's political significance increased over time. Following the fall of the Berlin Wall in November 1989 and the subsequent collapse of the Soviet Union, which occurred after Mikhail Gorbachev's resignation in December 1991, the Paul Lazarsfeld Society in Vienna established the New Democracies Barometer (NDB). This initiative aimed to monitor public responses to political and economic transformations in Central and Eastern Europe through nationwide representative sample surveys conducted first in the autumn of 1991.[9] Following that, four consecutive

[7] Diener et al. (1985) selected the following five items for SWLS items among 48 questions they asked in their survey: (1) In most ways my life is close to my ideal; (2) The conditions of my life are excellent; (3) I am satisfied with my life; (4) So far I have gotten the important things I want in life; and (5) If I could live my life over, I would change almost nothing. The scale common to these five are: 1 = strongly disagree; 2 = disagree; 3 = slightly disagree; 4 = neither agree nor disagree; 5 = slightly agree; 6 = agree; 7 = strongly agree.

[8] Defining hedonic approach as a pursuit of pleasure and the avoidance of pain, which had been the center of studies of well-being until that time, Ryff (1989a, 1989b)'s new approach is often categorized as the Eudaimonic approach, named after Eudaimonia of Aristotle. However, Aristotle's original concepts of Eudaimonia is on realizing the highest human good and what is "realized in the activity of the most divine part of man, functioning in accordance with its proper excellence" (Nagel, 1972, p. 252), as long as it "essentially involves not just the activity of the theoretical intellect, but the full range of human life and action, in accordance with the broader excellences of moral virtue and practical wisdom" (ibid., p. 252). Therefore, we express Ryff's approach as psychological approach.

[9] According to the NDB homepage, the first NDB survey was conducted between November 1991 and January 1992 in the following countries: Bulgaria, Czechoslovakia, Hungary, Poland, Romania, Slovenia, and, for comparison with a democratic market system, Austria. A total of 7,202 people

surveys were conducted between 1993 and 1998. Since they included life satisfaction items, they are later classified as large-scale surveys in the field of happiness studies. Rose and Haerpfer (1994) analyzed the mass response to transformation in post-communist societies, focusing on living standards and evaluations of political systems, using the first and second NDB surveys conducted in autumn 1991 and autumn/winter 1992. The work of Rose et al. (1998) wrapped up all five NDB surveys during 1991 to 1998.

Diener and Suh (1997) indicated that social indicators, SWB measures, and economic indices are needed in unison to understand human quality of life and to make informed policy decisions. With a background of long-term, steady decline in the GDP growth rates among high-income countries (Table 4.1), critics of using GDP as a primary metric and assertions of the need for using multiple metrics, including SWB, have become popular. In the 2000s, Diener suggested creating national accounts of SWB (Diener & Seligman, 2004). Hayo (2007) used the NDB surveys to analyze the determinants of life satisfaction in the transition economies. For forming social policies, Loewenstein and Ubel (2008) insist that the hybrid of one, conventional welfare based on ordinal utility and choice, and another, welfare based on Kahneman's notion of "experience utility,"[10] which is a revival of the original, hedonic conception of utility first proposed by Bentham, is needed. Politically and economically, the importance of SWB indicators rose, but as Frey and Stutzer (2002) describe, economic indicators and SWB indicators cannot be substitutes. The French-led commission on the measurement of economic performance and social progress published a report by Joseph Stiglitz, Amartya Sen, and Jean-Paul Fitoussi (Stiglitz et al., 2009), and it had a large impact on pursuing measures that complement GDP. The authors further studied how GDP overlooks economic inequality or environmental impacts in economic decisions (Fitoussi et al., 2011).

Graham et al. (2018) emphasize that survey-based happiness metrics are "democratic" because they are based on individual responses, not what scholars think influences happiness. They say these metrics also identify important trends in ill-being and mental illness. Being happy not only helps people to engage in productive activities or live vigorously but also promotes environmental protection. Kasser (2017) conducted a literature survey and found that frequent engagement in pro-ecological behaviors positively correlates with personal well-being.

Happiness is multidimensional. When analyzing SWB, we must specify the dimension of SWB under examination. Kahneman and Deaton (2010) separated emotional well-being, which refers to the emotional quality of an individual's everyday experience, from life evaluation, which refers to the thoughts people have about their life when they think about it. Marsh et al. (2020) emphasized the importance of psychological aspects (Ryan & Deci, 2001) to determine SWB. In their

---

were interviewed about household and national economic conditions, their evaluations of the new regime compared to the old Communist regime, as well as their social and demographic characteristics (https://www.cspp.strath.ac.uk/view_itemb7b8.html?id=204, retrieved on September 28, 2025).

[10] The concept of experience utility is not identical to SWB, but it consists of SWB together with cognitive and emotional evaluations.

Table 4.1 Ten-year averages of annual GDP growth rates (%)

	1960s	1970s	1980s	1990s	2000s	2010s	2020s
World	5.28	4.01	3.05	2.82	3.00	3.19	2.39
High-income countries	5.32	3.70	2.94	2.44	1.97	2.12	1.65

Notes

1. Gross domestic product (GDP) here represents the sum of value added by all its producers. Value added is the value of the gross output of producers less the value of intermediate goods and services consumed in production, before accounting for the consumption of fixed capital in production. The United Nations System of National Accounts calls for value added to be valued at either basic prices (excluding net taxes on products) or producer prices (including net taxes on products paid by producers but excluding sales or value added taxes). Both valuations exclude transport charges that are invoiced separately by producers. Total GDP is measured at purchaser prices
2. High-income economies are those in which the 2023 Atlas GNI per capita was more than $14,005
3. 2020s data is the average of 2020–2023

Source Calculated by the author from the data of the World Bank, World Development Indicators

life-course model of well-being derived from the British Cohort Study (BCS70),[11] Layard et al. (2014) assert that adult life satisfaction is directly affected by both adult circumstances and by childhood characteristics.[12]

In econometric analysis, we need to make SWB measures that include: (1) Hedonic: positive and negative feelings (e.g., momentary experiences of happiness or stress); (2) Life evaluations (e.g., life satisfaction); and (3) Eudaimonic[13]: feelings of having a life purpose (Nikolova & Graham, 2022). Our analysis uses CAO data that mainly measures life evaluations and also includes the third factor.

The determinants of SWB have certain tendencies. Individuals with higher income typically have higher SWB in a country. SWB tends to follow a U-shaped trajectory over the life course, with the lowest levels in middle age. Females often report greater life satisfaction than men, though they show emotional fluctuations. Psychological factors and mental health are also important. Lombardo et al. (2018) showed that life satisfaction was strongly associated with self-reported mental health, even after simultaneously considering factors such as income, general health, and gender. The poor self-reported mental health group had a particularly low life satisfaction. Also, human relationships (inverse of loneliness) are often raised (Powdthavee, 2007), and we would like to focus on them. The English Government emphasizes the importance

[11] The 1970 British Cohort Survey, BCS70, collected the information of 17,000 babies born in a single week in 1970. Then there have been ten further surveys of the BCS70 study members, at ages 5, 10, 16, 26, 30, 34, 38, 42, 46, and, in the latest "Life in your early 50s survey," ages 51–54. See BCS70 homepage for detailed information: https://bcs70.info/ (retrieved on August 31, 2025).

[12] Layard et al. (2014) added that even though childhood characteristics affect adult circumstances, their predicting power in adult life-satisfaction is limited.

[13] As noted in footnote 8, the category can be better described as "psychological" rather than "Eudaimonic."

of human relationships in a publication, *A Connected Society: A Strategy for tackling loneliness, Laying the foundations for change* (Department for Digital, Culture, Media and Sport, 2018). The Office for National Statistics has highlighted the importance of social support, connections, and relationships in measuring national and personal well-being.

Although life-course models such as those of Layard et al. (2014) and Giuntella et al. (2023) are ideal, we utilize Japan's national annual survey, which the Cabinet Office conducted for three years.

4.3 Overview of the Data

(1) The Surveys

Table 4.2 summarizes the "Survey on Satisfaction and Quality of Life" of the Cabinet Office. Although the survey has been conducted yearly since 2019, we only use the last three years (2022–2024) because psychological questions were introduced in 2022.

(2) Latent Components of SWB

The question that measures SWB comes first (Q1) in every survey as:

> Q1. How satisfied are you with your life as a whole? If "not satisfied at all" is 0 points and "very satisfied" is 10 points, what score would you give?[14]

Additionally, questions about the satisfaction of the following thirteen subjects are asked with the same 11-point scale:

- Household finances and assets
- Employment and wages
- Housing
- Work-life balance
- Health
- Your educational level and environment
- Social connections, such as friendships and communities
- Trust in politics, governments, and the judiciary
- Natural environments around you, such as air and water
- Safety in your surroundings
- Ease of child-raising
- Ease of nursing care
- Enjoyment and interests in life.

[14] The original message is in Japanese. The English translation is made by the author.

Table 4.2 Survey information

Purpose	To investigate overall subjective satisfaction and satisfaction by category and clarify the relationship with objective indicators
Survey method	Internet survey
Target	Internet-panel-registered monitors living in Japan aged 15–89
Number of targets	Approximately 10,000 people each year
Number of valid responses	Total: 31,883 Yearly respondents: 10,631 (2022), 10,619 (2023), 10,633 (2024) Past respondents: 4948 (2022 & 2023), 1322 (2022 & 2024), 3598 (2023 & 2024), 11,241 (all years) Single-year respondents: 3749 (2022), 2599 (2023), 4426 (2024), (10,774 in total)
Allocation of monitors	Stratified by prefecture, gender, and age group
Survey period	Thursday, February 10, 2022–Friday, February 25, 2022 Friday, February 10, 2023–Sunday, March 5, 2023 Friday, February 2, 2024–Wednesday, February 28, 2024
Survey content	• Overall subjective satisfaction • Categories that affect overall subjective satisfaction (important category for respondents) • Subjective satisfaction by category • Future concerns by category (sustainability) • Categories that are important for overall subjective satisfaction • Demographics and living conditions

Source Cabinet Office (2022, 2023, 2024)

Although these indices can be aggregated or made into composite variables as another variable of SWB, we select only Q1 as representative of SWB for this study. So, the variable *SWB* here is the response to Q1.

Using the Shapley decomposition,[15] we briefly check the contribution of these thirteen subquestions in Fig. 4.2. The percentage points in the figure are the contributions that each subsubject explains to the independent variable, *SWB*. We also show the contributions by gender (male and female percentage points are not displayed).

(3) **SWB Distributions**

The three-year overall satisfaction, SWB, is in Fig. 4.3. The averages are not statistically different between 2022 and 2023, but 2024 is significantly higher than either 2022 or 2023. Compared to the normal density curves, "7" and "8" have relatively high density.

(4) **SWB by Gender**

[15] The Shapley value is a mathematical tool from game theory that allocates payoffs fairly (Shapley, 1953). It evaluates the marginal contribution of a predictor by considering all possible subsets of predictors and how their inclusion changes the model's performance. This ensures a fair allocation of variance, even if predictors are correlated. See Shorrocks (2013) for a mathematical explanation.

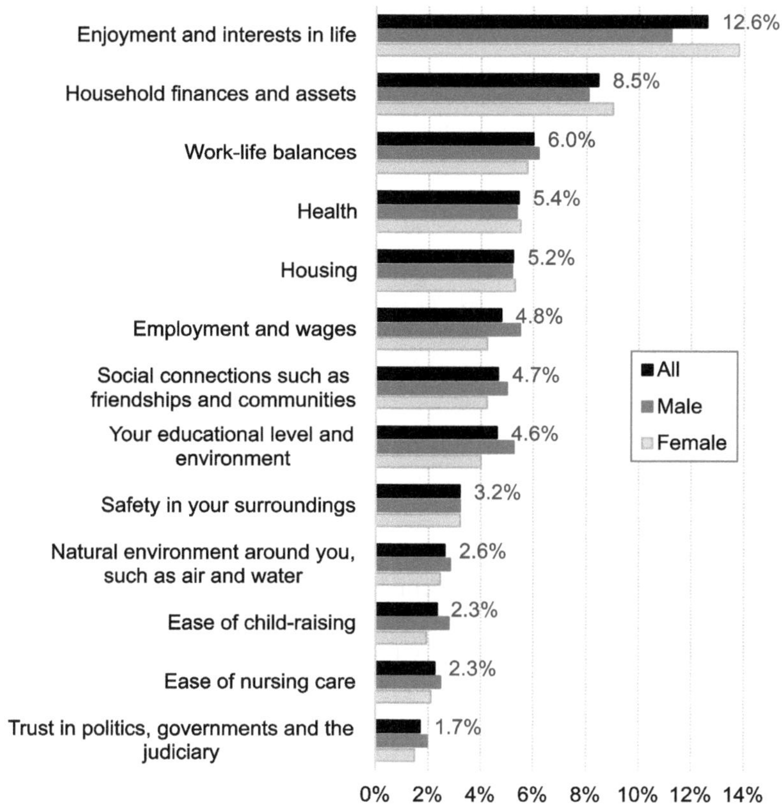

Fig. 4.2 Contributions of subquestions to SWB (Shapley value). *Note* $N = 31{,}883$, controlled with the year dummies (the years' contributions are not displayed because the effect was less than 0.01%). The sum of listed contributions for SWB is 63.95% for all respondents, 65.20% for males, and 63.03% for females

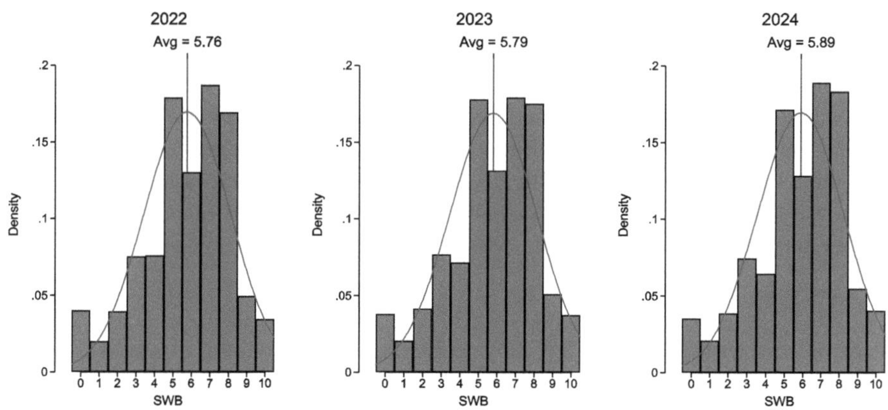

Fig. 4.3 Histogram of SWB scaled from 0 to 10. *Note* A normal density curve is added to each graph. *Source* The Cabinet Office and authors

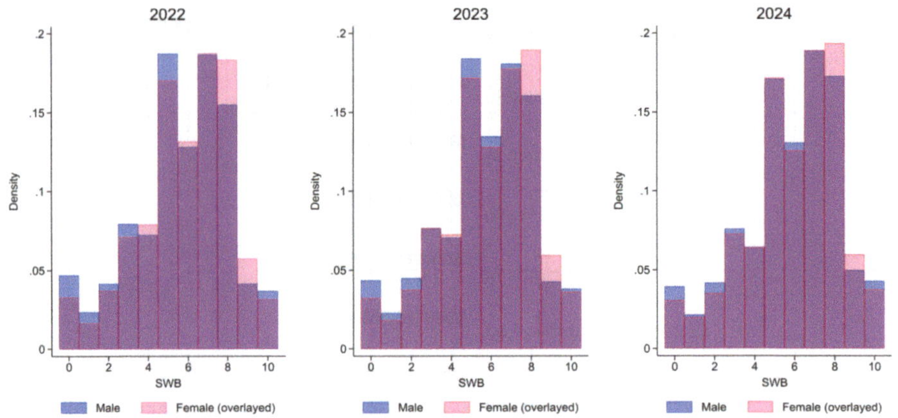

Fig. 4.4 Histogram of SWB by gender. *Note* The Purple area is common to both sexes. *Source* The Cabinet Office and authors

Let us compare the distributions of SWB by gender. Figure 4.4 is the histogram of SWB by gender. Blue is male, pink is female, and the purple overlaid area is common to both genders. Females tend to report higher SWB or feel happiness more strongly than males. Males mainly contributed to the overall improvement observed in 2024. The averages for the years 2022, 2023, 2024 of males were 5.63, 5.67, 5.81, and 2024 for males was statistically higher than the other two years. Female averages were 5.88, 5.90, 5.96, and the data between 2022 and 2024 did not show a statistical difference. The gender gap, in which female respondents report higher SWB than males, is widely observed (see Sect. 4.2).

As for the gender gaps, Montgomery (2022) shows that the gap is consistent with women and men systematically using different response scales and that once these scales have been normalized, women appear less happy than men on average. The possibility is observed in our study (Fig. 4.5). We found that, assuming lifestyle differences affect the scale, comparing the SWB of regularly employed persons showed specific results. The average SWB of the male regular worker is 5.81, and that of the female is 5.92, but they are not statistically different. Others' SWBs were 5.82 vs. 5.98, and the female average SWB was higher than the male SWB. Whether working as regular workers, although women's working regularly (5.92) is lower than others (5.98), they are statistically not different. However, Fig. 4.5 shows that the density of those responding to 3 and 4 is higher than that of other professions and the unemployed.

(5) **SWB by Prefecture**

To examine the differences in SWB by prefecture, we present three-year averages of SWB by prefecture ($N = 31{,}833$). The SWB scores and rankings are in Table 4.3; the score map is in Fig. 4.6. The average SWB for all regions is 5.811.

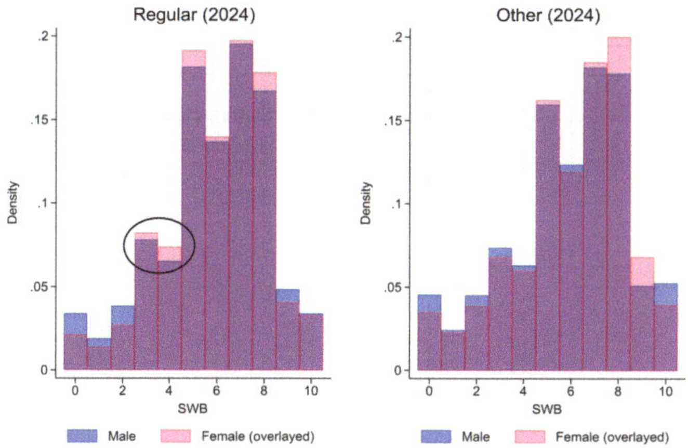

Fig. 4.5 Histogram of SWB by gender, regular workers, and others. *Note* The Purple area is common to both sexes. *Source* The Cabinet Office and authors

The top prefecture, Hyogo, is in the Kinki region, comprising Mie (6th) and Osaka (5th), and the region has a relatively high SWB. Generally, the Tohoku region has lower values of SWB. Those living in metropolitan Tokyo do not show the best SWB, although its SWB is higher than the average (5.911 > 5.811). We should note that these numbers are statistically insignificant and subject to change depending on the selection of respondents. Statistically, the highest group of Hyogo, Ooita, and Miyazaki (first to third) is higher than the lowest group of Akita, Aomori, and Iwate (47th to 45th). Other prefectures are transitional because they overlap with either one or both groups at 5% significance level. The relationship is not guaranteed to persist and should be revisited as new data or changing conditions emerge.

(6) **K6 and Loneliness**

The questions about the psychological aspects of happiness have been adopted in the CAO survey since 2022. Although some questions were abandoned, the K6 questions and those about loneliness and close colleagues remained for three consecutive years.

K6 scales are a set of six questions that were developed by Ronald C. Kessler, with support from the US government's National Center for Health Statistics, for use in the redesigned US National Health Interview Survey (NHIS) to measure psychological distress (Kessler et al., 2002). Its feasibility is widely investigated and ensured by researchers including Furukawa et al., (2003, 2008), Kessler et al., (2003, 2010), Green et al. (2010), Sunderland et al. (2012), Mewton et al. (2016), Lace et al. (2020), and Carter et al. (2024).

The questions ask about the frequency of having the following feelings[16]:

During the past 30 days, how often did you feel nervous?
During the past 30 days, how often did you feel hopeless?

[16] The questionnaire can be accessed at Harvard Medical School's National Comorbidity Survey Website (https://www.hcp.med.harvard.edu/ncs/k6_scales.php) as of 2025/1/12.

Table 4.3 Average SWB by region and prefecture

Region	Prefecture	**SWB**	Rank
Hokkaido	Hokkaido	5.664	41
Tohoku	Aomori	5.464	46
	Iwate	5.513	45
	Miyagi	5.682	38
	Akita	5.417	47
	Yamagata	5.579	42
	Fukushima	5.683	37
Kanto	Ibaraki	5.758	27
	Tochigi	5.870	19
	Gunma	5.534	44
	Saitama	5.915	13
	Chiba	5.950	10
	Tokyo	5.911	15
	Kanagawa	5.732	31
Chubu	Niigata	5.784	26
	Toyama	5.678	39
	Ishikawa	5.706	34
	Fukui	5.664	40
	Yamanashi	5.961	7
	Nagano	5.836	25
	Gifu	5.953	8
	Shizuoka	5.842	21
	Aichi	6.035	4
Kinki	Mie	5.965	6
	Shiga	5.913	14
	Kyoto	5.846	20
	Osaka	5.969	5
	Hyogo	6.182	1
	Nara	5.895	17
	Wakayama	5.737	29
Chugoku	Tottori	5.565	43
	Shimane	5.692	36
	Okayama	5.841	23
	Hiroshima	5.752	28
	Yamaguchi	5.842	22
Shikoku	Tokushima	5.728	32
	Kagawa	5.701	35
	Ehime	5.736	30
	Kochi	5.882	18
Kyushu & Okinawa	Fukuoka	5.952	9
	Saga	5.838	24
	Nagasaki	5.715	33
	Kumamoto	5.942	12
	Oita	6.128	2
	Miyazaki	6.075	3
	Kagoshima	5.91	16
	Okinawa	5.95	11

Note The average SWB is the average of all respondents for the three years 2022–2024 ($N = 31{,}883$)
Source The Cabinet Office (2024)

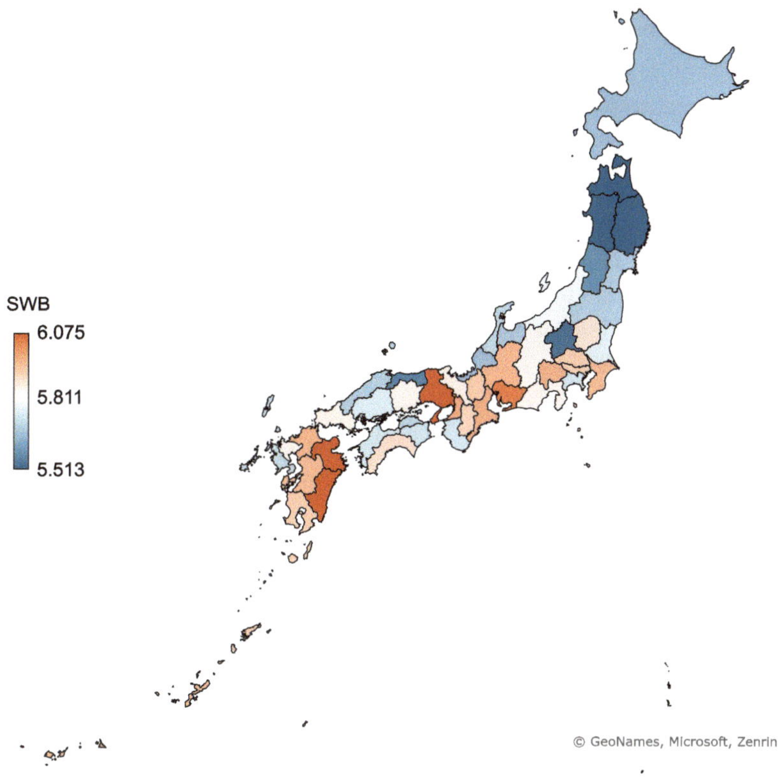

Fig. 4.6 SWB score map by prefecture. *Source* The Cabinet Office (2024, Table 3)

During the past 30 days, how often did you feel restless or fidgety?
During the past 30 days, how often did you feel so depressed that nothing could cheer you up?
During the past 30 days, how often did you feel that everything was an effort?
During the past 30 days, how often did you feel worthless?

Frequencies are recorded as scores using a five-category scale (0 = all of the time, 1 = most of the time, 2 = some of the time, 3 = a little of the time, and 4 = none of the time). Scores are then summed to give a total score out of 24, with higher scores indicating higher levels of psychological distress. In the CAO survey, the above questions were modified to "Recently" instead of "During the past 30 days," but we created a variable K6 by summing the six responses.

Also, there are two more questions asked with the same five-category scale: They are, "Recently, how often did you feel lonely?" and "Recently, how often did you feel that you do not have anyone to enjoy time with?" Since these two respondents have close meanings to represent loneliness or being alone, and the variables correlate highly (the correlation coefficient being 0.717 at the 0.1% significance level), we only use the former question and name the variable *Loneliness.*

Table 4.4 Correlation with SWB

	2022	2023	2024	All
Loneliness	−0.427	−0.465	−0.470	−0.452
K6	−0.456	−0.469	−0.472	−0.465

Note All values are significant at 1%

We used *K6* and *Loneliness* to estimate SWB because each correlates with *SWB* (Table 4.4). The correlation became slightly stronger over time. *Loneliness* and *K6* also highly correlate, but we will include both in the estimation because they did not cause multicollinearity.

4.4 Estimation Results

This section estimates pooled data (Sect. 4.4.1) and panel data (Sect. 4.4.2). Detailed descriptions of variables are in Table 4.5. Descriptive statistics are presented in the Appendix A.1.

4.4.1 Annual and Pooled Data

Loneliness lowers SWB and is alleviated through social connection. We hypothesize that if one does not have any relations with society other than coworkers and family members, loneliness deepens. To explore that, we take the interaction between *Loneliness* and *NoVolunteer* on SWB so that the regression model includes the interaction term *Loneliness* × *NoVolunteer*.

The estimation equation is:

$$
\begin{aligned}
SWB = \beta_0 + \beta_L Loneliness + \beta_{NV} NoVolunteer + \beta_{L\times NV}(Loneliness \times NoVolunteer) \\
+ \boldsymbol{X}\gamma + \varepsilon,
\end{aligned}
$$

where $\boldsymbol{X}$ is a vector of other variables (e.g., age, gender, income) included to adjust for potential confounding effects, and ε is the error term.

Table 4.6 lists the OLS estimation results for the three-year-pooled data and each year's data. In the Pooled model, the 2022 year dummy was significantly lower than 2024 (base), but that of 2023 was insignificant. Summary statistics of the variables are in the Appendix.

As we see from the simple distribution in Sect. 4.4, males have lower SWB than females in all models. It resonates with what existing studies indicate.

As for *Age*, the coefficients are compared to the age group "70s and over." There are differences yearly, but by looking at Fig. 4.7, which compares the coefficients

Table 4.5 Definitions of variables

Variables	Definition
SWB	The response to the question: How satisfied are you with your life as a whole? If "not satisfied at all" is 0 points and "very satisfied" is 10 points, what score would you give?
Male	Dichotomous variable: 1 = Male, 0 = Female
Age	
10s and under	Dichotomous variable: 10s and under = 1, 0 otherwise
20s	Dichotomous variable: 20s = 1, 0 otherwise
30s	Dichotomous variable: 30s = 1, 0 otherwise
40s	Dichotomous variable: 40s and under = 1, 0 otherwise
50s	Dichotomous variable: 50s and under = 1, 0 otherwise
60s	Dichotomous variable: 60s and under = 1, 0 otherwise
70s and over	Dichotomous variable: 70s and over = 1, 0 otherwise (base)
Education	Those who graduated from a University or Graduate School = 1, 0 otherwise
Household_Income	Household annual income. Originally, a seven-category scale. Natural log of the median of each range of categories
Unemployed	Unemployed (Not working and seeking jobs)
Household_Asset	Household assets. Originally, a seven-category scale. Natural log of the median of each range of categories
Good_Health	The response to the question: How do you feel about the current state of your health? (1 = Not good 2 = Not very good 3 = Average 4 = Fairly good 5 = Good)
K6	Kessler's K6. See Sect. 4.3 (6) for the definition
Sleeping_Hours (less than five hours)	Dichotomous variable: Less than five hours of sleeping time = 1, 0 otherwise
Loneliness	The response to the question: Recently, how often did you feel lonely? (0 = all of the time, 1 = most of the time, 2 = some of the time, 3 = a little of the time, and 4 = none of the time)
NoVolunteer	Those who selected choice 12 to the question: What kind of volunteer or community activities do you do? Please select all that apply (1 = Neighborhood association, 2 = Festivals, 3 = Clean-up activities, 4 = Welfare for the older adults, 5 = Child-rearing support, 6 = PTA, 7 = Disaster relief and reconstruction support, 8 = Music, dance, and sports activities, 9 = Support for people with disabilities, 10 = Voluntary donations and fundraising (including donations from the cafeteria menu and the purchase of fair trade products), 11 = Other, 12 = I do not engage in volunteer or community activities)
NoHobby	Those who selected choice 2 (No) to the question: Do you have any hobbies or anything that gives your life meaning? (1 = Yes, 2 = No)
No_worries_for_home	The response to the question: When you think about the future, how much anxiety do you feel about various aspects of your life? If you score 0 for "extremely anxious" and 10 for "not anxious at all," how much anxiety do you feel? / Housing

(continued)

Table 4.5 (continued)

Variables	Definition
No_worries_for_ work-life_balance	The response to the question: When you think about the future, how much anxiety do you feel about various aspects of your life? If you score 0 for "extremely anxious" and 10 for "not anxious at all," how much anxiety do you feel? / Work-life balance
Y2022	Dichotomous variable: Survey year is 2022 = 1, 0 otherwise
Y2023	Dichotomous variable: Survey year is 2023 = 1, 0 otherwise

and confidence intervals of four models, we see that the SWB of "10 s and under" is the highest, "20s" and "70s and over" are almost even, and "40s" and "50s" are low. The people in their forties and fifties are often referred to as having lower SWB; our result resonates with that.

Individuals with educational years equivalent to or exceeding those of university graduates tend to be better off than those with less education, although the coefficient is insignificant. "Household_Income" works positively to SWB. No professions showed statistical significance, so we excluded jobs from explanatory variables in the estimation, but being unemployed ("unemployment") lowered SWB, except for 2022. Looking into a stock variable, a unit change in the log of "Household_Assets" also works to increase SWB.

Being healthy naturally matters to SWB. Physical health ("Good_Health") increases SWB; mental distress, "K6," decreases "SWB." Moreover, those who sleep less than five hours on average have lower SWB.

Cross terms of "Loneliness" and "No_Volunteer" showed interesting results. The average marginal effect of change in SWB for the pooled and 2024 data is shown in Fig. 4.8. The result suggests that encouraging voluntary participation in activities with neighbors can help improve the SWB. For those who do not feel lonely any of the time, participation in volunteering does not make a difference in SWB, but for those who volunteer, the stronger the "Loneliness," the lower the SWB. For those who do not participate in volunteering, the decline in SWB due to loneliness is stronger. Especially for those who feel lonely all the time, participating in voluntary activities significantly improves SWB.

Having no hobbies lowers SWB. Concerning the future, having no worries about both home and work-life balance raises SWB.

Table 4.6 The result of the pooled and each year's estimation

	(1) Pooled	(2) 2022	(3) 2023	(4) 2024
Male	−0.270***	−0.316***	−0.259***	−0.238***
	(0.022)	(0.033)	(0.033)	(0.032)
Age				
10s and under	0.108	0.005	0.266*	0.065
	(0.069)	(0.112)	(0.118)	(0.105)
20s	−0.008	−0.003	−0.054	0.036
	(0.045)	(0.070)	(0.063)	(0.064)
30s	−0.137**	−0.114	−0.145*	−0.152*
	(0.045)	(0.070)	(0.064)	(0.064)
40s	−0.237***	−0.163*	−0.307***	−0.239***
	(0.046)	(0.069)	(0.064)	(0.065)
50s	−0.261***	−0.244***	−0.339***	−0.197**
	(0.049)	(0.073)	(0.067)	(0.068)
60s	−0.174***	−0.084	−0.247***	−0.193**
	(0.045)	(0.067)	(0.062)	(0.063)
Education (University and graduate school)	0.088***	0.121***	0.057	0.086*
	(0.023)	(0.034)	(0.034)	(0.034)
Household income (log)	0.077***	0.097***	0.074**	0.062**
	(0.015)	(0.023)	(0.023)	(0.023)
Unemployed	−0.245***	−0.189	−0.319**	−0.243*
	(0.071)	(0.120)	(0.124)	(0.103)
Household asset (log)	0.071***	0.069***	0.067***	0.077***
	(0.010)	(0.014)	(0.014)	(0.015)
Good health	0.287***	0.267***	0.289***	0.304***
	(0.013)	(0.020)	(0.020)	(0.019)
K6	−0.035***	−0.042***	−0.034***	−0.030***
	(0.003)	(0.004)	(0.005)	(0.004)
Sleeping hours (less than 5 h)	−0.181***	−0.128**	−0.192***	−0.225***
	(0.030)	(0.045)	(0.046)	(0.048)
Cross term (Loneliness × No_Volunteer)				
Loneliness (vs. None of the time)				
A little of the time	−0.225***	−0.193**	−0.271***	−0.217***
	(0.040)	(0.067)	(0.066)	(0.065)
Some of the time	−0.416***	−0.351***	−0.451***	−0.457***
	(0.045)	(0.074)	(0.073)	(0.073)
Most of the time	−0.606***	−0.448***	−0.690***	−0.694***
	(0.073)	(0.122)	(0.119)	(0.119)

(continued)

Table 4.6 (continued)

	(1) Pooled	(2) 2022	(3) 2023	(4) 2024
All of the time	−0.805***	−0.673***	−1.016***	−0.752***
	(0.111)	(0.185)	(0.190)	(0.185)
No_Volunteer	−0.040	−0.005	−0.079	−0.043
	(0.032)	(0.050)	(0.054)	(0.052)
Loneliness × No_Volunteer				
A little of the time × No_Volunteer	−0.032	−0.058	0.004	−0.037
	(0.049)	(0.083)	(0.084)	(0.082)
Some of the time × No_Volunteer	−0.108*	−0.094	−0.099	−0.118
	(0.050)	(0.084)	(0.082)	(0.082)
Most of the time × No_Volunteer	−0.199*	−0.289*	−0.159	−0.138
	(0.081)	(0.140)	(0.133)	(0.132)
All of the time × No_Volunteer	−0.521***	−0.457*	−0.303	−0.774***
	(0.118)	(0.199)	(0.201)	(0.195)
No hobby	−0.421***	−0.421***	−0.361***	−0.481***
	(0.027)	(0.041)	(0.041)	(0.042)
No worries for home	0.253***	0.257***	0.254***	0.250***
	(0.008)	(0.013)	(0.012)	(0.012)
No worries for work−life balance	0.301***	0.310***	0.305***	0.288***
	(0.008)	(0.013)	(0.013)	(0.013)
Y2022	−0.158***			
	(0.021)			
Y2023	−0.035			
	(0.020)			
Constant	2.078***	1.759***	2.132***	2.154***
	(0.103)	(0.156)	(0.155)	(0.155)
Statistics				
Adjusted R-squared	0.5185279	0.5117649	0.5218155	0.5213851
N	31,883	10,631	10,619	10,633
AIC	121,883.3	40,762.5	40,588.65	40,579.39
BIC	122,126	40,958.83	40,784.95	40,775.72

Note

1. $+p < 0.10$, $* p < 0.05$, $** p < 0.01$, $*** p < 0.001$
2. Standard errors are in parentheses

Source Authors' estimation

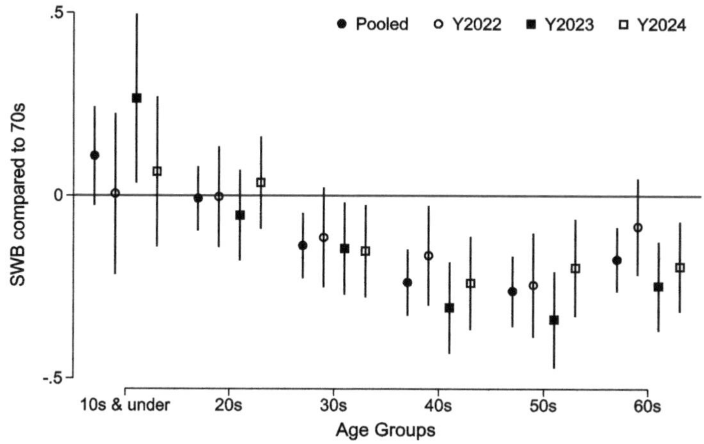

Fig. 4.7 Coefficients of age group with confidence interval. *Source* Authors' estimation

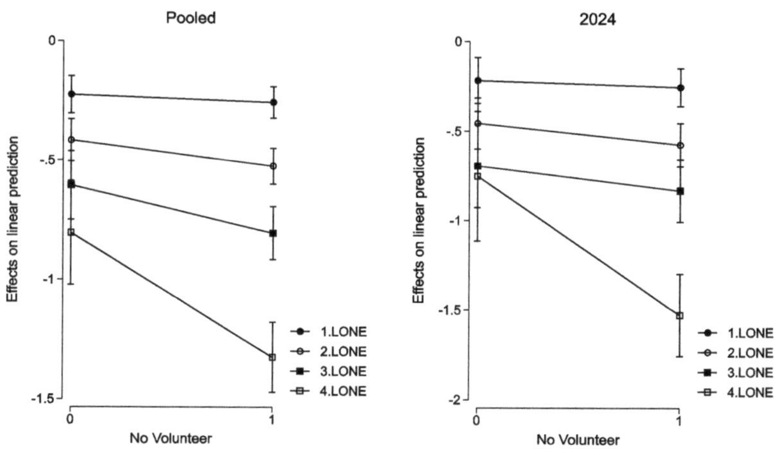

Fig. 4.8 Average marginal effects with 95% confidence interval. *Note* (1) "1.LONE" = A little of the time, "2.LONE" = Some of the time, "3.LONE" = Most of the time, "4.LONE = All of the time." (2) Effects are predicted compared to 0.LONE = None of the time

4.4.2 Panel Data

(1) **Factors Affecting SWB (All Respondents)**

The Hausman test suggested that a fixed effect under the assumption that the unobserved individual effects are uncorrelated with the explanatory variables is appropriate, so we took fixed effects that control all time-invariant factors. After testing autocorrelation in the Wooldridge test, we adopted the clustered variance–covariance estimator.

The panel regression results can be seen in Table 4.7. The standardized coefficients for both unbalanced and balanced panels are depicted together in Fig. 4.9, ranked by unbalanced-panel coefficients.

(2) **Factors Affecting SWB by Gender**

To distinguish the factors affecting SWB between males and females, we divided respondents into two groups and conducted the analysis separately. The results for males are shown in Table 4.8, and those for females are shown in Table 4.9.

To compare the effect of each variable, we standardized the coefficients and listed them in order of importance in Fig. 4.10 (unbalanced panel coefficients determine ranks).

Table 4.7 Results of panel fixed-effects regression models

	Unbalanced			Balanced		
	β	S.E.	Std. b	*β*	S.E.	Std. b
Good health	0.109***	(0.020)	0.049	0.096***	(0.025)	0.041
K6	−0.029***	(0.004)	−0.078	−0.023***	(0.022)	−0.062
Loneliness	−0.109***	(0.018)	−0.057	−0.118***	(0.005)	−0.060
No hobby	−0.165***	(0.038)	−0.031	−0.130***	(0.017)	−0.025
No worries for home	0.024*	(0.011)	0.022	0.025*	(0.015)	0.023
No worries for work-life balance	0.070***	(0.012)	0.063	0.071	(0.015)	0.061
No worries for wealth	0.081***	(0.012)	0.081	0.089***	(0.016)	0.088
No worries for wages and employment	0.029*	(0.013)	0.028	0.036***	(0.015)	0.033
No worries for friends	0.055***	(0.012)	0.048	0.067*	(0.015)	0.056
No worries for safety	0.047***	(0.011)	0.040	0.029***	(0.017)	0.024
No worries for joy	0.144***	(0.012)	0.131	0.162**	(0.048)	0.142
Y2022	−0.108***	(0.022)	−0.022	−0.091	(0.025)	−0.018
Y2024	−0.078***	(0.020)	−0.016	−0.068***	(0.025)	−0.014
Constant	3.532***	(0.115)	0.175	3.303***	(0.134)	0.182
Within R^2	0.175			0.182		
Adjusted within R^2	0.174			0.181		
Between R^2	0.580			0.730		
Overall R^2	0.564			0.622		
N	31,883			11,241		
N of groups	19,455			3747		

Notes
1. $+p < 0.10$, $* p < 0.05$, $** p < 0.01$, $*** p < 0.001$
2. Standard errors are in parentheses

Source Authors' estimation

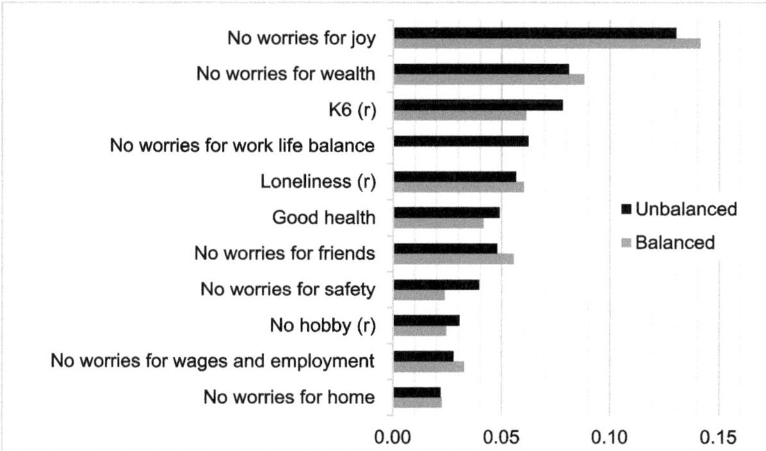

Fig. 4.9 The standardized coefficients of the fixed-effects model. *Note* The letter (r) indicates that the sign of the negative coefficient has been inverted

4.4.3 Linear Mixed-Effects Model

Our panel data is short (three years) and unbalanced, with one-third of respondents having data for only one year (10,774/31,883 = 33.8%, see Table 4.1); here, we adopt a linear mixed-effects model that allows for the inclusion of both time-varying and time-invariant predictors. The mixed-effects model has recently been widely used in a wide variety of research areas, including economics (see the survey of Asampana Asosega et al., 2024). Unlike fixed-effects models, which dropped key variables such as gender and age, the mixed model retained these predictors and enabled the estimation of cross-level interactions. Fixed-effects models estimate unit-specific parameters with no assumption of generalizability, but mixed models treat group effects as random draws from a common distribution. This treatment allows for partial pooling, which improves estimation stability and enables generalization to new units by relying on fixed effects.

Assume the variables as

X_{it}: time-varying predictors of individual i at year t.
Z_i: time-invariant predictors (e.g., gender, age group, and residence).[17]

The simplified and generalized expression of our pooled OLS estimation (Sect. 4.4.1) is:

$$SWB_{it} = \beta_0 + \beta_1 X_{it} + \beta_2 Z_i + \varepsilon_{it}.$$

[17] At the prefectural level, the narrowest geographical category we can collect from the Cabinet Office Survey, only 5.4% of total respondents moved to other prefectures during our analysis period, so residence can be considered time-invariant predictors. In the estimation, though, the prefectures were in-significant predictors.

Table 4.8 Results of panel fixed-effect model (male)

	Unbalanced			Balanced		
	β	S.E.	Std. b	β	S.E.	Std. b
Good health	0.107***	(0.028)	3.811	0.081*	(0.036)	2.254
K6	−0.021***	(0.006)	−3.669	−0.018**	(0.007)	−2.784
Loneliness	−0.108***	(0.024)	−4.459	−0.110***	(0.029)	−3.744
No hobby	0.086***	(0.019)	4.508	0.103***	(0.025)	4.185
No worries for home	0.048*	(0.020)	2.409	0.045*	(0.023)	1.968
No worries for work-life balance	0.036*	(0.017)	2.076	0.028	(0.022)	1.273
No worries for wealth	0.056**	(0.019)	2.993	0.058*	(0.023)	2.542
No worries for wages and employment	0.084***	(0.017)	4.900	0.091***	(0.021)	4.252
No worries for friends	0.036*	(0.016)	2.266	−0.011	(0.020)	−0.546
No worries for safety	0.135***	(0.019)	7.108	0.181***	(0.025)	7.247
No worries for joy	−0.159**	(0.054)	−2.922	−0.123	(0.064)	−1.936
Y2022	0.051	(0.027)	1.845	0.006	(0.035)	0.166
Y2024	0.151***	(0.030)	4.977	0.113**	(0.035)	3.197
Constant	3.094***	(0.156)	19.799	3.017***	(0.186)	16.195
Within R^2	0.181			0.182		
Adjusted within R^2	0.180			0.180		
Between R^2	0.598			0.754		
Overall R^2	0.581			0.641		
N	15,878			5907		
N of groups	9524			1969		

Notes
1. $+p < 0.10$, $*p < 0.05$, $**p < 0.01$, $***p < 0.001$
2. Standard errors are in parentheses
Source Authors' estimation

$\varepsilon_{it} \sim N(0, \sigma^2)$ are the residuals, and they are assumed to be uncorrelated across time and individuals, i.e., this model assumes all observations are independent. The same individual may appear multiple times in panel data, but intra-individual dependence is ignored when estimating coefficients. In our study, we set standard errors to be clustered at the individual level to adjust for repeated observations and intra-person correlation, which would otherwise lead to underestimated standard errors.

Fixed-effect panel analysis (Sect. 4.4.2) should be as follows:

$$SWB_{it} = \alpha_i + \beta_1 X_{it} + \varepsilon_{it}.$$

Here, α_i is an individual-specific intercept, representing a fixed effect for each person. Estimates are based on within-individual variation over time, and time-invariant

Table 4.9 Results of panel fixed−effect model (female)

	Unbalanced			Balanced		
	β	S.E	Std. b	β	S.E	Std. b
Good health	0.109***	(0.028)	3.905	0.109**	(0.035)	3.113
K6	−0.039***	(0.006)	−6.600	−0.03***	(0.008)	−3.971
Loneliness	−0.109***	(0.026)	−4.199	−0.129***	(0.033)	−3.898
No hobby	0.076***	(0.016)	4.675	0.072**	(0.022)	3.208
No worries for home	0.011	(0.016)	0.697	0.025	(0.021)	1.183
No worries for work-life balance	0.012	(0.015)	0.817	0.022	(0.019)	1.142
No worries for wealth	0.084***	(0.016)	5.330	0.085***	(0.021)	4.11
No worries for wages and employment	0.023	(0.016)	1.426	0.041*	(0.020)	2.053
No worries for friends	0.061***	(0.016)	3.914	0.074***	(0.021)	3.511
No worries for safety	0.153***	(0.016)	9.496	0.144***	(0.022)	6.532
No worries for joy	−0.171**	(0.052)	−3.272	−0.139	(0.073)	−1.911
Y2022	0.003	(0.028)	0.111	0.04	(0.036)	1.091
Y2024	0.058	(0.031)	1.840	0.069	(0.037)	1.87
Constant	3.785***	(0.169)	22.465	3.447***	(0.192)	17.943
Within R^2	0.173			0.189		
Adjusted within R^2	0.173			0.187		
Between R^2	0.562			0.702		
Overall R^2	0.549			0.599		
N	16,005			5334		
N of groups	9932			1778		

Notes
1. $+p < 0.10$, $* p < 0.05$, $** p < 0.01$, $*** p < 0.001$
2. Standard errors are in parentheses
Source Authors' estimation

predictors are absorbed into the fixed intercepts and excluded from estimation. It fully controls for unobserved, time-invariant heterogeneity across individuals. Observations from the same person are likely correlated over time, but we clustered standard errors at the respondent level to provide robust inference to deal with serial correlation and heteroskedasticity in the residuals over time within individuals. Its shortage is that it excludes between-person differences and is often inefficient for short and unbalanced panels like what we are using.

We selected the random intercept model, where individuals differ in terms of their intercept for the linear mixed effects model we applied.[18] The model includes both

[18] Precise explanations are available; these include Vonesh and Chinchilli (1997), Browne and Rsbash (2009), Snijders and Bosker (2012), and Nakagawa and Schielzeth (2013).

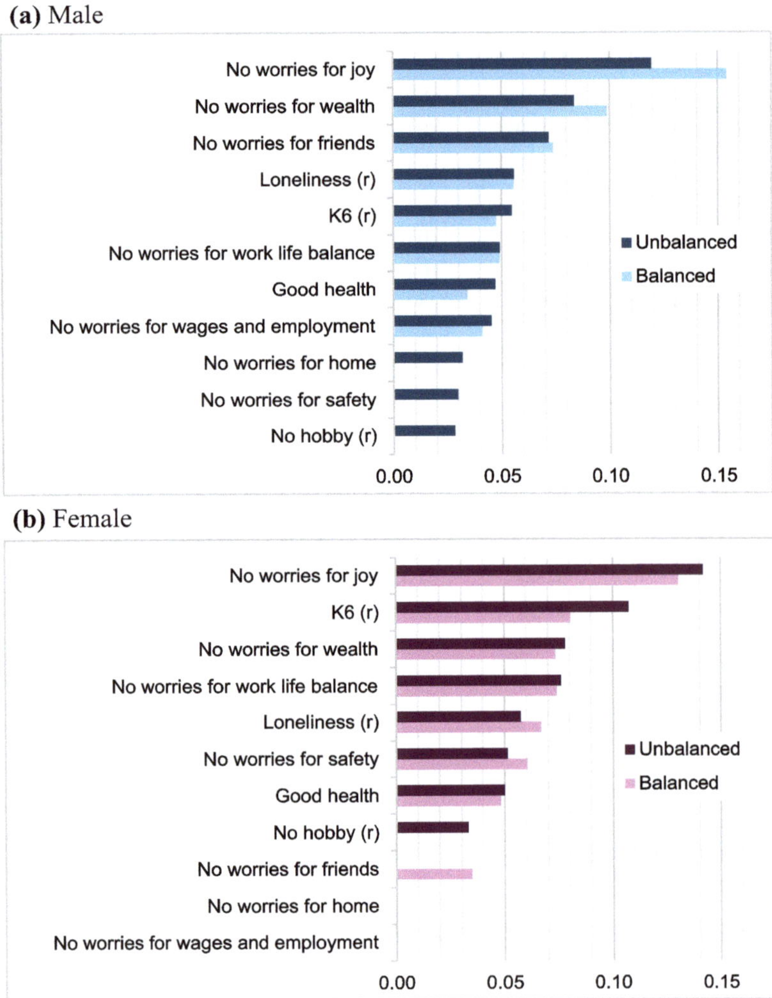

Fig. 4.10 The standardized coefficients of the fixed-effects model: **a** Male **b** Female. *Note* The letter (r) indicates that the sign of the negative coefficient has been inverted

fixed effects and random effects such that:

$$SWB_{it} = \beta_0 + \beta_1 X_{it} + \beta_2 Z_i + u_i + \varepsilon_{it},$$

where $u_i \sim N\left(0,\ \sigma_u^2\right)$ is a random intercept for individual i, which models the unexplained variance. Unlike fixed-effects models, which estimate individual-specific intercepts independently, mixed models estimate u_i using shrinkage estimators, which pull group means toward the population average depending on the amount of data available for each individual and the relative variance between and within groups. Theu_i is not estimated directly and is shrunk toward the group averages based on the number of observations for individual i and the variability within and between individuals. The estimated random intercept for person i is given by:

$$\hat{u}_i = B_i \cdot \left(\overline{SWB}_i - \hat{\beta}_0\right),$$

where $B_i = \frac{\sigma_u^2}{\sigma_u^2 + \frac{\sigma^2}{n_i}}$.

B_i determines how much the individual effect deviates from the overall mean. The term $\overline{SWB_i}$ represents the average observed SWB for individual i, while $\hat{\beta}_0$ is the estimated fixed, overall intercept of the model. Their difference reflects how much the individual's average deviates from the population mean. By weighting with B_i, we can get the estimated random effect $\hat{u}_i$. The larger the sample size for individual i, or the smaller the model-estimated overall residual variance, the more this deviation is preserved in the estimate. Otherwise, the estimate is pulled closer to the grand mean. Individuals with many observations or low within-person variance receive estimates close to their own sample mean, while those with limited data are more strongly adjusted toward the grand mean. This approach enables the model to retain individuals with sparse data and improves estimation efficiency in unbalanced panels.

The mixed model accommodates both time-varying and time-invariant predictors and allows for interaction effects such as gender × age group, which are otherwise unidentifiable in fixed-effects models. We formed a linear mixed-effects model of SWB on explanatory variables in Sect. 4.4.2, with random intercepts by individual IDs. Estimation is done by the software STATA version 18, using maximum likelihood under the assumption that both the residuals and random intercepts are normally distributed. This implies that the overall error structure of the model is Gaussian, a standard assumption in linear mixed-effects modeling.

The result is as in Table 4.10. In this estimation, the intra-class correlation (ICC) was 0.4603, indicating substantial variation exists between individuals. A mixed model application is justified to account for this clustering and to allow for both fixed and random effects.

From Table 4.10, we can find the determinants of the SWB.

The coefficient for Male was negative but not statistically significant, indicating that among the reference group (women aged 70 years and older), men reported slightly lower SWB on average. However, the difference was not statistically significant. Among women, SWB remained relatively stable across younger age groups but declined significantly in midlife. Compared with women aged 70 years and older, the SWB of women in their 40s, 50s, and 60s was lower by approximately 0.15, 0.23, and 0.15 points, respectively. The effects for women in their 40s and 60s were significant at the 5% level, and the impact for those in their 50s was significant at the 1% level. Gender differences in SWB varied considerably across age groups. The interaction terms for Male × 30s and Male × 40s were negative and statistically significant (−0.35 and −0.24, both are significant at less than 1%), indicating that men in their 30s and 40s reported substantially lower SWB than women of the same

Table 4.10 The result of the linear mixed effects model

	Coefficients	S.E
Male	−0.095	(0.078)
Age		
10s and under	0.040	(0.100)
20s	0.035	(0.065)
30s	0.016	(0.067)
40s	−0.151*	(0.067)
50s	−0.226**	(0.071)
60s	−0.147*	(0.067)
Cross term		
Male × 10s and under	0.113	(0.133)
Male × 20s	−0.144	(0.087)
Male × 30s	−0.346***	(0.090)
Male × 40s	−0.242**	(0.093)
Male × 50s	−0.130	(0.098)
Male × 60s	−0.042	(0.094)
Education (over university graduated)	0.099***	(0.023)
Household_Income (log)	0.075***	(0.013)
Unemployed	−0.243***	(0.057)
Household_Asset (log)	0.075***	(0.009)
Good_Health	0.286***	(0.010)
K6	−0.039***	(0.002)
Sleeping_Hours (less than 5 h)	−0.162***	(0.026)
Loneliness (vs. None of the time)		
A little of the time	−0.220***	(0.039)
Some of the time	−0.383***	(0.042)
Most of the time	−0.560***	(0.060)
All of the time	−0.755***	(0.077)
No_Volunteer	−0.067*	(0.032)
Cross Term		
A little of the time × No_Volunteer	0.010	(0.048)
Some of the time × No_Volunteer	−0.071	(0.047)
Most of the time × No_Volunteer	−0.145*	(0.068)
All of the time × No_Volunteer	−0.403***	(0.084)
No hobby	−0.408***	(0.023)
No worries for home	0.226***	(0.006)
No worries for work-life balance	0.267***	(0.006)
Y2022	−0.144***	(0.019)

(continued)

Table 4.10 (continued)

	Coefficients	S.E
Y2023	−0.048*	(0.019)
Regions (vs Hokkaido)		
Tohoku	0.040	(0.076)
Kanto	0.105	(0.074)
Chubu	0.101	(0.074)
Kinki	0.171*	(0.075)
Chugoku	0.066	(0.077)
Shikoku	0.099	(0.079)
Kyushu & Okinawa	0.153*	(0.074)
Constant	2.237***	(0.121)
Statistics		
Marginal $R^2 = 0.4811$, Conditional $R^2 = 0.7199$		
Number of obs. = 31,883; Number of groups = 19,455		
Obs. per group: min = 1, average = 1.6, max = 3		
ICC (Intra-Class Correlation) = 0.46		

Notes
1. $+p < 0.10$, * $p < 0.05$, ** $p < 0.01$, *** $p < 0.001$
2. Standard errors are in parentheses
Source Authors' estimation

age. By contrast, the interactions for the younger (10s–20s) and older (50s–60s) age groups were small and nonsignificant. When the main and interaction effects are combined, men in their 30s and 40s score roughly 0.43–0.49 points lower than the reference group (women aged 70 and above) and about 0.35–0.25 points lower than women of the same age group. The corresponding combined effects for men in their 50s (−0.45) and 60s (−0.28) are also negative but not statistically significant, while those for the youngest age groups are near zero. Taken together, the findings indicate that SWB declines in midlife for both genders but that the decline is considerably more pronounced among men. Men's SWB reaches its lowest point in the 30s–40s, whereas women's decline at the same ages is more moderate.

Those who have graduated from university or have a higher level of education report 0.1 points higher SWB than those with less education. Both household income and assets have a positive logarithmic relationship with SWB. The unemployed are less satisfied with life, reporting SWB that is 0.24 points lower than that of others. Physical health naturally has a positive effect on SWB, while psychological distress (measured by the K6 scale) has a negative impact. The number of sleeping hours affects SWB; sleeping for less than 5 h a day decreases SWB by 0.16 points. Having no hobby reduces SWB by as much as 0.4 points.

As discussed in Sect. 4.4.1, the ties to the community and loneliness relate. Both frequency of feeling lonely and lack of social engagement are strongly associated with lower SWB, and voluntary participation may partially soften the negative impact of intense loneliness. Compared with individuals who reported feeling lonely none of the time, those who experienced loneliness a little of the time scored lower SWB by 0.22 points, those lonely some of the time by 0.38 points, most of the time by 0.56 points, and all of the time by 0.76 points, all of which are significant at 0.1%. These results indicate that the more frequently individuals feel lonely, the lower their reported SWB. The coefficient for No Volunteer was negative ($-0.07, p < 0.05$), indicating that individuals who did not engage in volunteering reported slightly lower SWB than those who volunteered, after controlling for loneliness levels.

The interaction terms reveal that the adverse association between loneliness and SWB is even stronger among those who do not volunteer. Although the interactions for A little × No Volunteer and Some × No Volunteer were small and nonsignificant, the coefficients for Most × No Volunteer ($-0.15, p < 0.05$) and All × No Volunteer (-0.40) were negative and significant. Combining the main and interaction effects shows that, relative to individuals who never feel lonely and who volunteer, those who feel lonely most of the time and do not volunteer report SWB lower by about 0.7 points ($0.560 + 0.145$), while those who feel lonely all of the time and do not volunteer score nearly 1.2 points lower ($0.755 + 0.403$).

In this linear mixed model, the regional dummies,[19] which were not significant in the pooled OLS estimation, now showed significant effects as regional dummies collectively on SWB. Compared to the base region, Hokkaido (the most northern region), statistically significant positivity is observed in the Kinki region (+0.171) and the Kyushu & Okinawa region (+0.153).

Using the results above, we can predict SWB across age groups and regions (Fig. 4.11). The gender and region influence SWB in parallel but partially compensating ways. Males in each region have a U-shaped curve, while females in each region have a shallower quasi-U-shaped curve, with the left declining point starting in their 40s. Kinki and Kyushu and Okinawa have higher curves. Interestingly, the level of males in Kyushu & Okinawa is close to that of females in Tohoku, Chugoku, or Shikoku. If we move the curve of male in Kyushu and Okinawa to Tohoku, Chugoku, or Shikoku, we can see that it is almost as high as that of females in each region. This pattern indicates that the advantages associated with gender may partly offset the disadvantage linked to where people live, yet neither factor fully accounts for the other.

From a policy perspective, we should continue to investigate the effect of age group and the difference in the shape of curves by gender. Moreover, we emphasize the need to view SWB disparities in relation to both gender and region simultaneously. Measures that improve local living conditions—such as employment, public services, and social participation—are likely to support overall well-being. We also have to analyze how the role and opportunities for genders affect SWB in each region precisely. This insight is our novel contribution to the existing literature.

---

[19] The eight regions. See Table 4.3 for the prefectures comprised in each region.

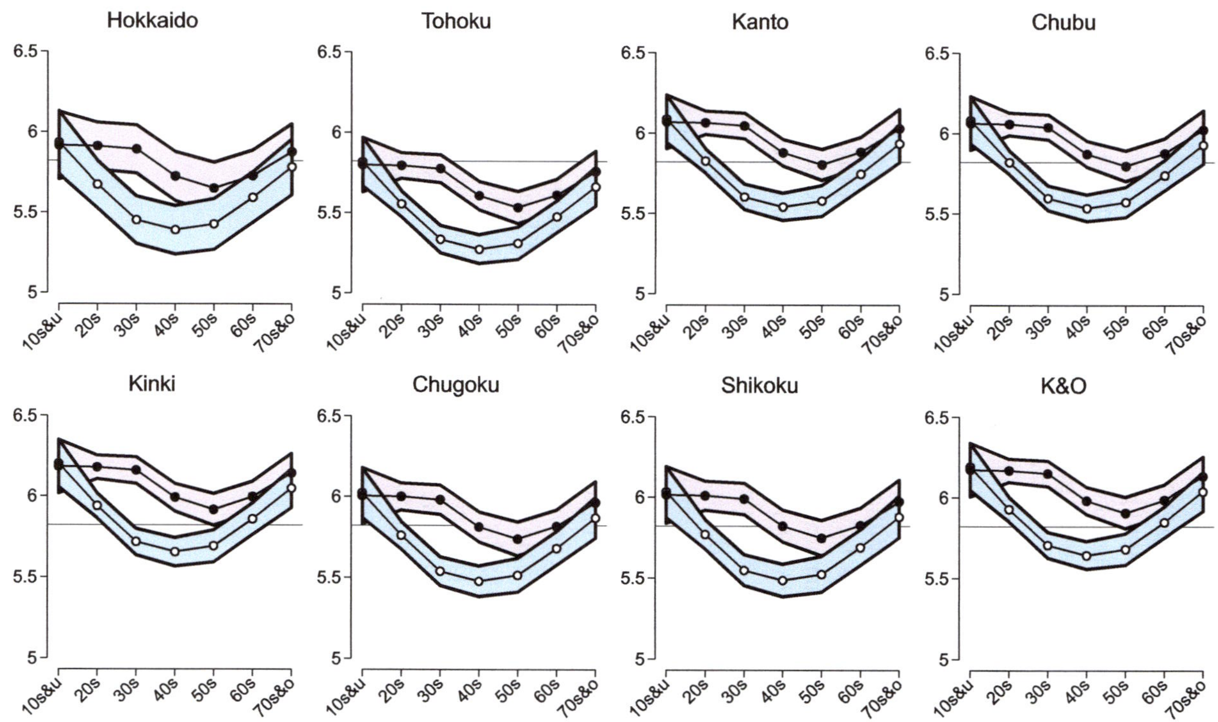

Fig. 4.11 Gender differences in predicted SWB across age groups and regions. *Note* (1) White dots are male and black dots are female. (2) Horizontal lines are the unweighted overall average SWB (5.811). (3) The shaded areas represent the 95% confidence interval for each predicted SWB

4.5 Concluding Remarks

SWB is an important metric that reveals consumers' utility and evaluates the wealth of nations, complementing GDP.

Using CAO data from 2022 to 2024, we analyzed the SWB of Japanese consumers. Simple averages of SWB showed gender gaps and prefectural gaps.

Econometric analysis extracted several factors that affect SWB. Log of household income, log of household assets, good physical condition, "educational years of university graduates and more," and "no worries of housing" work positively to SWB Contrarily, being unemployed, having psychological distress, having no hobby, and sleeping less than five hours every day lower SWB. Loneliness is one of the negative determinants of SWB, and encouraging voluntary participation in activities with neighbors can help decrease loneliness and improve SWB.

We could observe gender differences in predicted SWB across age groups and regions. The U-shaped trajectory over age is observed in males in all regions, but the shape is different for females. The gender discrepancies are not observed in the age groups of 15–19 and 70–89 and are widest in the 30s. We can conclude that we need not only national but also area-, gender-, and age-specific policies to improve the Japanese consumers' SWB.

The use of SWB as a measure of welfare is still a topic of debate (e.g., Hausman, 2012). Layard (2005), in his study of happiness, insists that "public policy can more easily remove misery than augment happiness" (p. 231). Futhermore, Sugden (2014) even criticizes the prevailing view that combines neo-classical preference-based economics with behavioral economics which suggests that individuals are not always rational and can make errors. He points out that the idea that "welfare economics then has the task of reconstructing the preferences that the individual would have revealed in the absence of error" (p. 13) is not sufficient. Despite the limitation, we cannot wait for the dispute to be resolved before continuing to conduct SWB studies. Instead, we should keep exploring whether SWB can complement traditional macroeconomic measures like GDP.

Appendix

Descriptive Statistics for pooled and annual data are provided in Sect. A.1, for panel data are in Sect. A.2, and for linear mixed effect model data in Sect. A.3.

A.1 Pooled and Annual Data

Table 4.11 shows the descriptive statistics for pooled and annual data analysis. Table 4.11 (a) is statistics of pooled data, (b) is that of year 2022, (c) is that of 2023, and (d) is that of 2024.

A.2 Panel Data

Descriptive statistics for the panel analysis is in Table 4.12. The standard deviations are shown for overall, between, and, within.

A.3 Linear Mixed Effect Model Data

Here we show the summary statistics of variables that added to the data for panel analysis in Table 4.12 (Table 4.13).

Table 4.11 Descriptive statistics for pooled and annual data analysis

(a) Pooled data

	Mean	S.D.	Min	Max
SWB	5.811	2.357	0	10
Male	0.498	0.500	0	1
Age				
10s and under	0.031	0.174	0	1
20s	0.250	0.433	0	1
30s	0.197	0.397	0	1
40s	0.179	0.383	0	1
50s	0.127	0.333	0	1
60s	0.138	0.345	0	1
Education (University and graduate school)	0.466	0.499	0	1
Household income (log)	6.065	0.864	3.912	7.824
Unemployed	0.026	0.160	0	1
Household asset (log)	5.895	1.374	3.912	7.824
Good health	3.273	1.060	1	5
K6	7.036	6.363	0	24
Sleeping hours (less than 5 h)	0.170	0.376	0	1
Cross term (Loneliness × No_Volunteer)				
Loneliness (vs. None of the time)				
A little of the time	0.223	0.416	0	1
Some of the time	0.263	0.440	0	1
Most of the time	0.095	0.293	0	1
All of the time	0.068	0.251	0	1
No_Volunteer	0.637	0.481	0	1
Loneliness × No_Volunteer				
A little of the time × No_Volunteer	0.139	0.346	0	1
Some of the time × No_Volunteer	0.175	0.380	0	1
Most of the time × No_Volunteer	0.064	0.244	0	1
All of the time × No_Volunteer	0.050	0.219	0	1
No hobby	0.259	0.438	0	1
No worries for home	5.420	2.195	0	10
No worries for work-life balance	5.208	2.099	0	10
Year 2022	0.333	0.471	0	1
Year 2023	0.333	0.471	0	1

(continued)

Table 4.11 (continued)

(b) 2022

	Mean	S.D.	Min	Max
SWB	5.758	2.352	0	10
Male	0.498	0.500	0	1
Age				
10s and under	0.030	0.172	0	1
20s	0.247	0.431	0	1
30s	0.201	0.400	0	1
40s	0.178	0.383	0	1
50s	0.127	0.332	0	1
60s	0.146	0.354	0	1
Education (University and graduate school)	0.470	0.499	0	1
Household income (log)	6.085	0.846	3.912	7.824
Unemployed	0.026	0.160	0	1
Household asset (log)	5.933	1.369	3.912	7.824
Good health	3.285	1.052	1	5
K6	6.839	6.360	0	24
Sleeping hours (less than 5 h)	0.178	0.382	0	1
Cross term (Loneliness × No_Volunteer)				
Loneliness (vs. None of the time)				
A little of the time	0.219	0.413	0	1
Some of the time	0.242	0.429	0	1
Most of the time	0.085	0.279	0	1
All of the time	0.061	0.240	0	1
No_Volunteer	0.635	0.481	0	1
Loneliness × No_Volunteer				
A little of the time × No_Volunteer	0.137	0.344	0	1
Some of the time × No_Volunteer	0.159	0.365	0	1
Most of the time × No_Volunteer	0.055	0.229	0	1
All of the time × No_Volunteer	0.047	0.212	0	1
No hobby	0.262	0.440	0	1
No worries for home	5.436	2.186	0	10
No worries for work-life balance	5.207	2.106	0	10

(continued)

Table 4.11 (continued)

(c) 2023

	Mean	S.D.	Min	Max
SWB	5.785	2.363	0	10
Male	0.498	0.500	0	1
Age				
10s and under	0.029	0.168	0	1
20s	0.253	0.435	0	1
30s	0.196	0.397	0	1
40s	0.180	0.384	0	1
50s	0.125	0.331	0	1
60s	0.134	0.341	0	1
Education (University and graduate school)	0.464	0.499	0	1
Household income (log)	6.048	0.868	4	8
Unemployed	0.024	0.154	0	1
Household asset (log)	5.839	1.372	4	8
Good health	3.242	1.054	1	5
K6	7.191	6.372	0	24
Sleeping hours (less than 5 h)	0.174	0.379	0	1
Cross term (Loneliness × No_Volunteer)				
Loneliness (vs. None of the time)				
A little of the time	0.224	0.417	0	1
Some of the time	0.280	0.449	0	1
Most of the time	0.098	0.298	0	1
All of the time	0.071	0.256	0	1
No_Volunteer	0.646	0.478	0	1
Loneliness × No_Volunteer				
A little of the time × No_Volunteer	0.139	0.346	0	1
Some of the time × No_Volunteer	0.189	0.392	0	1
Most of the time × No_Volunteer	0.068	0.252	0	1
All of the time × No_Volunteer	0.053	0.224	0	1
No hobby	0.263	0.441	0	1
No worries for home	5.386	2.202	0	10
No worries for work-life balance	5.179	2.096	0	10

(continued)

Table 4.11 (continued)

(d) 2024

	Mean	S.D.	Min	Max
SWB	5.890	2.355	0	10
Male	0.498	0.500	0	1
Age				
10s and under	0.034	0.182	0	1
20s	0.249	0.432	0	1
30s	0.193	0.395	0	1
40s	0.179	0.383	0	1
50s	0.128	0.334	0	1
60s	0.133	0.340	0	1
Education (University and graduate school)	0.464	0.499	0	1
Household income (log)	6.061	0.877	3.912	7.824
Unemployed	0.028	0.165	0	1
Household asset (log)	5.913	1.380	3.912	7.824
Good health	3.291	1.074	1	5
K6	7.079	6.354	0	24
Sleeping hours (less than 5 h)	0.158	0.365	0	1
Cross term (Loneliness × No_Volunteer)				
Loneliness (vs. None of the time)				
A little of the time	0.227	0.419	0	1
Some of the time	0.267	0.443	0	1
Most of the time	0.101	0.302	0	1
All of the time	0.071	0.256	0	1
No_Volunteer	0.631	0.483	0	1
Loneliness × No_Volunteer				
A little of the time × No_Volunteer	0.141	0.348	0	1
Some of the time × No_Volunteer	0.176	0.381	0	1
Most of the time × No_Volunteer	0.068	0.251	0	1
All of the time × No_Volunteer	0.051	0.220	0	1
No hobby	0.250	0.433	0	1
No worries for home	5.438	2.198	0	10
No worries for work-life balance	5.237	2.095	0	10

Table 4.12 Descriptive statistics for panel analysis

(a) Unbalanced: $N = 31{,}883$, $n = 19{,}455$, T-bar = 1.639

Variable		Mean	S.D.	Min	Max
SWB	Overall	5.811	2.357	0	10
	Between		2.267	0	10
	Within		0.774	−0.856	12.478
Good health	Overall	3.273	1.060	1	5
	Between		1.027	1	5
	Within		0.379	0.939	5.273
Loneliness	Overall	1.304	1.229	0	4
	Between		1.172	0	4
	Within		0.468	−1.362	3.971
K6	Overall	7.036	6.363	0	24
	Between		6.129	0	24
	Within		2.189	−8.297	23.036
No worries for wealth	Overall	4.777	2.357	0	10
	Between		2.270	0	10
	Within		0.831	−1.890	11.444
No worries for wages and employment	Overall	4.704	2.234	0	10
	Between		2.155	0	10
	Within		0.861	−1.963	11.371
No worries for home	Overall	5.420	2.195	0	10
	Between		2.109	0	10
	Within		0.832	−0.913	11.087
No worries for work-life balance	Overall	5.208	2.099	0	10
	Between		2.017	0	10
	Within		0.841	−1.459	11.875
No worries for friends	Overall	5.281	2.039	0	10
	Between		1.973	0	10
	Within		0.796	−0.719	11.614
No worries for safety	Overall	5.515	1.974	0	10
	Between		1.888	0	10
	Within		0.808	−1.152	10.848

(continued)

Table 4.12 (continued)

(a) Unbalanced: $N = 31{,}883$, $n = 19{,}455$, T-bar $= 1.639$

Variable		Mean	S.D.	Min	Max
No worries for joy	Overall	5.543	2.130	0	10
	Between		2.052	0	10
	Within		0.794	−0.790	11.543
No hobby	Overall	0.259	0.438	0	1
	Between		0.406	0	1
	Within		0.181	−0.408	0.925
Year	Overall	23	0.817	22	24
	Between		0.689	22	24
	Within		0.586	22	24

(b) Balanced: $N = 11{,}241$, $n = 3747$, $T = 3$

Variable		Mean	Std. dev.	Min	Max
SWB	Overall	5.718	2.378	0	10
	Between		2.169	0	10
	Within		0.974	−0.948	12.385
Good health	Overall	3.177	1.023	1	5
	Between		0.905	1	5
	Within		0.476	0.844	5.177
Loneliness	Overall	1.272	1.214	0	4
	Between		1.060	0	4
	Within		0.592	−1.394	3.939
K6	Overall	6.642	6.290	0	24
	Between		5.649	0	24
	Within		2.767	−8.691	22.642
No worries for wealth	Overall	4.824	2.345	0	10
	Between		2.102	0	10
	Within		1.038	−1.843	11.490
No worries for wages and employment	Overall	4.712	2.169	0	10
	Between		1.884	0	10
	Within		1.075	−1.955	11.378

(continued)

Table 4.12 (continued)

(b) Balanced: $N = 11{,}241$, $n = 3747$, $T = 3$					
Variable		Mean	Std. dev.	Min	Max
No worries for home	Overall	5.427	2.151	0	10
	Between		1.886	0	10
	Within		1.034	−0.907	11.094
No worries for work-life balance	Overall	5.229	2.034	0	10
	Between		1.738	0	10
	Within		1.058	−1.438	11.896
No worries for friends	Overall	5.206	1.963	0	10
	Between		1.687	0	10
	Within		1.004	−0.794	11.539
No worries for safety	Overall	5.563	1.922	0	10
	Between		1.627	0	10
	Within		1.024	−1.104	10.896
No worries for joy	Overall	5.471	2.081	0	10
	Between		1.833	0	10
	Within		0.986	−0.863	11.471
No hobby	Overall	0.279	0.448	0	1
	Between		0.382	0	1
	Within		0.234	−0.388	0.945
Year	Overall	23	0.817	22	24
	Between		0.000	23	23
	Within		0.817	22	24

Table 4.13 Descriptive statistics of variables added for the linear mixed-effect model

$N = 31{,}883$, $n = 19{,}455$, T-bar = 1.639

Variable		Mean	S.D.	Min	Max
Male	Overall	0.498	0.500	0	1
	Between		0.500	0	1
	Within		0.004	−0.002	0.998
Age group					
10s and under	Overall	0.031	0.174	0	1
	Between		0.205	0	1
	Within		0.033	−0.635	0.698
20s	Overall	0.250	0.433	0	1
	Between		0.456	0	1
	Within		0.063	−0.417	0.916
30s	Overall	0.197	0.397	0	1
	Between		0.397	0	1
	Within		0.087	−0.470	0.863
40s	Overall	0.179	0.383	0	1
	Between		0.359	0	1
	Within		0.093	−0.488	0.846
50s	Overall	0.127	0.333	0	1
	Between		0.303	0	1
	Within		0.083	−0.540	0.793
60s	Overall	0.138	0.345	0	1
	Between		0.314	0	1
	Within		0.083	−0.529	0.805
70s	Overall	0.079	0.270	0	1
	Between		0.242	0	1
	Within		0.062	−0.588	0.746
Education (over university graduated)	Overall	0.466	0.499	0	1
	Between		0.496	0	1
	Within		0.065	−0.201	1.133
Household_Income (log)	Overall	6.065	0.864	3.912	7.824
	Between		0.857	3.912	7.824
	Within		0.247	3.797	8.673
Unemployed	Overall	0.026	0.160	0	1
	Between		0.151	0	1
	Within		0.076	−0.640	0.693
Household_Asset (log)	Overall	5.895	1.374	3.912	7.824
	Between		1.314	3.912	7.824

(continued)

Table 4.13 (continued)

$N = 31{,}883$, $n = 19{,}455$, T-bar = 1.639					
Variable		Mean	S.D.	Min	Max
	Within		0.434	3.287	8.503
Sleeping_Hours (less than 5 h)	Overall	0.170	0.376	0	1
	Between		0.357	0	1
	Within		0.157	−0.497	0.837
Loneliness	Overall	1.304	1.229	0	4
	Between		1.172	0	4
	Within		0.468	−1.362	3.971
No_Volunteer	Overall	0.637	0.481	0	1
	Between		0.454	0	1
	Within		0.198	−0.030	1.304
No hobby	Overall	0.259	0.438	0	1
	Between		0.406	0	1
	Within		0.181	−0.408	0.925
Regions					
Hokkaido	Overall	0.023	0.151	0	1
	Between		0.151	0	1
	Within		0.015	−0.643	0.523
Tohoku	Overall	0.122	0.328	0	1
	Between		0.329	0	1
	Within		0.033	−0.544	0.789
Kanto	Overall	0.167	0.373	0	1
	Between		0.369	0	1
	Within		0.050	−0.499	0.834
Chubu	Overall	0.189	0.392	0	1
	Between		0.388	0	1
	Within		0.042	−0.478	0.856
Kinki	Overall	0.152	0.359	0	1
	Between		0.354	0	1
	Within		0.042	−0.515	0.818
Chugoku	Overall	0.102	0.303	0	1
	Between		0.300	0	1
	Within		0.031	−0.565	0.769
Shikoku	Overall	0.080	0.272	0	1
	Between		0.271	0	1
	Within		0.027	−0.587	0.747

(continued)

Table 4.13 (continued)

$N = 31{,}883$, $n = 19{,}455$, T-bar = 1.639					
Variable		Mean	S.D.	Min	Max
Kyushu & Okinawa	Overall	0.164	0.371	0	1
	Between		0.374	0	1
	Within		0.035	−0.502	0.831

References

Abramovitz, M. (1959). The welfare interpretation of secular trends in national income and product. In M. Abramovitz et al. (Eds.), *The allocation of economic resources* (pp. 1–22). Stanford University Press.

Andrews, F. M., & Withey, S. B. (1974). Developing measures of perceived life quality: Results from several national surveys. *Social Indicators Research, 1*(1), 1–26. https://doi.org/10.1007/BF00286419

Andrews, F. M., & Withey, S. B. (1976). *Social indicators of well-being: Americans' perceptions of life quality*. Plenum Press. Reprinted in 2012, Springer Science & Business Media.

Arrow, K. J. (1951). *Social choice and individual values*. Wiley.

Asampana Asosega, K., Adebanji, A. O., Aidoo, E. N., & Owusu-Dabo, E. (2024). Application of hierarchical/multilevel models and quality of reporting (2010–2020): A systematic review. *The Scientific World Journal, 2024*(1), 4658333. https://doi.org/10.1155/2024/4658333

Barschak, E. (1951). A study of happiness and unhappiness in the childhood and adolescence of girls in different cultures. *The Journal of Psychology, 32*(2), 173–215.

Bentham, J. (1776). *A fragment on government* (Reprinted in R. Harrison, ed., 1988, *Bentham: A fragment on government*. Cambridge University Press).

Bentham, J. (1789). *An introduction to the principles of morals and legislation*. T. Payne and Son. Retrieved from BLTC Research homepage on August 7, 2025. https://www.utilitarianism.com/jeremy-bentham/index.html#one

Bradburn, N. M., & Caplovitz, D. (1965). *Reports on happiness: A pilot study of behavior related to mental health*. Aldine.

Bradburn, N. M., & Noll, C. E. (1969). *The structure of psychological well-being*. Aldine Pub. Co.

Browne, W., & Rsbash, J. (2009). Multilevel modelling. In M. A. Hardy & A. Bryman, *Handbook of data analysis* (Chap. 20, pp. 459–479). Sage.

Cabinet Office. (2022). *2022-nen jisshi gaiyō/chōsahyo* [Survey information and questionnaire of 2022] [PDF]. https://www5.cao.go.jp/keizai2/wellbeing/manzoku/index.html (in Japanese)

Cabinet Office. (2023). *2023-nen jisshi gaiyō/chōsahyo* [Survey information and questionnaire of 2023] [PDF]. https://www5.cao.go.jp/keizai2/wellbeing/manzoku/index.html (in Japanese)

Cabinet Office. (2024). *2024-nen jisshi gaiyō/chōsahyo* [Survey information and questionnaire of 2024] [PDF]. https://www5.cao.go.jp/keizai2/wellbeing/manzoku/index.html (in Japanese)

Campbell, A. (1976). Subjective measures of well-being. *American Psychologist, 31*(2), 117–124. https://doi.org/10.1037/0003-066X.31.2.117

Cantril, H. (1965). *The pattern of human concerns*. Rutgers University Press. https://cir.nii.ac.jp/crid/1130282270933054080

Carter, S. R., Collins, J. C., Hu, J., O'Reilly, C. L., Wheeler, A. J., McMillan, S. S., & El-Den, S. (2024). Confirmatory factor analysis of the Kessler-6 psychological distress (k6) scale in a community sample of people living with severe and persistent mental illness: A bifactor model. *International Journal of Mental Health and Addiction, 22*(4), 2210–2228. https://doi.org/10.1007/s11469-022-00981-0

Colander, D. (2007). Retrospectives: Edgeworth's hedonimeter and the quest to measure utility. *The Journal of Economic Perspectives, 21*(2), 215–226.

Department for Digital, Culture, Media and Sport. (2018). *A connected society: A strategy for tackling loneliness: Laying the foundations for change.* https://assets.publishing.service.gov.uk/government/uploads/system/uploads/attachment_data/file/936725/6.4882_DCMS_Loneliness_Strategy_web_Update_V2.pdf

Diener, E. (1984). Subjective well-being. *Psychological Bulletin, 95*(3), 542–575. https://doi.org/10.1037/0033-2909.95.3.542

Diener, E., Emmons, R. A., Larsen, R. J., & Griffin, S. (1985). The satisfaction with life scale. *Journal of Personality Assessment, 49*(1), 71–75. https://doi.org/10.1207/s15327752jpa4901_13

Diener, E., & Seligman, M. E. P. (2004). Beyond money: Toward an economy of well-being. *Psychological Science in the Public Interest, 5*(1), 1–31. https://doi.org/10.1111/j.0963-7214.2004.00501001.x

Diener, E., & Suh, E. (1997). Measuring quality of life: Economic, social, and subjective indicators. *Social Indicators Research, 40*(1), 189–216. https://doi.org/10.1023/A:1006859511756

Easterlin, R. A. (1974). Does economic growth improve the human lot? Some empirical evidence. In P. A. David & M. W. Reder (Eds.), *Nations and households in economic growth* (pp. 89–125). Academic Press. https://doi.org/10.1016/B978-0-12-205050-3.50008-7

Easterlin, R. A., & O'Connor, K. J. (2020). *The Easterlin paradox.* In K. F. Zimmermann (Ed.), *Handbook of labor, human resources and population economics* (pp. 1–25). Springer. https://doi.org/10.1007/978-3-319-57365-6_184-1

Edgeworth, F. Y. (1881). *Mathematical psychics: An essay on the application of mathematics to the moral sciences.* C. Kegan Paul & Co.

Fitoussi, J.-P., Stiglitz, J. E., & Sen, A. K. (2011). *Mismeasuring our lives: Why GDP doesn't add up.* The New Press.

Frey, B. S., & Stutzer, A. (2002). *Happiness and economics: How the economy and institutions affect human well-being.* Princeton University Press.

Furukawa, T. A., Kawakami, N., Saitoh, M., Ono, Y., Nakane, Y., Nakamura, Y., Tachimori, H., Iwata, N., Uda, H., Nakane, H., Watanabe, M., Naganuma, Y., Hata, Y., Kobayashi, M., Miyake, Y., Takeshima, T., & Kikkawa, T. (2008). The performance of the Japanese version of the K6 and K10 in the World Mental Health Survey Japan. *International Journal of Methods in Psychiatric Research, 17*(3), 152–158. https://doi.org/10.1002/mpr.257

Furukawa, T. A., Kessler, R. C., Slade, T., & Andrews, G. (2003). The performance of the K6 and K10 screening scales for psychological distress in the Australian National Survey of Mental Health and Well-being. *Psychological Medicine, 33*(2), 357–362. https://doi.org/10.1017/S0033291702006700

Giuntella, O., McManus, S., Mujcic, R., Oswald, A. J., Powdthavee, N., & Tohamy, A. (2023). The midlife crisis. *Economica, 90*(357), 65–110. https://doi.org/10.1111/ecca.12452

Glatzer, W., & Gulyas, J. (2014). Affect balance scale. In A. C. Michalos (Ed.), *Encyclopedia of quality of life and well-being research.* Springer. https://doi.org/10.1007/978-94-007-0753-5_40

Goldings, H. J. (1954). On the avowal and projection of happiness. *Journal of Personality, 23*, 30–47. https://doi.org/10.1111/j.1467-6494.1954.tb02336.x

Graham, C., Laffan, K., & Pinto, S. (2018). Well-being in metrics and policy. *Science, 362*(6412), 287–288. https://doi.org/10.1126/science.aau5234

Green, J. G., Gruber, M. J., Sampson, N. A., Zaslavsky, A. M., & Kessler, R. C. (2010). Improving the K6 short scale to predict serious emotional disturbance in adolescents in the USA. *International Journal of Methods in Psychiatric Research, 19*(Suppl. 1), 23–35. https://doi.org/10.1002/mpr.314

Gurin, G., Veroff, J., & Feld, S. (1960). *Americans view their mental health: A nationwide interview survey* (pp. xxxv, 444). Basic Books.

Hausman, D. M. (2012). *Preference, value, choice, and welfare.* Cambridge University Press.

Hayo, B. (2007). Happiness in transition: An empirical study on Eastern Europe. *Economic Systems, 31*(2), 204–221. https://doi.org/10.1016/j.ecosys.2006.08.003

Helliwell, J. F., Layard, R., Sachs, J. D., De Neve, J.-E., Aknin, L. B., & Wang, S. (Eds.). (2024). *World Happiness Report 2024*. Well-Being Research Centre.

Hicks, J. R., & Allen, R. G. D. (1934). A reconsideration of the theory of value. Part II. A mathematical theory of individual demand functions. *Economica, 1*(2), 196–219. https://doi.org/10.2307/2548749

Kahneman, D., & Deaton, A. (2010). High income improves evaluation of life but not emotional well-being. *Proceedings of the National Academy of Sciences of the United States of America (PNAS), 107*(38), 16489–16493. https://doi.org/10.1073/pnas.1011492107

Kahneman, D., & Krueger, A. B. (2006). Developments in the measurement of subjective well-being. *Journal of Economic Perspectives, 20*(1), 3–24. https://doi.org/10.1257/089533006776526030

Kahneman, D., & Sugden, R. (2005). Experienced utility is a standard of policy evaluation. *Environmental and Resource Economics, 32*(1), 161–181. https://doi.org/10.1007/s10640-005-6032-4

Kahneman, D., Wakker, P. P., & Sarin, R. (1997). Back to Bentham? Explorations of experienced utility. *Quarterly Journal of Economics, 112*(2), 375–406. https://doi.org/10.1162/003355397555235

Kasser, T. (2017). Living both well and sustainably: A review of the literature, with some reflections on future research, interventions and policy. *Philosophical Transactions of the Royal Society A: Mathematical, Physical and Engineering Sciences, 375*(2095). https://doi.org/10.1098/rsta.2016.0369

Kessler, R. C., Andrews, G., Colpe, L. J., Hiripi, E., Mroczek, D. K., Normand, S.-L.T., Walters, E. E., & Zaslavsky, A. M. (2002). Short screening scales to monitor population prevalences and trends in non-specific psychological distress. *Psychological Medicine, 32*(6), 959–976. https://doi.org/10.1017/S0033291702006074

Kessler, R. C., Barker, P. R., Colpe, L. J., Epstein, J. F., Gfroerer, J. C., Hiripi, E., Howes, M. J., Normand, S.-L.T., Manderscheid, R. W., Walters, E. E., & Zaslavsky, A. M. (2003). Screening for serious mental illness in the general population. *Archives of General Psychiatry, 60*(2), 184. https://doi.org/10.1001/archpsyc.60.2.184

Kessler, R. C., Green, J. G., Gruber, M. J., Sampson, N. A., Bromet, E., Cuitan, M., Furukawa, T. A., Gureje, O., Hinkov, H., Hu, C., Lara, C., Lee, S., Mneimneh, Z., Myer, L., Oakley-Browne, M., Posada-Villa, J., Sagar, R., Viana, M. C., & Zaslavsky, A. M. (2010). Screening for serious mental illness in the general population with the K6 screening scale: Results from the WHO World Mental Health (WMH) survey initiative. *International Journal of Methods in Psychiatric Research, 19*(S1), 4–22. https://doi.org/10.1002/mpr.310

Lace, J. W., Merz, Z. C., Grant, A. F., Emmert, N. A., Zane, K. L., & Handal, P. J. (2020). Validation of the K6 and its depression and anxiety subscales for detecting nonspecific psychological distress and need for treatment. *Current Psychology, 39*(5), 1552–1561. https://doi.org/10.1007/s12144-018-9846-2

Layard, R. (2005). *Happiness: Lessons from a new science*. Penguin Books.

Layard, R., Clark, A. E., Cornaglia, F., Powdthavee, N., & Vernoit, J. (2014). What predicts a successful life? A life-course model of well-being. *Economic Journal, 124*(580), F720–F738. https://doi.org/10.1111/ecoj.12170

Loewenstein, G., & Ubel, P. A. (2008). Hedonic adaptation and the role of decision and experience utility in public policy. *Journal of Public Economics, 92*(8), 1795–1810. https://doi.org/10.1016/j.jpubeco.2007.12.011

Lombardo, P., Jones, W., Wang, L., et al. (2018). The fundamental association between mental health and life satisfaction: Results from successive waves of a Canadian national survey. *BMC Public Health, 18*, 342. https://doi.org/10.1186/s12889-018-5235-x

Marsh, H. W., Huppert, F. A., Donald, J. N., Horwood, M. S., & Sahdra, B. K. (2020). The well-being profile (WB-Pro): Creating a theoretically based multidimensional measure of well-being to advance theory, research, policy, and practice. *Psychological Assessment, 32*(3), 294–313. https://doi.org/10.1037/pas0000787

Marshall, A. (1890). *Principles of economics*. Macmillan.

Mewton, L., Kessler, R. C., Slade, T., Hobbs, M. J., Brownhill, L., Birrell, L., Tonks, Z., Teesson, M., Newton, N., Chapman, C., Allsop, S., Hides, L., McBride, N., & Andrews, G. (2016). The psychometric properties of the Kessler Psychological Distress Scale (K6) in a general population sample of adolescents. *Psychological Assessment, 28*(10), 1232–1242. https://doi.org/10.1037/pas0000239

Mill, J. S. (1863). *Utilitarianism*. Parker, Son, and Bourn.

Montgomery, M. (2022). Reversing the gender gap in happiness. *Journal of Economic Behavior and Organization, 196*, 65–78. https://doi.org/10.1016/j.jebo.2022.01.006

Nagel, T. (1972). Aristotle on eudaimonia. *Phronesis, 17*(3), 252–259.

Nakagawa, S., & Schielzeth, H. (2013). A general and simple method for obtaining R^2 from generalized linear mixed-effects models. *Methods in Ecology and Evolution, 4*(2), 133–142. https://doi.org/10.1111/j.2041-210x.2012.00261.x

Nikolova, M., & Graham, C. (2022). The economics of happiness. In K. F. Zimmermann (Ed.), *Handbook of labor, human resources and population economics*. Springer. https://doi.org/10.1007/978-3-319-57365-6_177-2

Nilsson, A. H., Eichstaedt, J. C., Lomas, T., Schwartz, A., & Kjell, O. (2024). The Cantril ladder elicits thoughts about power and wealth. *Scientific Reports, 14*(1), 2642. https://doi.org/10.1038/s41598-024-52939-y

OECD. (1976). *Measuring social well-being: A progress report on the development of social indicators*. OECD Publications Center.

Pareto, V. (1971). *Manual of political economy* (A. S. Schwier, Trans.). Augustus M. Kelley (original work published as Manuale di economia politica, 1906).

Pigou, A. C. (1920). *The economics of welfare*. Macmillan.

Powdthavee, N. (2007). Putting a price tag on friends, relatives, and neighbours: Using surveys of life satisfaction to value social relationships. *The Journal of Socio-Economics*. https://doi.org/10.1016/j.socec.2007.04.004

Robbins, L. (1932). *An essay on the nature and significance of economic science*. Macmillan.

Rose, R., & Haerpfer, C. (1994). Mass response to transformation in post-communist societies. *Europe-Asia Studies, 46*(1), 3–28. https://doi.org/10.1080/09668139408412147

Rose, R., Mishler, W., & Haerpfer, C. W. (1998). *Democracy and its alternatives: Understanding post-communist societies*. Polity Press.

Ryan, R. M., & Deci, E. L. (2001). On happiness and human potentials: A review of research on hedonic and eudaimonic well-being. *Annual Review of Psychology, 52*(1), 141–166. https://www.annualreviews.org/doi/10.1146/annurev.psych.52.1.141

Ryff, C. D. (1989a). Beyond Ponce de Leon and life satisfaction: New directions in quest of successful ageing. *International Journal of Behavioral Development, 12*(1), 35–55. https://doi.org/10.1177/016502548901200102

Ryff, C. D. (1989b). Happiness is everything, or is it? Explorations on the meaning of psychological well-being. *Journal of Personality and Social Psychology, 57*(6), 1069–1081. https://doi.org/10.1037/0022-3514.57.6.1069

Samuelson, P. A. (1938). A note on the pure theory of consumer's behaviour. *Economica, 5*(17), 61–71. https://doi.org/10.2307/2548836

Samuelson, P. A. (1948). Consumption theory in terms of revealed preference. *Economica, 15*(60), 243–253. https://doi.org/10.2307/2549561

Shapley, L. (1953). A value for n-person games. In H. W. Kuhn & A. W. Tucker (Eds.), *Contributions to the theory of games* (Vol. 2). Princeton University Press.

Smith, A. (1776). *The wealth of nations*. W. Strahan and T. Cadell.

Snijders, T. A. B., & Bosker, R. J. (2012). *Multilevel analysis: An introduction to basic and advanced multilevel modeling* (2nd ed.). Sage.

Shorrocks, A. F. (2013). Decomposition procedures for distributional analysis: A unified framework based on the Shapley value. *The Journal of Economic Inequality. Society for the Study of Economic Inequality, 11*(1), 99–126.

Stiglitz, J. E., Amartya, S., & Fitoussi, J.-P. (2009). *Report by the commission on the measurement of economic performance and social progress*. The Commission on the Measurement of Economic Performance and Social Progress (formed by the initiative of the French Government). https://ec.europa.eu/eurostat/documents/8131721/8131772/Stiglitz-Sen-Fitoussi-Commission-report.pdf

Sugden, R. (2014). *The community of advantage: A behavioural economist's defence of the market*. Oxford Economic Press.

Sunderland, M., Mahoney, A., & Andrews, G. (2012). Investigating the factor structure of the Kessler Psychological Distress Scale in community and clinical samples of the Australian population. *Journal of Psychopathology and Behavioral Assessment, 34*(2), 253–259. https://doi.org/10.1007/s10862-012-9276-7

Vonesh, E., & Chinchilli, V. M. (1997). Linear mixed-effects models for repeated measurements. In *Linear and nonlinear models for the analysis of repeated measurements* (Chapter 6). CRC Press.

Watson, G. (1930). Happiness among adult students of education. *Journal of Educational Psychology, 21*(2), 79–109. https://doi.org/10.1037/h0070539

Wilson, W. R. (1967). Correlates of avowed happiness. *Psychological Bulletin, 67*(4), 294–306. https://doi.org/10.1037/h0024431

Chapter 5
Economic Growth and Internal Migration

Takayuki Yamashita and Tamaki Morita

Abstract Population decline has recently become a significant issue in Japan's regional economies. The population has become increasingly concentrated only in the capital, Tokyo. This chapter incorporates a geographical and economic analysis to clarify the issues of this population movement. It focuses on Shizuoka Prefecture as a case study from a national and regional perspective. Our study, which takes a non-hierarchical approach, delves into the migration dynamics between the 47 prefectural capitals and the 46 prefectural capitals, using the 2020 Census data.

Keywords Laws of migration · Hierarchical urban structure · Urban migration · Gravity model · Out migration · Gender differences

5.1 Introduction

Japan's population is concentrated in large cities, especially Tokyo Metropolis. Briefly looking at the numbers of people who moved outside of their prefectures in 2020 (Fig. 5.1), Tokyo (#13) and other prefectures nearby (#11 Saitama, #12 Chiba, and #14 Kanagawa) in the Kanto region experienced both flow-ins (vertical lines) and flow-outs (horizontal lines), but colors of flow-ins are slightly thicker (i.e., larger numbers) than flow-outs.

From an analysis of the British population censuses of 1871 and 1881, Ernst Georg Ravenstein (1834–1913) conceptualized the interregional migration of populations. The laws are summarized as follows (Ravenstein, 1885, pp. 198–199):

T. Yamashita (✉)
School of Global Studies and Collaboration, Aoyama Gakuin University, Sagamihara City, Kanagawa, Japan
e-mail: yamashita.takayuki@gsc.aoyama.ac.jp

T. Morita
Faculty of Aviation Management, J. F. Oberlin University, Tama City, Tokyo, Japan
e-mail: morita_t01@obirin.ac.jp

T. Yamashita and T. Morita (eds.), *On the Structural Transformation of the Japanese Economy 1985-2023*, Advances in Japanese Business and Economics 38,
https://doi.org/10.1007/978-981-95-7230-4_5

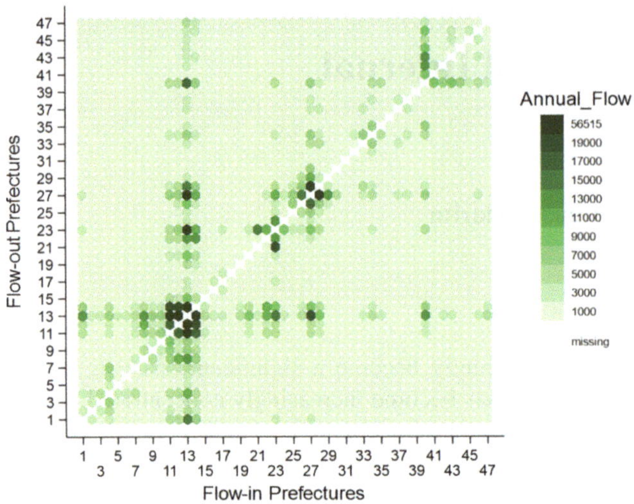

Region	No.	Prefecture	Region	No.	Prefecture
*	1	**Hokkaido**	Kinki	24	Mie
Tohoku	2	Aomori		25	Shiga
	3	Iwate		26	Kyoto
	4	**Miyagi**		27	**Osaka**
	5	Akita		28	Hyogo
	6	Yamagata		29	Nara
	7	Fukushima		30	Wakayama
Kanto	8	Ibaraki	Chugoku	31	Tottori
	9	Tochigi		32	Shimane
	10	Gunma		33	Okayama
	11	Saitama		34	**Hiroshima**
	12	Chiba		35	Yamaguchi
	13	**Tokyo**	Shikoku	36	Tokushima
	14	Kanagawa		37	Kagawa
Chubu	15	Niigata		38	Ehime
	16	Toyama		39	Kouchi
	17	Ishikawa	Kyushu & Okinawa	40	**Fukuoka**
	18	Fukui		41	Saga
	19	Yamanashi		42	Nagasaki
	20	Nagano		43	Kumamoto
	21	Gifu		44	Ooita
	22	Shizuoka		45	Miyazaki
	23	**Aichi**		46	Kagoshima
				47	Okinawa

Fig. 5.1 Number of persons moved: outflows and inflows by prefecture. *Notes* 1. This data excludes the moves inside a prefecture. 2. Numbers in the legend are the median of each category. 3. Prefectural numbers with regions are listed in the tables at the right. 4. Prefectures shaded in the list include seven major metropolitan areas. * The region name for Hokkaido is "Hokkaido Region." *Source* Compiled by the author with data from the National Population Census

(1) The majority of migrants only move short distances. As a result, there is a universal migration of the population, and this creates a "migration flow" that is set to move towards large commercial and industrial centers that absorb migrants. When creating this estimate of migration, the number of people born in each prefecture that supplies migrants, as well as the population of the towns that absorb them, must also be taken into account.

(2) Residents living in the immediate vicinity of a rapidly growing town will flock to it. The gaps that arise in the rural population will be filled by migrants from even more distant regions, insofar as the appeal of the rapidly growing town gradually reaches the furthest reaches.

(3) The dispersal process of the population is the reverse of the absorption process and shows similar characteristics.

(4) The main flow of migration creates a counter-current that offsets it.

(5) Those who move long distances generally prefer to go to one of the larger commercial or industrial centers.

(6) Those born in towns do not move as much as those born in rural areas.

(7) Women are more mobile than men.

The following law was added in the 1989 paper (Ravenstein, 1889, pp. 287–288):

(8) If you rely only on natural increase (of the population), the population of large cities will increase very slowly, and in some cases even decrease.
(9) Women predominate among short-distance migrants.
(10) The increase in means of transport and the development of industry and commerce increase the number of migrants.

Walter Christaller (1893–1969), a German geographer, observed the spatial distribution of cities and towns in southern Germany and found that a hierarchical structure can be observed in spatial market areas according to the distance reached by goods and services. According to his central place theory, each city is divided into a hierarchy from the highest to the lowest, with the lower cities following only one higher city.

In Japan, people began moving from the surrounding prefectures to large cities such as Tokyo and Osaka during the Meiji period (Takahashi, 2006). After World War II, the concentration of the population in cities progressed at a rapid pace during the period of high economic growth (1955–1973). Research based on central place theory became active to clarify urban functions. The relationship among cities in Japan is considered to show a hierarchy consisting of multiple layers.

This chapter discusses the internal migration in Japan after 1990. Section 5.2 reveals the hierarchical structure of internal migration, Sect. 5.3 raises the current issue of over-concentration of the population in Tokyo, Sect. 5.4 explores the economic factors of out-migration, and Sect. 5.5 discusses the factors that encourage in-migration.

5.2 Internal Migration Under Hierarchical Structure

Population migration along the hierarchical structure is analyzed using a robust and widely accepted method. Morikawa found a four-level hierarchy examining domestic migration (Morikawa, 1985, 2016). He further attempted to classify cities by adding a study of population size and urban functions to the study of population movement zones and obtained a six-level hierarchy (Morikawa, 2022).

The hierarchical structure of Japanese cities is generally thought to be arranged in the following order: municipalities with a declining population at the bottom, followed by small and medium-sized cities, prefectural capitals, regional capitals, and the special wards of Tokyo. The order reflects the population size but is often connected to the central management function. In this chapter, we use a four-level hierarchy (Fig. 5.2).

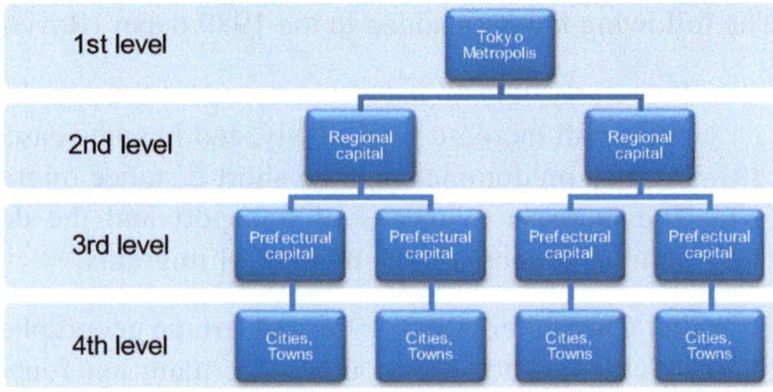

Fig. 5.2 Hierarchical structure of the Japanese urban system

The 2nd level consists of Osaka City, Nagoya City, and four regional capitals[1]: Sapporo City, Sendai City, Hiroshima City, and Fukuoka City. The 3rd level consists of 40 prefectural capitals.

5.3 Current Issues in Internal Migration

According to the *2016 Report on Internal Migration in Japan Derived from the Basic Resident Registration*, Shizuoka City, the 3rd level recorded an excess of outgoing transfers for the first time. Shizuoka City is the prefectural capital of Shizuoka Prefecture and a Government Ordinance Designated City,[2] so this report shocked not only residents but nationwide.

If we look into the characteristics of this population outflow, we will see that the outflow of women has had a strong impact (Yamashita, 2019). Many young people from Shizuoka City attend universities in Tokyo, Aichi, and other prefectures, but it has always been the case that they return when they finish their studies. However, the situation has changed because young women no longer return. A similar situation was observed in Hiroshima Prefecture. Since then, the exodus of women from regional cities has spread nationwide.

Table 5.1 shows the breakdown of population movement from prefectural capitals. The population migration used to follow a step-by-step hierarchical structure. However, the female population now prefers to move directly from the 3rd to the 1st level of the hierarchy, skipping the 2nd level.

Figure 5.3 shows a migration from the 3rd to the 1st level that does not go through the 2nd level.

A gravity model is used in empirical research on population movement. A gravity model is a model that explains population migration in terms of the concept of the law

[1] According to Hino (2017), the term "regional central city" started to be used as the 2nd level in the 1960s in Japanese geography.

[2] Twelve Government Ordinance Designated Cities are large cities with a population of 500,000 or more. They are given special authority by the national government to provide administrative services over a wide area.

Table 5.1 Destinations from migration (%)

		From prefectural capitals (40 cities)		
		To Tokyo	To regional capitals	To other areas
Male	1990	16.4	14.7	68.9
	2000	13.6	16.4	70.0
	2010	13.2	15.8	71.0
	2015	13.4	15.7	70.8
	2020	14.7	15.5	69.8
Female	1990	14.2	15.0	70.8
	2000	15.4	16.0	68.6
	2010	15.1	15.7	69.2
	2015	15.8	14.9	69.3
	2020	17.6	15.5	66.9

Source Compiled by the author based on the Population Census

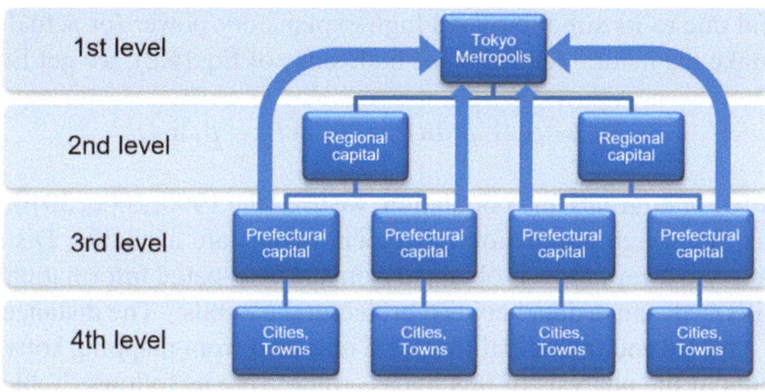

Fig. 5.3 Hierarchical structure of the urban system and bypass to the second level

of universal gravitation in physics. It relates the law of universal gravitation discovered by Sir Isaac Newton (1642–1727) to economic activity. This model allows us to understand the dynamics of population movement between each level of the hierarchy with confidence and precision: a statistical tool commonly used in economics to predict the movement of people or goods between two locations,

$$M_{ij} = \alpha \frac{P_i P_j}{D_{ij}} \tag{5.1}$$

where M_{ij} is the number of people moving from region i to region j, P_i is the population of region i, P_j is the population of region j, and D_{ij} is the distance between the two regions. Regional population is the basis for the supply and demand of goods and services and is thought to explain the interregional movement of goods and people. This framework is consistent with Lavenstein's law.

If we generalize Eq. (5.1), we get the following equation:

$$M_{ij} = \alpha \frac{P_i^{\beta_1} P_j^{\beta_2}}{D_{ij}^{\beta_3}} \tag{5.2}$$

where β_i $(i = 1, 2, 3)$ is a parameter. Physical, time, and economic distance can be used as distance. The larger the population size of the place of origin, the more people will migrate. The population size of the destination is generally considered to be a proxy variable for the labor market, and the larger the size of the labor market, the more likely it is that both the number and variety of available employment opportunities will be large (Greenwood, 1975, p. 419). In cases where the industrial base differs, such as when moving from a rural area to a city, the population of the place of departure acts as a push factor, while the population of the destination acts as a pull factor.

Although the gravity model is not necessarily an excellent theoretical model, it is highly useful due to its simplicity and high explanatory power for actual aggregate data. If we take the natural logarithm of both sides of Eq. (5.2), we get Eq. (5.3).

$$\ln M_{ij} = \beta_0 + \beta_1 \ln P_i + \beta_2 \ln P_j - \beta_3 \ln D_{ij} \tag{5.3}$$

For the number of migrants and population, we used the 1990, 2000, 2010, 2015, and 2020 census, for which population movement counts are available. Distance (km) between prefectural capitals was obtained from the Geospatial Information Authority of Japan (GSI)'s distance data between prefectural capitals.[3] The distances between prefectural capitals and municipalities were obtained from mapping software.

The results of the analysis of this bypass route were as follows (Table 5.2). The values in parentheses below the coefficients are t-values and $\boldsymbol{R}^2_{adj}$ is the adjusted coefficient of determination for the degrees of freedom.

Table 5.2 indicates the force of the current residential population pushing out-migration. The upward trend is shown for both men and women, indicating a stronger tendency to move directly to Tokyo 23 special wards without taking a hierarchical route. In addition, β_3, which implies hindrance by distance traveled, is higher for females, which is consistent with the discussion of Rabenstein's law.

For comparison, the migration from the 3rd to the 2nd level that does not go through the 2nd level is as follows. Interestingly, when comparing Tables 5.2 and 5.3, the resistance to the distance from the prefectural capitals to Tokyo is lower than that from the prefectural capitals to the regional centers.

[3] https://www.gsi.go.jp/.

Table 5.2 Migration from prefectural capitals to Tokyo

Year		β_0	β_1	β_2	β_3	R^2_{adj}
1990	Male	0.0477 (0.029)	0.764 (6.398)	–	0.247 (3.062)	0.616
	Female	0.349 (0.191)	0.7436 (5.507)	–	0.320 (3.586)	0.574
2000	Male	−2.091 (−1.987)	0.966 (12.725)	–	0.335 (6.795)	0.886
	Female	−1.849 (−1.443)	0.957 (10.271)	–	0.409 (6.872)	0.845
2010	Male	−3.209 (−3.005)	1.017 (13.647)	–	0.303 (6.130)	0.904
	Female	−3.302 (−2.640)	1.031 (11.722)	–	0.352 (6.129)	0.875
2015	Male	−4.055 (−3.801)	1.069 (14.373)	–	0.291 (6.027)	0.911
	Female	−3.807 (−2.999)	1.064 (11.931)	–	0.356 (6.269)	0.880
2020	Male	−5.859 (−6.503)	1.163 (18.560)	–	0.218 (5.288)	0.940
	Female	−6.103 (−5.533)	1.191 (15.460)	–	0.261 (5.181)	0.915

Source Estimated by the author based on the Population Census

5.4 Factors that Push Women to Migrate

Why are women increasingly moving to Tokyo? Hayashi (2016) attributes this trend to women's higher education and increasing opportunities to play an active role. Table 5.4 compares persons engaged in three economic sectors. One characteristic of the Tokyo special wards is the high proportion of people engaged in the tertiary industry. This employment opportunity may be affecting the internal migration of women.

Yamashita (2019) noted that an economy centered on service industries facilitated the out-migration of female workers. While female workers often work in the service industry, this sector has a high rate of turnover. Prefectural capitals serve as hubs for retail, medical/welfare, lodging, and food service industries within regional economies. However, compared to the Tokyo metropolitan area, they offer fewer attractive workplaces, leading to an outflow of the female population.

We will use a modified gravity model to see the impact of industrial structure.[4] It is easy to add the explanatory variables on the right-hand side of Eq. (5.3) as Eq.

[4] The model that adds various variables related to the decision to move to the basic gravity model is called the "modified gravity model" or "extended gravity model" (Greenwood, 2016, p. 33). Income, unemployment rate, degree of urbanization, and climate are additional variables.

Table 5.3 Migration from prefectural capitals to regional capitals

Year		β_0	β_1	β_2	β_3	R^2_{adj}
1990	Male	−7.048 (−5.261)	1.051 (14.071)	0.472 (7.740)	1.080 (18.617)	0.751
	Female	−8.006 (−5.788)	1.069 (12.780)	0.540 (8.069)	1.095 (17.201)	0.724
2000	Male	−7.653 (−5.830)	1.067 (15.172)	0.481 (7.727)	1.065 (19.384)	0.766
	Female	−8.820 (−6.191)	1.058 (13.737)	0.559 (8.347)	1.095 (18.770)	0.751
2010	Male	−7.940 (−6.338)	1.066 (16.272)	0.478 (7.876)	1.036 (20.070)	0.779
	Female	−9.825 (−7.385)	1.028 (15.487)	0.634 (9.999)	1.087 (20.235)	0.780
2015	Male	−8.766 (−6.639)	1.110 (16.010)	0.466 (7.353)	0.973 (18.197)	0.757
	Female	−10.383 (−7.100)	1.096 (14.181)	0.587 (8.442)	1.023 (17.540)	0.740
2020	Male	−4.792 (−2.459)	1.109 (17.246)	0.149 (1.190)	0.940 (19.225)	0.742
	Female	−8.730 (−4.003)	1.083 (14.875)	0.470 (3.362)	1.031 (18.886)	0.719

Source Estimated by the author based on the Population Census

Table 5.4 Percentage of workers engaged in economic sector (%, 2020)

	Japan		Tokyo	
	Male	Female	Male	Female
Primary sector	3.9	3.0	0.2	0.1
Secondary sector	31.6	14.2	18.5	9.6
Tertiary sector	64.4	82.8	81.3	90.3

Source Compiled by the author from the Census

(5.4).

$$\ln M_{ij} = \beta_0 + \beta_1 \ln P_i + \beta_2 \ln P_j - \beta_3 \ln D_{ij} + \beta_4 X_i \tag{5.4}$$

We will add the percentage of employment in the tertiary industry in prefecture i as an explanatory variable and see the impact on population migration. The analysis results are summarized in Table 5.5.

Regarding population movement from the third level to Tokyo, the rise in the ratio of tertiary industry in the place of departure has a positive effect on migration. In

Table 5.5 Migration from prefectural cities to Tokyo

Year		β_0	β_1	β_2	β_3	β_4	R^2_{adj}
1990	Male	2.388 (1.419)	0.7249 (6.618)	–	0.376 (4.395)	2.870 (2.936)	0.626
	Female	3.367 (1.857)	0.691 (5.806)	–	0.484 (5.315)	3.680 (3.502)	0.674
2000	Male	0.257 (0.284)	0.910 (15.676)	–	0.440 (10.509)	3.009 (5.414)	0.935
	Female	1.112 (1.040)	0.886 (12.798)	–	0.539 (10.984)	3.811 (5.750)	0.917
2010	Male	−0.524 (−0.529)	0.922 (15.086)	–	0.395 (9.251)	3.158 (4.990)	0.886
	Female	0.0686 (0.0611)	0.911 (13.090)	–	0.464 (9.728)	3.958 (5.458)	0.930
2015	Male	−1.380 (−1.339)	0.953 (14.721)	–	0.363 (8.710)	3.139 (4.648)	0.943
	Female	−0.669 (−0.532)	0.926 (11.663)	–	0.437 (8.752)	3.672 (4.406)	0.920
2020	Male	−15.931 (−7.127)	1.068 (19.953)	–	0.278 (7.920)	2.661 (4.756)	0.960
	Female	−18.524 (−6.575)	1.072 (16.022)	–	0.333 (7.694)	3.290 (4.643)	0.942

Source Estimated by the author based on the Population Census

other words, the more the service economy develops in the prefectural capital cities, the more people move to Tokyo.

In nineteenth-century Britain, when Ravenstein was considering the "law of migration," "the majority of (female) migrants came in search of domestic service," but at the same time, "they hoped to find employment in shops and factories" (Ravenstein, 1885, p. 197). Today, women in Japan also tend to work in the tertiary industry. However, the fact that the value is more significant for women than for men may suggest that population movement is more effortless in the tertiary industry. The more the tertiary industry grows, the more migration will increase.

We will further subdivide the tertiary sector to examine which economic activities are related to mobility. We will utilize a modified gravity model that captures the economic characteristics of prefectures,

$$\ln M_{ij} = \beta_0 + \beta_1 \ln P_i + \beta_2 \ln P_j - \beta_3 \ln D_{ij} + \sum_{k=1}^{14} \gamma_k LQ_k + TECH_i \qquad (5.5)$$

where LQ_k is a location quotient in the departure prefecture and $TECH_i$ is the technological progress of the departure prefecture in Chap. 3. Without limiting ourselves to hierarchical frameworks, we analyzed migration between the 47 prefectural capitals and the 46 prefectural capitals using 2020 Census data.[5]

Table 5.6 provides important insights for understanding population migration. We found that specialization in the information and communications industry, the accommodation industry, the food and beverage service industry, and the medical, health, and welfare service industry are factors inducing population outflow. On the other hand, although the statistical significance is low, we obtained an interesting result: the finance and insurance industry, which has strong ties to the regional economy, negatively impacts population migration. This finding has significant implications for regional economic planning, making it a crucial area for further research and policy development.

Furthermore, the results suggest that technical progress affects men and women differently. While technical progress in the regional economy leads to labor-saving effects, it also becomes a factor encouraging men's migration. This finding underscores the necessity for a nuanced understanding of technology's influence on population movement. Given that the impact of the location quotient in the service industry is generally higher for women than for men, this suggests that women are more likely to find economic opportunities in sectors such as interpersonal services, where the effects of technological progress are less significant.

5.5 Factors that Induce Migration

In this section, using the year 2020 data, we consider two external factors of arrival prefectures that may invite migration—one is the relative wage rates, and the other is the average subjective well-being (SWB) of residents. SWB represents the quality of life in the arrival prefectures. The prefectures that include seven major metropolitan areas (7MMA)[6] are also included. The equation for the estimation here becomes Eq. (5.6).

$$\ln M_{ij} = \beta_0 + \beta_1 \ln P_i + \beta_2 \ln P_j - \beta_3 \ln D_{ij} + \beta_{WAGE} WAGE_j + \beta_{SWB} SWB_j + \varepsilon \tag{5.6}$$

We have tried other possible explanatory variables, but only two of the variables above were significant.

Wage rates have been considered an important factor in determining internal migrations. Harris and Todaro (1970) modeled migrations according to expected incomes. Economic costs such as migration typically explain the remaining regional

[5] The number of observations is $47 \times 46 = 2162$. However, the number of observations for females is 2152, as there is missing data on migration.

[6] The seven major metropolitan areas are: Tokyo, Nagoya, Osaka, Sapporo, Sendai, Hiroshima, and Fukuoka. The prefectures that comprise them (and used as variables in the estimations) are Tokyo, Aichi, Osaka, Hokkaido, Miyagi, Hiroshima, and Fukuoka, respectively.

Table 5.6 Push factors of internal migration

	Male	Female
β_0	17.76675*** (8.09)	−41.98894*** (−8.48)
β_1	0.9634159*** (18.98)	0.9737742*** (18.34)
β_2	1.076366*** (65.92)	1.170799*** (68.06)
β_3	−0.9699986*** (−50.86)	−1.037028*** (−51.91)
γ_1: Agriculture and forestry	0.5817997** (3.32)	0.6828963** (3.72)
γ_2: Fisheries	0.0352467+ (1.68)	0.0316266 (1.42)
γ_3: Mining and quarrying of stone and gravel	0.0227181 (0.84)	.0516623+ (1.82)
γ_4: Construction	2.264478*** (5.87)	2.149029*** (5.31)
γ_5: Manufacturing	3.241416*** (4.35)	3.697373*** (4.74)
γ_6: Electricity, gas, heat supply and water	0.03577 (0.36)	0.141057 (1.36)
γ_7: Information and communications	0.7233629*** (3.96)	0.8805864*** (4.62)
γ_8: Transport and postal activities	1.74128*** (4.1)	1.876434*** (4.22)
γ_9: Wholesale and retail trade	3.049409*** (3.71)	3.157953*** (3.63)
γ_{10}: Finance and insurance	−0.1752832 (−0.43)	−0.303441 (−0.72)
γ_{11}: Real estate and goods rental and leasing	1.076533** (3.4)	1.203367*** (3.62)
γ_{12}: Scientific research, professional and technical services	1.273413** (3.39)	1.367406** (3.47)
γ_{13}: Accommodations, eating and drinking services	1.442401** (3.39)	1.649212*** (3.68)
γ_{14}: Living-related and personal services and amusement services	−0.1249009 (−0.30)	−0.1796603 (−0.42)
γ_{15}: Education, learning support	1.175907** (2.71)	1.257915** (2.77)
γ_{16}: Medical, health care and welfare	2.774506*** (4.18)	3.398705*** (4.88)
γ_{17}: Compound services	0.3247815* (2.34)	0.3287721* (2.25)

(continued)

Table 5.6 (continued)

	Male	Female
γ_{18}: Services, n.e.c	1.547678* (2.31)	1.876882** (2.67)
γ_{19}: Government, except elsewhere classified	1.600786*** (6.24)	1.844434*** (6.86)
Tech	4.776755 (0.61)	−6.917646 (−0.84)
R^2_{adj}	0.8401	0.8409

Note 1. $^{+}$ $p < 0.10$, * $p < 0.05$, ** $p < 0.01$, *** $p < 0.001$
2. t-values are in parentheses

differences (Redding & Rossi-Hansberg, 2017), so basic momentum to move to higher-wage areas always exists fundamentally. Our data was taken from the prefectural average of scheduled cash earnings per person/month in 2023 (source: "Monthly Labour Survey," Statistics and Information Department, Minister's Secretariat, Ministry of Health, Labour, and Welfare of Japan). We made the variable *WAGE* as the ratio of average wage rates of the departure prefecture to that of the arriving prefecture.

SWB here is a proxy of amenities. Moro et al., (2008, p. 455) provided findings that "simple SWB averages per (Ireland's) county reflect the 'objective' level of environmental endowment in those counties." We used *SWB* represented by the prefectural average to a survey question: "How satisfied are you with your life as a whole? If 'not satisfied at all' is 0 points and 'very satisfied' is 10 points, what score would you give?" collected by the Cabinet Office of Japan in 2022. Details of the survey are explained in Chap. 4.

The Pearson product-moment correlation coefficient between *WAGE* and *SWB* is 0.1530 ($p < 0.001$), and the two variables are not correlated.

Equation (5.6) now becomes:

$$\ln M_{ij} = \beta_0 + \beta_1 \ln P_i + \beta_2 \ln P_j - \beta_3 \ln D_{ij} + \beta_{WAGE} WAGE_j + \beta_{SWB} SWB_j + \sum_{k=1}^{7} \gamma_k Z_k + \varepsilon \quad (5.7)$$

In Eq. (5.7), Z_k is the seven prefectures dummies, and γ_k is its coefficients.

Table 5.7 shows the estimation results. The left column (Model 1) is the result of the estimation of the total number of migrations, and the middle column (Model 2a) is the result of the migrations among prefectural capitals (both departments and arrivals are in prefectural capitals). The right column (Model 2b) is the result for the migrations other than among prefectural capitals, i.e., areas other than prefectural capitals and migrations that either depart from or arrive at prefectural capitals but not both. To compare the coefficients between the two models, we used seemingly

Table 5.7 Factors affecting migration in 2020 (All migrations)

		(1) All migrations	(2a) Among prefectural capitals	(2b) Among other areas
β_0		-20.806^{***} (1.033)	-18.804^{***} (1.121)	-19.218^{***} (1.131)
β_1		1.116^{***} (0.049)	1.070^{***} (0.048)	1.066^{***} (0.058)
β_2		0.978^{***} (0.046)	0.954^{***} (0.024)	0.972^{***} (0.054)
β_3		-0.935^{***} (0.063)	-0.919^{***} (0.066)	-0.952^{***} (0.064)
β_{WAGE}		0.878^{+} (0.443)	0.925^{**} (0.318)	0.431 (0.661)
β_{SWB}		0.441^{***} (0.106)	0.329^{**} (0.115)	0.495^{***} (0.105)
γ_1	Tokyo	0.336^{***} (0.065)	0.316^{***} (0.059)	1.023^{***} (0.114)
γ_2	Nagoya	-0.236^{***} (0.056)	-0.048 (0.063)	-0.215^{***} (0.058)
γ_3	Osaka	-0.251^{**} (0.082)	-0.360^{***} (0.065)	-0.125 (0.092)
γ_4	Sapporo	0.656^{***} (0.049)	0.629^{***} (0.061)	0.759^{***} (0.056)
γ_5	Sendai	0.379^{***} (0.082)	0.670^{***} (0.098)	0.431^{***} (0.092)
γ_6	Hiroshima	0.286^{**} (0.090)	0.290^{**} (0.085)	0.419^{***} (0.089)
γ_7	Fukuoka	0.485^{***} (0.083)	0.763^{***} (0.072)	0.429^{***} (0.081)
R^2		0.8190	0.8053	0.7972

Note 1. $+ p < 0.10$, $^{*} p < 0.05$, $^{**} p < 0.01$, $^{***} p < 0.001$
2. Standard errors are in parentheses. The standard errors have been clustered by departure prefectures to account for intra-group correlation
3. For γ_k, the names of seven major metropolitan areas are listed, but the prefecture is used as the estimation unit. See Footnote 5

unrelated estimations (SUEST) on Model 2a and 2b as Model 2.[7] After SUEST, we can test whether the coefficients differ significantly between two equations (or groups).

Although it is not in the Tables, a gender comparison is also made (the table is available upon request). The migration flow increases by approximately 0.1 more

[7] SUEST is designed for testing. It combines the estimation results of separate models and constructs a joint variance–covariance matrix that captures both the individual estimation variability and any potential correlation between the models.

than proportional to the population sizes of departure cities, with this increase being significantly more prominent for females than males (the difference is −0.04). The flow grows less but is almost proportional to the size of the arrival cities for males, and more but almost proportional to the size of the arrival cities for females (−0.06 gap). Females tend to migrate to large cities compared to males. Distance matters significantly more to females (−0.967) than to males (−0.901), with a 0.07 difference.

Wage rates of arrival prefectures did not affect males on average (variance is substantial) but affected females. Although the males' wage coefficient is insignificant, the gender difference is significant at a −0.48 gap. Females tend to pursue higher incomes more than males.

In both genders, the higher the residents' average SWB in prefectures, the more people migrate to the prefectures. Females may attach more importance to amenities, or males may have more official transfers by large companies.

Among migrations to 7MMA, Tokyo, Sapporo, Sendai, Hiroshima, and Fukuoka are positive. The impact is larger for males in Sapporo, Sendai, and Hiroshima. Tokyo and Fukuoka did not show statistical gender differences. Nagoya and Osaka are negative, with Nagoya's negativity for females (−0.379) being more than twice that of males (−0.159). Osaka was −0.291 for each gender (the p-value of the coefficient equality test is 0.9870 and they cannot be different to each other).

When focusing on the movement between capital cities, the result can be seen in Table 5.8.

Looking into the pattern of immigration between capital cities, the migration flow increases by approximately 0.7 more than proportional to the population sizes of departure cities, with this increase being significantly more prominent for females than males (the difference is −0.05). The flow decreases but is almost proportional to the size of the arrival cities for males (0.939), and increases, but is nearly proportional to the size of the arrival cities for females (1.033, with a −0.09 gap). Females tend to migrate to large cities compared to males. Distance discourages movements for both genders but significantly more for females than for males, with a 0.05 difference.

Wage rates of arrival prefectures affect both genders, with a significant gender difference of −0.43. Females tend to pursue higher incomes more than males.

In both genders, the higher the residents' average SWB in prefectures, the more people migrate to the prefectures. Females have higher coefficients (0.282) than males (0.341), but the difference was not significant.

Among migrations to 7MMA, coefficients of Tokyo, Sapporo, Sendai, Hiroshima, and Fukuoka are positive. The impact is larger for males than for females in all of them. The coefficients for Nagoya and Osaka are negative, while the male's coefficient for Nagoya is insignificant. Females' negativity towards Osaka (−0.459) is stronger than that of males (−0.368) when moving between capital cities.

To summarize this section, we incorporated independent variables such as the 7MMA dummy variable, relative wages, and subjective well-being (SWB) as a proxy for amenities into the basic gravity models using single-year data from 2020. Overall, the coefficients for both relative wages and SWB were positive. This finding indicates that people tend to migrate to prefectures with relatively higher wages compared

Table 5.8 Factors affecting migration in 2020 (between capital cities, by gender)

		(2) Among prefectural capitals	(3a) Male	(3b) Female	Differences (3a)–(3b)
β_0		-18.804^{***} (1.121)	-17.915^{***} (1.129)	-20.620^{***} (1.125)	
β_1		1.070^{***} (0.048)	1.060^{***} (0.048)	1.107^{***} (0.050)	-0.05^{***}
β_2		0.954^{***} (0.024)	0.939^{***} (0.027)	1.033^{***} (0.023)	-0.09^{***}
β_3		-0.919^{***} (0.066)	-0.894^{***} (0.062)	-0.943^{***} (0.071)	$+0.05^{***}$
β_{WAGE}		0.925^{**} (0.318)	0.701^{*} (0.327)	1.126^{***} (0.320)	-0.43^{***}
β_{SWB}		0.329^{**} (0.115)	0.282^{*} (0.119)	0.341^{**} (0.116)	-0.06
γ_1	Tokyo	0.316^{***} (0.059)	0.283^{***} (0.061)	0.167^{**} (0.061)	$+0.12^{***}$
γ_2	Nagoya	-0.048 (0.063)	-0.012 (0.064)	-0.174^{**} (0.063)	$+0.16^{***}$
γ_3	Osaka	-0.360^{***} (0.065)	-0.368^{***} (0.071)	-0.459^{***} (0.063)	$+0.09^{**}$
γ_4	Sapporo	0.629^{***} (0.061)	0.653^{***} (0.062)	0.496^{***} (0.064)	$+0.16^{***}$
γ_5	Sendai	0.670^{***} (0.098)	0.749^{***} (0.088)	0.527^{***} (0.110)	$+0.22^{***}$
γ_6	Hiroshima	0.290^{**} (0.085)	0.334^{***} (0.083)	0.184^{*} (0.088)	$+0.15^{***}$
γ_7	Fukuoka	0.763^{***} (0.072)	0.761^{***} (0.070)	0.685^{***} (0.076)	$+0.08^{**}$
R^2		0.8059	0.8275	0.8342	
N		4313	2162	2151	

Note 1. $+p < 0.10$, $^{*}\ p < 0.05$, $^{**}\ p < 0.01$, $^{***}\ p < 0.001$
2. Standard errors are in parentheses. The standard errors have been clustered by departure prefectures to account for intra-group correlation
3. For γ_k, the names of seven major metropolitan areas are listed, but the prefecture is used as the estimation unit. See Footnote 5

Source Authors' estimation

to their departure prefectures and to those with higher average SWB. Migration is particularly pronounced toward Tokyo, Sapporo (Hokkaido Prefecture), Sendai (Miyagi Prefecture), Hiroshima, and Fukuoka, while it is less toward Nagoya (Aichi Prefecture) and Osaka.

When comparing "migration among prefectural capitals" to "migration among other areas," it appears that people are more likely to move to higher SWB prefectures when relocating "among other areas." The movement toward Tokyo is exceptionally substantial among areas outside of prefectural capitals.

When examining gender differences, the relative wages and SWB were more significant for females than for males. Among the 7MMAs, the gender disparity is most considerable in Nagoya (Aichi Prefecture), where there are less female immigrants than their male counterparts.

5.6 Conclusion

The concentration of population and business activities in the metropolitan capital poses many problems in developed countries and emerging economies. Overpopulation in the metropolis leads to high house prices, traffic congestion, and an imbalance in the country's development. COVID-19 reminds us of the weakness of over-concentration.

The Japanese government proposed the *Renkei Chūsū Toshiken Kōsō* (cooperative core urban areas vision), which promoted the formation of a "dam of population" in prefectural capitals and large rural cities to correct the uneven distribution of population since 2014.[8] Resistance to geographic distance to Tokyo seems to be getting smaller yearly, while resistance to regional capitals is the same. The development of a service economy, i.e., employment in the service sector, tends to facilitate mobility. People are interested in quality of life. It should be noted that there may be holes in the dam depending on the direction of local economic development.

Appendix

The summary statistics of data used in Sect. 5.4 are in Table 5.9.

[8] The central concepts of this vision are compact and networked. In order to ensure effective service delivery, the settlement of Japan should become more compact. In order to offset the loss of agglomeration due to the shrinking population, cities and towns will need to be networked (Masuda, 2014).

Table 5.9 Summary statistics of data used in Sect. 5.4

Variable		Mean	Std. dev.	Min.	Max.
Number of persons moved (log)	(1) All	5.847	1.604	1.609	11.450
	(2a) Cities	3.913	1.703	0.000	10.229
	(2b) Other	5.638	1.618	1.099	11.130
	(3a) Males	6.014	1.556	2.197	11.431
	(3b) Females	5.680	1.633	1.609	11.450
Number of persons leaving the prefecture (log)	(1) All	13.748	0.787	12.485	15.783
	(2a) Cities	12.521	0.872	11.423	15.417
	(2b) Other	13.353	0.789	12.061	15.158
	(3a) Males	13.715	0.794	12.485	15.747
	(3b) Females	13.781	0.780	12.574	15.783
Number of persons arriving the prefecture (log)	(1) All	13.749	0.787	12.485	15.783
	(2a) Cities	12.521	0.872	11.423	15.417
	(2b) Other	13.355	0.786	11.988	14.971
	(3a) Males	13.715	0.794	12.485	15.747
	(3b) Females	13.783	0.779	12.574	15.783
Distance between the two prefectures (log)		5.982	0.806	2.351	7.716
WAGE		1.007	0.124	0.678	1.475
SWB		5.753	0.213	5.254	6.282
D_1: TOKYO	(Tokyo)	0.021	0.144	0	1
D_2: NAGOYA	(Aichi)	0.021	0.144	0	1
D_3: OSAKA	(Osaka)	0.021	0.144	0	1
D_4: SAPPORO	(Hokkaido)	0.021	0.144	0	1
D_5: SENDAI	(Miyagi)	0.021	0.144	0	1
D_6: HIROSHIMA	(Hiroshima)	0.021	0.144	0	1
D_7: FUKUOKA	(Fukuoka)	0.021	0.144	0	1
Number of observations	(1) All	4324			
	(2a) Cities	4313			
	(2b) Other	4311			
	(3a) Males	2162			
	(3b) Females	2162			

References

Christaller, W. (1933). *Die zentralen Orte in Süddeutschland*. Gustav Fischer.

Greenwood, M. J. (1975). Research on Internal Migration in the United States: A Survey. *Journal of Economic Literature, 13*(2), 397–433.

Greenwood, M. J. (2016). Perspectives on migration theory—Economics. In M. J. White (Ed.), *International Handbook of Migration and Population Distribution* (pp. 31–40). Springer.

Harris, J. R., & Todaro, M. P. (1970). Migration, unemployment and development: A two-sector analysis. *American Economic Review, 60*(1), 126–142.

Hayashi, R. (2016). Chihō shōmetsu no kagi wo nigiru jyosei to idō [Women and mobility is the Key to regional decline: An analysis of "urban concentration of young women"]. *Yomiuri Quarterly, 36*, 70–78.

Hino, M. (2017). Yōgo 'Kouiki chushin toshi,' 'Chihō chusu toshi,' 'Sassenhirofuku' no tōjō to teichaku (Appearance and diffusion of three terms concerning with regional capital: Kouiki chushin toshi, Chihō chusu toshi and Sassenhirofuku). In *2017 nendo Nihon Chiri Gakkai Syunki Gakujyutu Taikai* [Proceedings of the General Meeting of the Association of Japanese Geographers, Springer 2017]. https://doi.org/10.14866/ajg.2017s.0_100046

Masuda, H. (Ed.). (2014). *Chihō shōmetsu—Tokyo ikkyoku shūchū ga maneku Jinkō kyūgen [Regional disappearance: Rapid population decline caused by concentration of population in Tokyo*]. Chuokoron Shinsha, Inc.

Morikawa, H. (1985). Jinkō idō kara mita waga kuni no toshi sisutemu [The Japanese urban system based on the analysis of internal migration]. *Jinbun Chiri* [*Japanese Journal of Human Geography*], *37*(1), 20–38. https://doi.org/10.4200/jjhg1948.37.20

Morikawa, H. (2016). 2010 nen no jinkō idō kara mita nihon no toshi sisutemu to chiiki seisaku [An overview of Japanese urban systems based on an analysis of internal migration in 2010 and regional development policies]. *Jinbun Chiri* [*Japanese Journal of Human Geography*], *68*(1), 22–43. https://doi.org/10.4200/jjhg.68.1_22

Morikawa, H. (2022). Nihon no toshi no kinō to toshi bunrui [A study of urban functions and city classification in Japan]. *Chiri Kagaku* [*Geographical Sciences*], *77*(4), 1–15. https://doi.org/10.20630/chirikagaku.77.4_191

Moro, M., Brereton, F., Ferreira, S., & Clinch, J. P. (2008). Ranking quality of life using subjective well-being data. *Ecological Economics, 65*(3), 448–460. https://doi.org/10.1016/j.ecolecon.2008.01.003

Ravenstein, E. G. (1885). The laws of migration. *Journal of the Statistical Society of London, 48*(2), 167–235.

Ravenstein, E. G. (1889). The laws of migration. *Journal of the Royal Statistical Society, 52*(2), 241–305.

Redding, S. J., & Rossi-Hansberg, E. (2017). Quantitative spatial economics. *Annual Review of Economics, 9*(1), 21–58. https://doi.org/10.1146/annurev-economics-063016-103713

Takahashi, S. (2006). Meiji zenki no chiiki jinkō dōtai to jinkō idō [Regional changes of vital and migration rates in the early Meiji era]. *Kokumin Keizai Zasshi* [*Journal of Economics & Business Administration, Kobe University*], *194*(5), 31–46.

Yamashita, T. (Ed.). (2019). *Jinkō Idō no keizaigaku* [*Economics of Internal Migration*]. Koyo Shobo.

Chapter 6
Reconsideration of the Quantity and Quality Analysis of the Japanese and U.S. Economy

Tamaki Morita

Abstract This chapter examines the divergent technological change in the Japanese and the United States (U.S.) economies, demonstrating that improving factor productivity efficiency is essential for Japan. To ensure methodological consistency with the authors' prior research on the period from 1960 to 2004, the authors first re-estimate growth rates for this period using a new dataset. By providing updated insights into long-term growth dynamics based on the latest measurement standards and presenting a consistent analytical framework that bridges historical and contemporary growth analysis, this study contributes to a deeper understanding of recent economic trends. The primary focus of this study is the period from 1980 to 2020, marked by significant structural changes, including globalization, technological advancements, and demographic shifts. The findings underscore Japan's need to enhance both capital and labor efficiency, particularly in the context of population decline. This study also emphasizes the robust stability of the U.S. economy while addressing the belatedness in Japan's stability.

Keywords Biased technical change · Factor efficiency · Growth stability · Japan · Productivity · United States

6.1 Introduction

6.1.1 Motivation and Background

Economic stagnation in Japan, which began in the 1990s, persists in the 2020s at the time of writing this book. Due to the prolonged economic stagnation in Japan and declining birth rates, concerns about the future of the Japanese economy have been emerging. The labor force in Japan had been increasing from 63.84 million in 1990

T. Morita (✉)
Faculty of Aviation Management, J. F. Oberlin University, Tama City, Tokyo, Japan
e-mail: morita_t01@obirin.ac.jp

T. Yamashita and T. Morita (eds.), *On the Structural Transformation of the Japanese Economy 1985-2023*, Advances in Japanese Business and Economics 38,
https://doi.org/10.1007/978-981-95-7230-4_6

to 69.02 million in 2022,[1] but it is expected to decline to 65.56 million in 2030 and 60.02 million in 2040 under the zero growth and unchanged labor participation per capita scenario (Japan Institute for Labour Policy and Training, 2024).

We need to investigate how the Japanese economy can recover and transition to a stable growth path. Sato and Morita (2009) compared the economic structures of Japan and the United States (U.S.) from 1960 to 2004 by examining the rates of factor-augmenting technical change,[2] revealing that the efficient utilization of capital and labor significantly influences economic growth. As fifteen years have passed since then, we need to confirm recent changes in the economic structure. Ideally, we should use the recent data of the series used in Sato and Morita (2009). However, due to recent changes and discontinuities in official data, we were unable to continue the original series. Therefore, we utilize the data from Penn World Table 10.01 (Feenstra et al., 2015) and apply the methods employed in the previous study.

The introduction follows with a summary of the previous study in Sect. 6.1.2, discusses the problem of data discontinuity in Sect. 6.1.3, and outlines the structure of this chapter in Sect. 6.1.4.

6.1.2 Summary of the Previous Study

In "Quantity or Quality: The Impact of Labour Saving Innovation on U.S. and Japanese Growth Rates, 1960–2004," Sato and Morita (2009) state that although Japan's post-World War II economic growth was remarkable, concerns have arisen regarding future macroeconomic growth due to the country's declining population. Similarly, while the United States saw substantial growth following the war, fueled by President Kennedy's policies, capital accumulation, and population growth, the influx of immigrants has, at the time of writing, led to mixed feelings about continued population growth due to concerns about assimilation and overpopulation.

Building on the work of Sato and Ramachandran (1987) and Sato (1970), the study examines changes in total factor productivity (TFP) and the separate efficiencies of capital and labor, leading to policy recommendations for enhancing TFP growth. To analyze these efficiencies, the study applies the elasticity of factor substitution to the data from both countries. They found that the two economies' labor-saving technical change stressed the importance of the elasticity of substitution. They also showed equilibrium growth and stability under biased technical change theoretically.

Then, applications are made to the U.S. and Japanese data to estimate production functions and present the simulations. Over a 44-year period, from 1960 to 2004, Sato and Morita (2009) found that the Japanese economy experienced notably stronger growth despite lower labor force growth rates. The increase in capital and technical

[1] Ministry of Health, Labour and Welfare.

[2] A technical change is defined as "biased" if it alters the relative marginal products of production factors. Factor-augmenting technical change is a functional form that can generate biased technical change.

change fueled this high economic growth. The key drivers of Japan's economic growth were substantial capital investment and the effective combination of technical change in both capital and labor efficiency.[3]

Japan's economic growth was driven by improvements in the quality of its population and workforce rather than an increase in their numbers. In contrast, the U.S. experienced economic growth primarily due to an increase in the size of its population and labor force, rather than improvements in quality. In fact, the GDP growth rate per unit of labor in the U.S. was only 38% of that in Japan. Technological advancements and an expanding labor force sustained U.S. economic growth. With its abundance of land and natural resources, population growth played a significant role in the economic expansion of the U.S., allowing for growth without a significant increase in the efficiency of its production factors.

Sato and Morita (2009) provided several policy recommendations. First, investing in education and training would enhance labor efficiency, and Japan must improve the performance of its education system. Additionally, the Japanese government needs to prepare for its aging population in two keyways. One is that it should consider significant reforms to the social security system, which was initially designed with the assumption that the population would continue to grow. Reforming this system is an urgent matter. The other is to explore the possibility of allowing immigration for lower-skilled workers who could assist those in need. Although increasing immigration may have potential social repercussions, it could also help mitigate the effects of the anticipated population decline.

Regarding the macroeconomy, the decline in labor has not been the leading cause of problems in Japan. More significantly, the bursting of the bubble economy diminished companies' ability to foster technical change. Here, technical change does not solely refer to the development of information technology or the introduction of entirely new, innovative technologies. Instead, it encompasses all creative solutions that can enhance the efficiency of capital and labor.

In concluding remarks, Sato and Morita (2009) emphasized that innovation has been—and will continue to be—the driving force behind the development and growth of the Japanese economy. Therefore, Japan does not need to be excessively pessimistic about its declining birth rate. Innovation can be promoted through policies that boost people's motivation and expectations.

[3] They also contrasted the response of the two economies toward the oil crisis. The Japanese response to the oil crisis was more effective than that of the U.S. In 1974 and 1975, Japan experienced significantly positive growth rates in capital efficiency, indicating that the country effectively responded to price pressures by substituting capital for energy. Japan, being an energy-scarce country, quickly developed energy-saving measures. In contrast, the U.S., which has abundant energy resources, saw a decline in factor efficiencies following the crisis. It is important to note that had factor efficiencies not declined due to the crisis, both economies would likely have experienced faster growth.

6.1.3 *The Problem of Data Discontinuity in Long-Run Growth Analysis*

When updating results by connecting previous analyses with current data, losing data connectivity is fatal. Recent significant changes in the System of National Accounts (SNA), the Balance of Payments Manual (BPM), and the International Standard Industrial Classification (ISIC) affected the continuity of historical macroeconomic data.

Each time international manuals are revised, the criteria for what qualifies as production, income, or cross-border flow are redefined. New asset types may be recognized, and industries may be reclassified. Because those revisions are implemented prospectively, most statistical offices restart their official series when the new standard takes effect, leaving earlier figures in the old framework.

The shift to chain-volume indices after the 1990s added a serious break: observations prior to the revisions are not strictly comparable with those afterward. Long-run data contains unidentified jumps that reflect accounting reforms rather than genuine economic change. To explain the large impact of SNA2008 on historical analysis, here, we begin by explaining SNA1993 and the related changes in ISIC and BPM, which help us understand how SNA2008 was developed.

(1) **SNA1993 and Related Changes**

Major revisions began with ISIC Revision 3 in 1989 (United Nations, 1990), which aimed to harmonize various international classifications. ISIC Rev. 3 introduced a four-level hierarchy consisting of Section, Division, Group, and Class, replacing the previous two-level hierarchy of Major Division and Division used in Rev. 2. It reflects the increasing complexity of economies at the time. For example, new categories such as "mixed farming (growing of crops combined with farming of livestock)," "recycling" in mining and manufacturing areas," "renting and leasing," "computer-related activities," and "motor vehicles trade and repair" are introduced.

ISIC Rev. 3 provided the necessary detail for sectoral breakdowns in SNA1993. SNA1993 modernized economic measurement by expanding the production boundary to include activities such as own-account productions and original entertainment works. It improved the classification of financial transactions, introduced detailed sectoral accounts, and incorporated the International Investment Position to track cross-border assets and liabilities. Government and nonprofit activities were more clearly defined, while satellite accountings for tourism, the environment, and unpaid work were encouraged (United Nations, 1996). Overall, SNA1993 provided a broader, internationally harmonized framework better suited to analyzing a globalized and service-oriented economy. Aligning with the SNA revision, BPM introduced the international investment position (IIP), detailed foreign direct investment, and reclassified capital transfers from financial accounts (International Monetary Fund, 2004).

SNA1993 makes an excuse for the possible drawback of using the chain-type price index and warns of the lack of additive consistency of chained price data. (The next subsection, "SNA2008 and related changes," details the lack of consistency.)

> Although the preferred measure of real growth and inflation for GDP is a chain Fisher index, or alternatively a chain Laspeyres or Paasche index, it must be recognized that the lack of additive consistency can be a serious disadvantage for many types of analysis in which the interrelationships between various flows in the economy are the main focus of interest. Most macroeconometric models fall into this category. It is therefore recommended that disaggregated constant price data should be compiled and published in addition to the chain indices for the main aggregates. The need to publish two sets of data that may appear to conflict with each other should be readily appreciated by analysts engaged in macroeconometric modelling and forecasting. Users whose interests are confined to a few global measures of real growth and inflation can be advised to utilize the chain indices and ignore the more detailed constant price estimates. (United Nations, 1990, paragraph 16.75)

The Bureau of Economic Analysis (BEA) in the United States was the first among OECD countries to publish official chain-type GDP measures in 1996 (U.S. Bureau of Economic Analysis, 1996). Other OECD countries, especially in Europe, transitioned more gradually during the early 2000s. This transition was driven by harmonization efforts from Eurostat, the OECD, and the IMF, with most countries completing the switch by the mid-2000s. Japan adopted chain-type GDP measures in December 2004 when the government published the second preliminary quarterly estimates of GDP for July–September 2004 and the annual revision for Fiscal 2003 GDP (Cabinet Office, 2004).

(2) **SNA2008 and Related Changes**

Overall, the SNA2008 revision aimed to better represent a globalized, financialized, and intangible-asset-driven economy within the national account's framework. Annex 3 of SNA2008 details the change from the SNA1993 (European Communities et al., 2009). The most influential revision in SNA2008 was the use of chain price measures for real GDP and other real aggregates. On the one hand, it ensures more accurate growth comparisons over time; on the other hand, it makes data connection and sectoral aggregation difficult. In a fixed-price system adopted before SNA2008, prices from a single base year are used for all periods, and the sum of real GDP by sector equals total real GDP. However, as time passes, the fixed prices grow outdated, and the measurements no longer reflect the current structure of the economy. Due to fixed prices, sector shares do not adjust. Generally, a new, fast-growing sector tends to be undervalued because a large quantity is multiplied by an outdated, low price.[4] Conversely, a shrinking sector often remains overvalued since the old high price is still applied to a considerably smaller quantity.

In contrast, chain indices update the base year frequently (usually every year), adjusting for changes in prices and products. It makes growth estimates more accurate and realistic over time. The trade-off is the loss of additivity. When real GDP by

---

[4] In rare cases, the introduction of a new high-priced product in the base year may initially create an outsized share in fixed-price GDP, then may grow even more bloated and distorted as production expands. However, this is an exception rather than the main source of distortion.

sector is added, it may not exactly match the total real GDP, and the overall real growth may fall outside the range suggested by the sectors individually. This non-additivity is acknowledged and warned by European Communities et al., (2009, p. 298, subsection 15.59) for adopters of SNA2008, stating that "Whether published in monetary terms or indices, it is advisable to inform users via a footnote or other metadata that chain volume series are not additive." As a result, observations before the revisions are not strictly comparable to those afterward. Long-run data contains silent jumps reflecting accounting reforms rather than genuine economic change.

Other notable conceptual and practical changes are introduced since SNA1993. Jorgenson and Schreyer (2013) note that SNA2008 made a decisive step by recognizing capital services as an integral element in the new system of national accounts. They fully articulated sets of output, input, and productivity statistics. Examples of changes are as follows: (1) The capitalization of Research and Development (R&D), recognizing it as fixed investment instead of being categorized as intermediate consumption. This change highlights the increasing importance of knowledge assets; (2) Military weapons systems are also classified as fixed assets, improving the comparability of defense-related expenditures; (3) The treatment of financial derivatives is expanded, and new financial instruments like employee stock options were introduced; (4) Pension entitlements are more comprehensively recorded, including those arising from unfunded schemes; (5) Cross-border activities are revised to better reflect globalization: ownership in merchanting and goods for processing is emphasized, rather than the mere physical movement of goods; (6) Public sector delineation is improved, clarifying the boundary between general government and public corporations based on the distinction between market versus non-market production; (7) Household accounts are strengthened, particularly on pension rights and imputed rents.

Aligned with SNA2008, ISIC Revision 4 (United Nations, 2008) evolved from a goods-based structure to a more service- and knowledge-intensive classification system. This revision expanded categories related to Information and Communication, Financial Services, Professional, Scientific, and Technical Activities, as well as Administrative and Support Services. Additionally, new categories for waste management remediation were established. The revision also clarified the distinctions between outsourcing and core versus support functions.

BPM was also revised to BPM6 (International Monetary Fund, 2009), aligning with SNA2008 and addressing globalization, enhancing the elaboration of balance sheet issues, and promoting financial innovation.

Users seeking a continuous history must interweave fragments based on different definitions, deflators, and industry classifications while documenting any residual statistical discrepancies that arise. As of May 2025, Japan's Real GDP data, in chained 2015 Yen, aligning with the SNA2008, is estimated only from 1994. The official provisional estimates of GDP connectable to the present data are reported only for the period from January–March 1980 to October–December 1993. As we have seen, drastic changes in macroeconomic data have occurred, and researchers should address these transitions.

6.1.4 Research Objectives and Study Structure

The primary objective of this study is to analyze the biased technical changes of Japan and the U.S. from 1980 to 2024. This period encompasses significant structural changes, including globalization, technological advancements, asset price bubbles and bursts, and demographic shifts, making it crucial to understand the underlying drivers of growth during these decades. In this chapter, we dare to stick to macroeconomic observation to avoid the fallacy of composition and verify the macroeconomic impacts of these structural changes.

First, we compare the new data with the previous data. We re-estimate and quantify the discrepancies between the new results and the original fixed-price series for 1960–2004 and 1980–2004. Next, we analyze the period from 1980 to 2020 using the new data. Third, we have discussions using renewed data.

Although this study revisits a previously published analysis for 1960–2004, its primary contribution lies in extending that analysis using internationally comparable data from the Penn World Table 10.01 (Feenstra et al., 2015). Recognizing the challenges posed by definitional shifts in GDP and input measurement, the study first re-estimates the earlier period within the updated framework. This step ensures consistency and comparability, but the emphasis is on the detailed examination of growth patterns in the 1980–2024 period, where contemporary dynamics and policy relevance are most pronounced.

Section 6.2 provides an overview of the literature, while Sect. 6.3 discusses the relevant theories and data. In Sect. 6.4, we re-estimate the period from 1960 to 2004 using PWT data and compare these results with those of Sato and Morita (2009). Section 6.5 analyzes the period from 1980 to 2024, using PWT data for both Japan and the U.S. In this section, we estimate factor productivity and compare the simulation results of applying Hicks-neutral technical change to those of applying biased technical change. We also test the stability of each economy. Finally, Sect. 6.6 concludes the study and discusses its limitations.

6.2 Overview of the Literature

The early development of the theory of biased technical change can be found in Hicks (1932/1963), which discusses the types of inventions: neutral, labor-saving, and capital-saving, where the ratio of the marginal product of capital to that of labor is unchanged, increased, and decreased accordingly at the original factor proportion. The neutral invention here is named after him and called Hicks neutral. He epitomized Wicksell's (1934) idea that there are kinds of inventions that favor one factor over another. Then, Harrod (1948) noted the technical change that increases labor efficiency and is essential for maintaining a constant capital-output ratio in dynamic growth models. This technical change is referred to as labor-augmenting technical change or Harrod neutrality. Later, Solow (1956) constructed the neoclassical growth model with exogenous technical change, and later (Solow, 1957), he introduced the empirical method of growth accounting, defined as disembodied improvements that raise output while holding factor proportions constant. It was later named capital-augmenting technical change or Solow neutrality. Solow (1962) focused on how capital-augmenting innovation affects capital formation and growth.

In a neoclassical growth model with Cobb–Douglas production function, only Harrod-neutral (labor-augmenting) technical change allows a steady-state equilibrium, as Uzawa (1961) presented. However, Sato and Beckmann (1968) generalized Uzawa's condition to CES production functions, enabling the formal analysis of capital- and labor-augmenting technical change.

Beginning in the 1960s, economists began treating the direction of technical change as an endogenous outcome. Kennedy (1964) and Samuelson (1965) developed the theory of induced innovation, which posits that relative factor prices guide the direction of innovation. Innovations would thus tend to be biased toward the more expensive or scarce factor, as firms seek cost-saving technologies and relative factor prices influence where firms direct R&D. If labor becomes relatively expensive, innovation may favor labor-saving techniques and create a bias endogenously.

Sato and Beckman (1968) and Rose (1968) constructed the conditions for the factor-augmenting technical change theoretically.

Particularly from the 1990s onward, following the academic trend to provide a microeconomic foundation for macroeconomic analysis, economists have tried to endogenize the direction of technical change by introducing innovators, R&D sectors, or profit incentives. These micro-founded frameworks link factor prices and innovation choices, allowing the bias of technical change to evolve endogenously. Acemoglu (2002) shows that market incentives and resource scarcities determine whether innovation is capital- or labor-biased. He also showed that the elasticity of substitution between inputs determines whether technical change tends to reinforce or offset factor abundance. In Acemoglu (2003), he further analyzed the long-run implications of capital- and labor-augmenting progress.

These micro-foundational analyses have increased the empirical verification of biased technical change in the literature. Jin and Jorgenson (2010) pioneered new econometric methods that utilized unobservable (latent) variables as a factor-augmenting technical change index. They found heterogeneous bias across U.S. industries. Doraszelski and Jaumandreu (2018) aggregated microdata that accounts for firm-level heterogeneity in the components of productivity. Labor skills heterogeneity has recently been included in the analysis of biased technical change (Cui et al., 2024; Zhang et al., 2023).

Recognizing these developments, this chapter reevaluates macro models that extend beyond strict micro-foundations that include the fallacy of composition. Microfoundations may be subject to the risks of the fallacy of composition and over-reliance on stylized assumptions. Micro-based models may overlook institutional constraints, social norms, or intersectoral rigidities that influence macro dynamics. Purely optimizing agents might overstate biased responses compared to real-world inertia.

We also note that for the measurement of the structural change in an economy, in growth theory, there has been a field of the multisector model that divides an economy into more than two, for example, agriculture, manufacturing, and services to examine the long-term structural transformation (Herrendorf et al., 2014; Ngai & Pissarides, 2007). This chapter focuses not on sectoral differences but on the biases of technical changes in factors (capital and labor). We provide multi-sector analysis in Chap. 7.

When dealing with macroeconomic-biased technical change, as Diamond et al. (1978) suggest, researchers face the "impossibility theorem" that identifying both the elasticity of capital-labor substitution and the direction of nonneutral technical change simultaneously is infeasible. This theorem highlights the inherent difficulties in accurately measuring and interpreting biased technical changes. León-Ledesma et al. (2010) jointly modeled the production function and first-order conditions to identify the elasticity of substitution. Oberfield and Raval (2021) estimated the elasticity of the manufacturing sector by summing up industry-level micro elasticities. Although several ways may be the candidates, they have not yet been established for overcoming the impossibility theorem. Therefore, we adopted the traditional assumption used by Sato and Morita (2009) and compared the results.

6.3 Theoretical Framework and Data Description

6.3.1 Theoretical Framework

When we estimate the production function F of year t with a general index of technical change T, output Y can be expressed as:

$$Y(t) = F[K(t), L(t), T(t)] \tag{6.1}$$

If technical change is of the factor-augmenting type (or Sato-Beckman-Rose neutral type),[5] Eq. (6.1) takes the form,

$$Y(t) = F[A(t)K(t), B(t)L(t)] = F\left[\bar{K}(t), \bar{L}(t)\right], \tag{6.2}$$

where $A(t)$ and $B(t)$ are efficiencies of capital and labor respectively; and $\bar{K}(t) = A(t)K(t)$ and $\bar{L}(t) = B(t)L(t)$ or the effective capital and the effective labor. The production function $F[\cdot]$ satisfies the usual regularity conditions. When $A(t) \equiv B(t) \equiv T(t)$, Eq. (6.2) is reduced to the case of Hicks-neutral technical change, while when $A(t) \equiv 1 \neq B(t) \equiv T(t)$, it is reduced to the Harrod-neutral type and when $A(t) \equiv T(t) \neq B(t) \equiv 1$ it is reduced to the Solow-Ranis-Fei type. We empirically compare

[5] See Sato and Beckman (1968) and Rose (1968) for the conditions for the factor-augmenting technical change.

the assumption of factor-augmenting type technical change to the Hicks-neutral type technical change.

Before we estimate factor-augmenting type technical change, we must ensure that the production functions are not Cobb–Douglas, for if the function is Cobb–Douglas, there is no way to separate A and B. Also, if technical change is Hicks-neutral, A should always be equal to B, so we do not need to estimate the biased technical growth. Using the method introduced by Sato and Morita (2009), we have conducted tests of the non-unity of σ and confirmed the non-unity (Appendix 6.1). The results of the test of Hicks neutrality are in Appendix 6.2. Although some results did not observe non-Hicks neutrality, we separated A and B.

We must set several assumptions for empirical analysis and estimate biased technical change growth rates. Sato and Morita (2009) describe the minute process, which we here concisely describe.

6.3.1.1 Estimation of Hicks-Neutral Technical Change

We should first derive Solow-Kendrick TFP (T) for each country. With the share of capital $\alpha(t) = r(t)K(t)/Y(t)$ and that of labor $\beta(t) = w(t)L(t)/Y(t)$, the growth rate of Y is, by definition, expressed as

$$\frac{\dot{Y}(t)}{Y(t)} = \frac{\dot{T}(t)}{T(t)} + \alpha(t)\frac{\dot{K}(t)}{K(t)} + \beta(t)\frac{\dot{L}(t)}{L(t)} \tag{6.3}$$

The period averages of the growth rate of T for the period $t = [0, S]$ are calculated as $\left(\dot{T}/T\right)_{AVG} = (1/S)\sum_{t=0}^{S}\left(\dot{T}(t)/T(t)\right)$.

6.3.1.2 Deriving the Average Elasticity of Substitution σ^N

Next, we estimate the average of the "elasticity of substitution under the assumption of Hicks-neutral technical change, σ^N."

For a year t, σ^N is estimated using,

$$\sigma^N(t) = \frac{d\left(\frac{K(t)}{L(t)}\right)/\frac{K(t)}{L(t)}}{d\left(\frac{w(t)}{r(t)}\right)/\frac{w(t)}{r(t)}} = \frac{\frac{\dot{K}(t)}{K(t)} - \frac{\dot{L}(t)}{L(t)}}{\frac{\dot{w}(t)}{w(t)} - \frac{\dot{r}(t)}{r(t)}}.$$

The average elasticity of substitution for the period $[0, S]$ is calculated as

$$\sigma^N_{AVG} = \frac{1}{S}\sum_{t=0}^{S}\sigma^N(t). \tag{6.4}$$

The estimated σ^N_{AVG} for the period 1980–2019 is 0.45 for Japan and 0.46 for the U.S.[6]

6.3.1.3 Estimation of CES Functions with Hicks-Neutral Technical Change

Before estimating the production function with factor-augmenting technical change, we estimate the production function with Hicks-neutral technical change to compare it with a biased technical change.

With Hicks-neutral technical change, the function should take the form of

$$Y^N(t) = T(t)\left[\alpha K(t)^{-\rho^N} + \beta L(t)^{-\rho^N}\right]^{-1/\rho^N} \tag{6.5}$$

where $\sigma^N = 1/(1+\rho^N)$. $T(t)$ is assumed to grow constantly, given the average of each $\dot{T}(t)/T(t)$ estimated in Eq. (6.3). We also assume that α and β are constant throughout the period, and we apply period averages of observed α and β.

6.3.1.4 Estimation of CES Functions with Factor-Augmenting Technical Change

Finally, we can estimate the CES function with biased technical change. $A(t)$ and $B(t)$ have the relationships as Eqs. (6.3) and (6.7) (Sato & Morita, 2009, pp. 410–411).

$$\frac{\dot{A}(t)}{A(t)} = \frac{\sigma(t)\frac{\dot{r}(t)}{r(t)} - \left(\frac{\dot{Y}(t)}{Y(t)} - \frac{\dot{K}(t)}{K(t)}\right)}{\sigma(t) - 1} \tag{6.6}$$

$$\frac{\dot{B}(t)}{B(t)} = \frac{\sigma(t)\frac{\dot{w}(t)}{w(t)} - \left(\frac{\dot{Y}(t)}{Y(t)} - \frac{\dot{L}(t)}{L(t)}\right)}{\sigma(t) - 1} \tag{6.7}$$

We substitute the estimated elasticity σ^N into Eqs. (6.6) and (6.7) to derive $\dot{A}/A$ and $\dot{B}/B$. Theoretically, the elasticity of substitution of factor-augmenting technical change has to be stated as an Eq. (6.8) because when technical change is nonneutral, the elasticity's value is influenced by capital and labor efficiencies.[7]

$$\sigma^B = \frac{d\left(\frac{AK}{BL}\right)/\frac{AK}{BL}}{d\left(\frac{\frac{\partial F}{\partial BL}}{\frac{\partial F}{\partial AK}}\right)/\frac{\frac{\partial F}{\partial BL}}{\frac{\partial F}{\partial AK}}} \tag{6.8}$$

---

[6] To calculate period averages of σ^N, we excluded negatives and those over 1 from the summation of Eq. (6.4) because σ in developed countries are known to range $0 < \sigma < 1$.

[7] See Sato (1970) for a detailed discussion on the elasticity of substitution under factor-augmenting technical change.

Because we cannot observe σ^{B} directly, we use σ^N instead in the simulation of $Y^B(t)$.[8]

Then, the CES function takes the form of

$$Y^B(t) = \left[\alpha(A(t)K(t))^{-\rho^N} + \beta(B(t)L(t))^{-\rho^N}\right]^{-\frac{1}{\rho^N}}. \tag{6.9}$$

Estimated $Y^B(t)$ summarizes our model. It represents both the form of the production function and the bias of the technical change. In this way, we will obtain two series, Y^N and Y^B.

6.3.1.5 Stability Under Biased Technical Change

An economy with *endogenous* biased technical change exhibits a stable balanced growth path under a *general* factor-augmenting type of technical change, i.e., one characterized by positive growth rates of technical change for both capital and labor. Sato and Morita (2009) showed it as follows.

Let $Y(t) = F[K(t), L(t)]$ be the production function before the technical change. To distinguish the production function after the factor-augmenting type of technical change from the production function before the technical change, we may denote the function as $\bar{Y}(t)$ so that,

$$\bar{Y}(t) = F\left[\bar{K}(t), \bar{L}(t)\right] \tag{6.2'}$$

where $\bar{K}(t) = A(t)K(t)$, $\bar{L}(t) = B(t)L(t)$, and $\bar{Y}(t)$ is the output *after* the technical change. This equation can be viewed as the production function after K has been transformed to $\bar{K}$ and L transformed to $\bar{L}$.

Then the growth rate of Y may be expressed as

$$\begin{aligned}\frac{\dot{Y}(t)}{Y(t)} &= \frac{\partial F(t)}{\partial \bar{K}(t)}\frac{\bar{K}(t)}{Y(t)}\left(\frac{\dot{\bar{K}}(t)}{\bar{K}(t)}\right) + \frac{\partial F(t)}{\partial \bar{L}(t)}\frac{\bar{L}(t)}{Y(t)}\left(\frac{\dot{\bar{L}}(t)}{\bar{L}(t)}\right)\\ &= \frac{\partial F(t)}{\partial K(t)}\frac{K(t)}{Y(t)}\left(\frac{\dot{A}(t)}{A(t)} + \frac{\dot{K}(t)}{K(t)}\right) + \frac{\partial F(t)}{\partial L(t)}\frac{L(t)}{Y(t)}\left(\frac{\dot{B}(t)}{B(t)} + \frac{\dot{L}(t)}{L(t)}\right)\end{aligned} \tag{6.10}$$

where $\frac{\partial F(t)}{\partial K(t)}\frac{K(t)}{Y(t)}$ = the relative income share of capital $= \alpha\left(\bar{k}(t)\right)$, $\frac{\partial F(t)}{\partial L(t)}\frac{L(t)}{Y(t)}$ = the relative income share of labour $= \beta\left(\bar{k}(t)\right)$, $\alpha\left(\bar{k}(t)\right) + \beta\left(\bar{k}(t)\right) = 1$, and $\bar{k}(t) = \frac{\bar{K}(t)}{\bar{L}(t)} = \frac{A(t)K(t)}{B(t)L(t)}$.

Let labor efficiency improvement depend on the expenditure devoted to education and training. Then, the growth rate of the effective labor is given by Eq. (6.11) as,

---

[8] We demonstrated that the variational changes of σ around σ^N did not significantly deviate from their results. Thus, we decided that σ^N qualifies to be the proxy of σ^B. See Appendix 6.2.

$$\frac{\dot{\bar{L}}}{\bar{L}} = \frac{\frac{d}{dt}(BL)}{BL} = \frac{\dot{B}}{B} + \frac{\dot{L}}{L} = s_B \frac{\bar{Y}}{\bar{L}} + n, \tag{6.11}$$

where s_B is a fraction of output devoted to education and training.

Also, assume $\dot{\bar{K}}$ is endogenously determined by

$$\frac{\dot{\bar{K}}}{\bar{K}} = \frac{\frac{d}{dt}(AK)}{AK} = \frac{\dot{A}}{A} + \frac{\dot{K}}{K} = s_A \frac{\bar{Y}}{\bar{K}} + s_K \frac{\bar{Y}}{\bar{K}} = s \frac{\bar{Y}}{\bar{K}} = s\bar{y}, \tag{6.12}$$

where $\bar{y} = \bar{Y}/AK$, s_A is a fraction of output (or income) $\bar{Y}$ devoted to increasing the efficiency of capital, s_K is a fraction of output devoted to increasing physical capital, $s = s_A + s_K$ is a fraction of output used to create additional effective capital, and $1 > s > 0$.

Using the capital-labor ratio in efficiency units

$$\bar{k}(t) = \frac{\bar{K}(t)}{\bar{L}(t)} = \frac{A(t)K(t)}{B(t)L(t)}, \tag{6.13}$$

we may write

$$\begin{aligned} \frac{\dot{\bar{k}}}{\bar{k}} &= \frac{\dot{\bar{K}}}{\bar{K}} - \frac{\dot{\bar{L}}}{\bar{L}} = \frac{s\bar{Y}}{\bar{K}} - \frac{s_B\bar{Y}}{\bar{L}} - n = sF\left(1, \frac{1}{\bar{k}}\right) - s_B F\left(\bar{k}, 1\right) - n \\ &= sf\left(\bar{k}\right) - s_B g\left(\bar{k}\right) - n, \end{aligned} \tag{6.14}$$

where $1 > s + s_B > 0$.

The stability condition is satisfied if

$$\frac{d\left(\frac{\dot{\bar{k}}}{\bar{k}}\right)}{d\bar{k}} = s\frac{df}{d\bar{k}} - s_B\frac{dg}{d\bar{k}} < 0. \tag{6.15}$$

The first term $s \cdot df/d\bar{k}$ is negative. The second term is always positive because $dg/d\bar{k}$ is the marginal product of effective capital. Hence, Eq. (6.15) is automatically satisfied. The growing economy is dynamically stable under the *endogenous* factor-augmenting type of technical change.

To apply the balanced growth condition to the data, we rearrange Eq. (6.10) as

$$\frac{\dot{\bar{Y}}}{\bar{Y}} = \alpha\left(\frac{\dot{A}}{A} + \frac{\dot{K}}{K}\right) + \beta\left(\frac{\dot{B}}{B} + \frac{\dot{L}}{L}\right) = \alpha\frac{\dot{\bar{K}}}{\bar{K}} + \beta\frac{\dot{\bar{L}}}{\bar{L}} \tag{6.16}$$

At steady state $\bar{k} = \bar{k}^*$, $\left(\frac{\dot{\bar{K}}}{\bar{K}}\right)^* = \left(\frac{\dot{\bar{L}}}{\bar{L}}\right)^*$ holds. Because $\alpha + \beta = 1$, if we put $\left(\frac{\dot{\bar{K}}}{\bar{K}}\right)^* = \left(\frac{\dot{\bar{L}}}{\bar{L}}\right)^* = G^*$, Eq. (6.16) becomes

$$\left(\frac{\dot{\bar{Y}}}{\bar{Y}}\right)^* = \alpha\left(\frac{\dot{\bar{K}}}{\bar{K}}\right)^* + \beta\left(\frac{\dot{\bar{L}}}{\bar{L}}\right)^* = \alpha G^* + \beta G^* = G^*$$

such that

$$\left(\frac{\dot{\bar{Y}}}{\bar{Y}}\right)^* = \left(\frac{\dot{\bar{K}}}{\bar{K}}\right)^* = \left(\frac{\dot{\bar{L}}}{\bar{L}}\right)^* = G^* \tag{6.17}$$

is the condition for stable growth.

We examine the economies of Japan and the U.S. to see whether they satisfy this condition. From Eqs. (6.12) and (6.16), we can derive the following two equations.

$$\begin{cases} \frac{\dot{\bar{Y}}}{\bar{Y}} = as\bar{y} + \beta\frac{\dot{\bar{L}}}{\bar{L}} \\ \frac{\dot{\bar{K}}}{\bar{K}} = s\bar{y} \end{cases}$$

There exists a steady-state growth rate G_i^* that satisfies Eq. (6.17) and the optimal output per effective capital, $\bar{y}^* = \left(\frac{\bar{Y}}{\bar{K}}\right)^* = \left(\frac{\bar{Y}}{AK}\right)^*$.

6.3.2 *Overview of Data Sources*

The data sources of the previous study (Sato & Morita, 2009) and this study (PWT 10.01) are presented in Tables 6.1 and 6.2, respectively.

Key distinctions include: (1) This study's Real GDP encompasses the public sector; and (2) The share of labor compensation in the PWT is calculated as the total labor income of employees alongside self-employed workers in the GDP.

6.4 Quantitative Comparison: Original Versus PWT Results

Sato and Morita (2009) analyzed biased technical change using OECD data and national data covering 1960–2004, based on fixed-price GDP measures and labor and capital aggregates. To extend this framework to the period 1980–2020 using more recent data, we replicated the original model using the Penn World Table (PWT, version 10.01) for the overlapping period of 1960–2000.

Although the fundamental methodological framework remains unchanged, the updated data provides numerically different estimates for the period from 1960 to 2004. We cannot determine whether the observed discrepancies arise from a categorical change or a real price change. Nevertheless, these results do not revise the

Table 6.1 Data sources: Japan

	Previous study	This study
Y	**Real Gross Domestic Products excluding Government Consumption** (OECD National Accounts Database, OECD, http://new.sourceoecd.org/vl=1563494/cl=22/nw=1/rpsv/home.htm)	**Real GDP at constant 2017 national prices** (in bil. 2017JPY) (Source: PWT 10.01)
K	**Real Private Capital Stock** (Annual Report on Gross Capital Stock of Private Enterprises, Systems of National Accounts, Cabinet Office Homepage, Japan, http://www.esri.cao.go.jp/jp/sna/toukei.html#s-kakuho)	**Capital stock at constant 2017 national prices** (in bil. 2017JPY) (Source: PWT 10.01)
L	**Labor Force** (Labor Force Survey, Source: OECD Main Economic Indicators, OECD, http://new.sourceoecd.org/vl=1563494/cl=22/nw=1/rpsv/home.htm) multiplied by **Hours worked per worker** (Systems of National Accounts, Cabinet Office Homepage, Japan, http://www.esri.cao.go.jp/jp/sna/toukei.html#s-kakuho)	**Number of persons engaged** (in millions) multiplied by **Average annual hours worked by persons engaged** (Source: PWT 10.01)
w	**Real Compensation of Employees** (OECD National Accounts Database, OECD, http://new.sourceoecd.org/vl=1563494/cl=22/nw=1/rpsv/home.htm) divided by labor force ***L***	**Share of labor compensation in GDP at current national prices** divided by labor force ***L***, multiplied by real GDP ***Y*** (Source: PWT 10.01)

Table 6.2 Data sources: United States

	Previous study	This study
Y	**Real Gross Domestic Products of Private Sector** (National Income and Product Accounts Tables, Bureau of Economic Analysis, U.S. Department of Commerce, http://www.bea.gov/national/nipaweb/Index.asp)	**Real GDP at constant 2017 national prices** (in mil. 2017US$) (Source: PWT 10.01)
K	**Real Private Fixed Assets (Fixed Asset Tables,** Bureau of Economic Analysis, U.S. Department of Commerce, http://www.bea.gov/national/FA2004/SelectTable.asp#S6)	**Capital stock at constant 2017 national prices** (in mil. 2017US$) (Source: PWT 10.01)
L	**Total Hours Worked, Private** (National Income and Product Accounts Tables, Bureau of Economic Analysis, U.S. Department of Commerce, http://www.bea.gov/national/nipaweb/Index.asp)	**Number of persons engaged** (in millions) multiplied by **Average annual hours worked by persons engaged** (Source: PWT 10.01)
w	**Real Compensation of Employees** (OECD National Accounts Database, OECD, http://new.sourceoecd.org/vl=1563494/cl=22/nw=1/rpsv/home.htm) divided by labor force ***L***	**Share of labor compensation in GDP at current national prices** divided by ***L***, multiplied by ***Y*** (Source: PWT 10.01)

earlier findings; rather, they serve as a bridge that allows for a consistent extension into the primary focus period of 1980 to 2020.

6.4.1 *Original Periods (1960–2004, 1960–1989, 1990–2004)*

Firstly, we compare the periods used in the previous study: the period from 1960 to 2004. It is further divided into two as original: 1960–1989 and 1990–2004. The results are in Table 6.3 (Japan) and Table 6.4 (the U.S.).

6.4.2 *Overlapping Periods (1980–2004)*

Secondly, we compare the overlapping 1980–2004 periods. The estimated variables are in Table 6.5 (Japan) and Table 6.6 (the U.S.).

The replication based on PWT produced results that differ from the original analysis. For instance, in Japan, the average share of capital increased by 14.3 percentage points, from 26.43 to 40.72%. Meanwhile, the growth rate of capital is lower by 0.71 points, and the growth rate of capital efficiency is lower by 1 point. Also, labor efficiency is higher by 1.77 points in the new data, so the data revision elevates the base of labor efficiency. These discrepancies are likely due to differences in data construction, such as using chained-price GDP, purchasing power parity (PPP)-adjusted income measures, and imputed labor hours and capital services in the PWT. However, we cannot determine the extent of each contribution.

Despite these differences, given the methodological improvements and increased consistency, we will use the PWT-based results as the baseline for our analysis of the extended period from 1980 to 2020. We will keep the original estimates as a comparative benchmark, acknowledging the impact of evolving data definitions on macroeconomic interpretations as discussed in Sect. 6.1.3.

6.5 Analysis of 1980–2024

This chapter deals with the period from 1980 to 2024, which is our central theme. As shown in the last subsection, the PWT data, which differs significantly from the data used in the previous study, compels us to prioritize a thorough examination of recent developments in Japan and the United States, rather than historical analysis from the 1950s (available from PWT) to present.

Section 6.5.1 presents the growth of the fundamental variables, Sect. 6.5.2 simulates the output growth, and Sect. 6.5.3 evaluates the stability of the two economies.

Table 6.3 Comparison of average relative shares of factors and growth rates of main indicators: Japan

	Previous study			This study			Difference		
	1960–2004	1960–1989	1990–2004	1960–2004	1960–1989	1990–2004	1960–2004	1960–1989	1990–2004
Average relative share of capital, α	29.34	31.6	24.82	39.49	38.46	41.53	+10.15	+6.86	+16.71
Average relative share of labor, β	70.66	68.4	75.17	60.51	61.54	58.47	−10.15	−6.86	−16.70
Total $(\boldsymbol{\alpha} + \boldsymbol{\beta})$	100	100	100	100	100	100	–	–	–
Growth rate of output, $\dot{Y}/Y$	4.65	6.35	1.03	4.75	6.45	1.48	+0.10	+0.10	+0.45
Growth rate of capital, $\dot{K}/K$	7.32	9.25	3.18	6.56	8.48	2.85	-0.76	-0.77	-0.33
Growth rate of labor, $\dot{L}/L$	0.28	0.56	-0.31	0.33	0.83	-0.62	+0.05	+0.27	-0.31
Growth rate of output per labor, $\dot{z}/z$	4.35	5.76	1.34	4.39	5.57	2.11	+0.04	-0.19	+0.77
Growth rate of Hicks neutral technical change, $\dot{T}/T$	2.13	2.91	0.45	2.00	2.69	0.67	−0.13	-0.29	+0.22
Estimated elasticity of substitution, σ^{N}_{AVG}	0.57	0.63	0.50	0.85	0.94	0.69	+0.28	+0.31	+0.19
Growth rate of capital efficiency, $\dot{A}/A$	−1.61	−1.63	−1.36	−3.76	−7.75	−2.15	−2.15	−6.12	−0.79
Growth rate of labor efficiency, $\dot{B}/B$	3.86	5.11	1.01	5.83	9.59	2.70	+1.97	+4.48	+1.69

Source Sato and Morita (2009), Penn World Table 10.01, and authors

Table 6.4 Comparison of average relative shares of factors and growth rates of main indicators: United States

	Previous study			This study			Difference		
	1960–2004	1960–1989	1990–2004	1960–2004	1960–1989	1990–2004	1960–2004	1960–1989	1990–2004
Average relative share of capital, α	31.33	30.80	32.39	37.70	37.53	38.06	+6.37	+6.73	+5.67
Average relative share of labor, β	68.67	69.20	67.61	62.30	62.47	61.94	−6.37	−6.73	−5.67
Total $(\alpha + \beta)$	100	100	100	100	100	100	–	–	–
Growth rate of output, $\dot{Y}/Y$	3.08	3.05	3.13	3.46	3.67	3.05	+0.38	+0.62	−0.08
Growth rate of capital, $\dot{K}/K$	3.31	3.58	2.72	3.03	3.26	2.58	−0.28	−0.32	−0.14
Growth rate of labor, $\dot{L}/L$	1.39	1.49	1.19	1.40	1.67	0.88	+0.01	+0.18	−0.31
Growth rate of output per labor, $\dot{z}/z$	1.66	1.54	1.92	2.03	1.97	2.16	+0.37	+0.43	+0.24
Growth rate of Hicks neutral technical change, $\dot{T}/T$	1.07	0.90	1.43	1.45	1.41	1.53	+0.38	+0.51	+0.10
Estimated elasticity of substitution, σ_{AVG}^{N}	0.46	0.51	0.38	0.50	0.55	0.39	+0.04	+0.04	+0.01
Growth rate of capital efficiency, $\dot{A}/A$	−0.41	−0.59	0.08	0.28	0.08	0.51	0.69	0.67	0.43
Growth rate of labor efficiency, $\dot{B}/B$	1.74	1.56	1.97	2.10	2.14	2.12	0.36	0.58	0.15

Source Sato and Morita (2009), Penn World Table 10.01, and authors

Table 6.5 Japan

	Previous study	This study	Difference
Average relative share of capital, α	26.43	40.72	14.3
Average relative share of labor, β	73.57	59.28	−14.3
Total ($\alpha + \beta$)	100	100	–
Growth rate of output, $\dot{Y}/Y$	2.39	2.62	+0.23
Growth rate of capital, $\dot{K}/K$	4.32	3.61	−0.71
Growth rate of labor, $\dot{L}/L$	0.26	−0.07	−0.33
Growth rate of output per labor, $\dot{z}/z$	2.12	2.69	0.57
Growth rate of Hicks neutral technical change, $\dot{T}/T$	1.03	1.20	0.17
Estimated elasticity of substitution, σ_{AVG}^{N}	0.55	0.67	0.12
Growth rate of capital efficiency, $\dot{A}/A$	−1.35	−2.35	−1.00
Growth rate of labor efficiency, $\dot{B}/B$	1.87	3.65	1.77

Table 6.6 United States

	Previous study	This study	Difference
Average relative share of capital, α	31.92	38.36	6.4
Average relative share of labor, β	68.08	61.64	−6.4
Total ($\alpha + \beta$)	100	100	–
Growth rate of output, $\dot{Y}/Y$	2.79	3.08	+0.29
Growth rate of capital, $\dot{K}/K$	2.91	2.68	−0.22
Growth rate of labor, $\dot{L}/L$	1.28	1.20	−0.08
Growth rate of output per labor, $\dot{z}/z$	1.49	1.86	+0.37
Growth rate of Hicks neutral technical change, $\dot{T}/T$	1.00	1.32	0.32
Estimated elasticity of substitution,σ_{AVG}^{N}	0.45	0.49	0.04
Growth rate of capital efficiency, $\dot{A}/A$	−0.44	0.31	0.75
Growth rate of labor efficiency, $\dot{B}/B$	1.63	1.89	0.26

6.5.1 *Growth Rates of Key Variables*

Table 6.7 summarizes the series we have from PWT for the years 1980–2019. Although Japan's output, labor, and technical growth are lower than those of the U.S., capital growth is higher. Japan's economic growth was driven by capital growth during the period.

The average relative contributions of TFP, T, and input factors in Eq. (6.9) are shown in Table 6.8. Because Japan experienced a labor decline (−0.08% in Table 6.7), the labor contribution was also negative. So, the growth of T supported about half of the output growth, and the growth of physical capital, multiplied by its capital share, supported the other half. In the U.S., the growth of T supported 43% of GDP growth.

Table 6.7 Summary of variables (1980–2019)

	Japan	United States
Growth rate of output, $\dot{Y}/Y$ (%)	1.91	2.64
Growth rate of capital, $\dot{K}/K$ (%)	2.46	2.27
Growth rate of labor, $\dot{L}/L$ (%)	−0.08	1.03
Growth rate of Hicks neutral technical change, $\dot{T}/T$ (%)	0.96	1.13
Relative share of capital, α	0.42	0.39
Relative share of labor, β	0.58	0.61

Source Penn World Table and author's estimates for T and its growth

Table 6.8 Average relative contribution to the growth rate of real GDP (1980–2019)

	Japan	United States
$(\dot{T}/T)/(\dot{Y}/Y)$	50.1	43.0
$\alpha(\dot{K}/K)/(\dot{Y}/Y)$	53.7	33.7
$\beta(\dot{L}/L)/(\dot{Y}/Y)$	−2.4	23.7
Statistical adjustment	−1.4	-0.3
Total	100.0	100.0

Source Estimated by authors

Table 6.9 Summary growth rates of technical changes (1980–2019)

	Japan	United States
Growth rate of Hicks neutral technical change, $\dot{T}/T$ (%)	0.96	1.13
Growth rate of capital efficiency, $\dot{A}/A$ (%)	−0.84	0.21
Growth rate of labor efficiency, $\dot{B}/B$ (%)	2.19	1.69

Source Estimated by authors

The growth of physical capital times capital share was 33.7%, and the growth of labor times labor share was 23.7%. The contributions are more evenly distributed compared to those in Japan.

Tables 6.9 and 6.10 present the average growth rates of TFP and factor efficiencies. In both countries, the growth rate of capital efficiency is lower than that of labor efficiency, i.e., $\dot{A}/A < \dot{B}/B$. Under the condition that the elasticity of substitution σ is less than one, both countries experienced labor-saving technical change.[9]

[9] When the elasticity of substitution is less than unity, and the efficiency of labor increases faster than that of capital at the constant capital-labor ratio, technical change is labor saving. In this case, the initial effects of the technical change are to increase the ratio of the marginal product of capital to that of labor at the constant capital-labor ratio. Such technical changes increase the marginal product of capital more than they increase the marginal product of labor; thus, they raise the relative share of capital and reduce the relative share of labor. See Sato (1970) for details and other classifications.

Table 6.10 Relative contributions to Hicks-neutral technical change by biased technical change

	Japan	United States
$\alpha(\dot{A}/A)/(\dot{T}/T)$	-36.5	7.2
$\beta(\dot{B}/B)/(\dot{T}/T)$	133.0	90.7
Statistical Adjustment	3.5	2.1
Total	100.0	100.0

The growth rate of capital efficiency is, on average, negative in Japan. What supported the growth of Hicks neutral technical change ($\dot{T}/T$) was the growth of labor productivity, $\dot{B}/B$, which compensated for the decline in capital efficiency growth, $\dot{A}/A$. The physical capital investment that supported half of Japan's economic growth (Table 6.8) was inefficient.

In the case of the U.S., labor productivity growth contributed 90% of the TFP growth, while capital productivity growth added 7.2%.

Figure 6.1 illustrates the annual and ten-year average growth rates of capital efficiency in Japan and the U.S., while Fig. 6.2 illustrates those of labor efficiency.

In Japan, although capital efficiency was negative from 1980 to 2009, we observe an improvement in the 2010s. There is hope for reducing dormant assets that had long accumulated during the bubble and its burst.

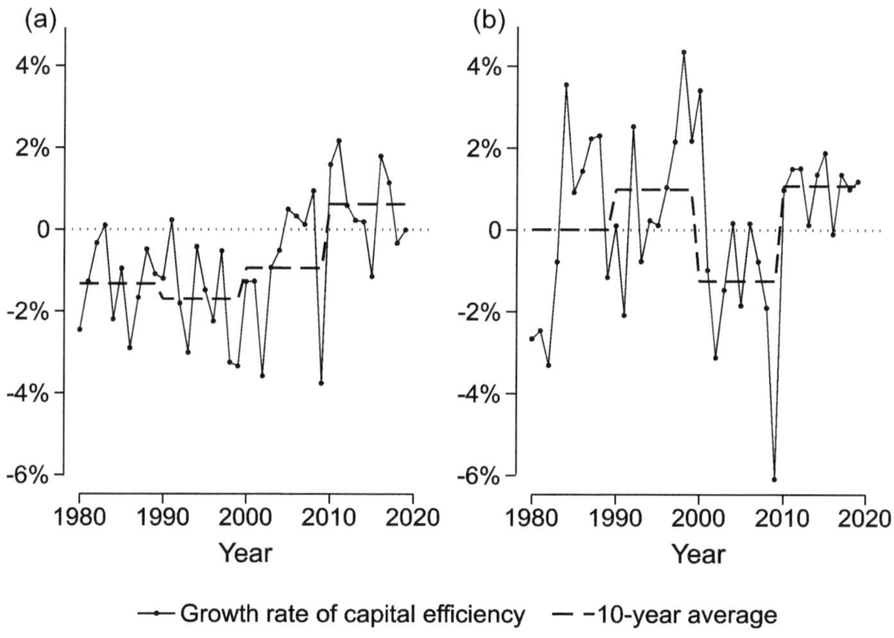

Fig. 6.1 Growth rate of capital efficiency (annual and decade average): **a** Japan, **b** the U.S. *Source* Estimated by authors

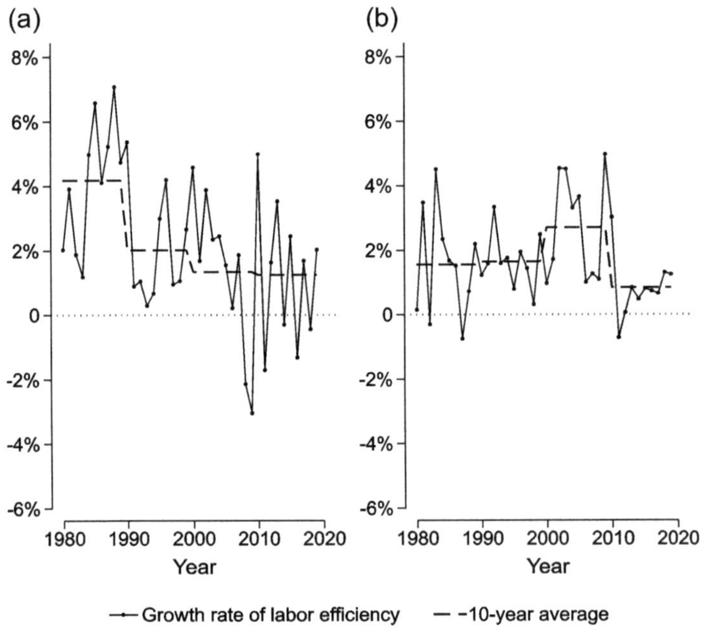

Fig. 6.2 Growth rate of labor efficiency (annual and decade average): **a** Japan, **b** the U.S. *Source* Estimated by authors

Japan's positive labor efficiency experienced a gradual decline throughout the entire period. In the 1980s, labor efficiency surpassed that of the United States. However, this advantage did not persist, and in the 2000s, the average labor efficiency in Japan was lower than that of the U.S. Additionally, fluctuations in labor efficiency became apparent, raising questions about the sustainability of Japan's earlier productivity gains. After Sato and Morita (2009) wrote, labor efficiency was not as supportive as they had expected at that time. Figure 6.1 illustrates the annual growth rate of capital efficiency in Japan and the U.S., while Fig. 6.2 illustrates that of labor efficiency. In Japan, although capital efficiency was negative from 1980 to 2009, we observe an improvement in the 2010s. There arouses a hope of the decrease of long-accumulated dormant assets.

Japan's positive labor efficiency experienced a gradual decline throughout the entire period. In the 1980s, labor efficiency surpassed that of the United States. However, this advantage did not persist, and in the 2000s, the average labor efficiency in Japan was lower than that of the U.S. Additionally, fluctuations in labor efficiency became apparent, raising questions about the sustainability of Japan's earlier productivity gains. After the writing of Sato and Morita (2009), labor efficiency was not as supportive as they had expected at that time.

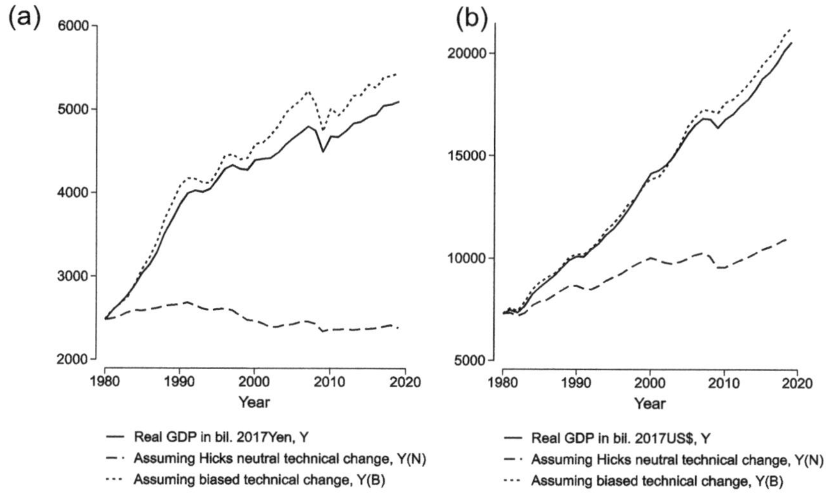

Fig. 6.3 Estimated output (1980–2019): **a** Japan, **b** the U.S. Source: Estimated by authors

6.5.2 Simulation Results

In this subsection, using observed capital (K) and labor (L), we simulate the CES production functions assuming that the total or factor efficiencies, elasticity of substitution, and factor shares had been estimated as in Sect. 6.5.1.

The two series, Y^N (derived in Eq. (6.5) under Hicks-neutral technical change) and Y^B (Eq. (6.9) under biased technical change), are contrasted in Fig. 6.3 with the actual real GDP, Y. The estimated value of biased Y^B demonstrates a closer alignment with actual Y than the Hick-neutral Y^N in both countries. This tendency was also marked by Sato and Morita (2009). It is marked again that we should not conclude by estimating TFP (T); instead, we must continue examining the biased technical changes A and B.

Comparing the two countries, the discrepancy between Y^N and actual Y is higher in Japan, especially after the 1990s. The possibility of considerable structural changes can be observed.

6.5.3 Stability of Economic Growth

To verify the stability, following the discussion in Sect. 6.3.1.5, simulated results are illustrated in Fig. 6.4.

In the steady state, by restating Eq. 6.17, the growth rates of effective capital $\bar{K} = AK$, effective labor $\bar{L} = BL$, and production under biased technical change $\bar{Y}$ should satisfy, $\left(\frac{\dot{\bar{Y}}}{\bar{Y}}\right)^* = \left(\frac{\dot{\bar{K}}}{\bar{K}}\right)^* = \left(\frac{\dot{\bar{L}}}{\bar{L}}\right)^* = G^*$, where G^* is the steady-state growth

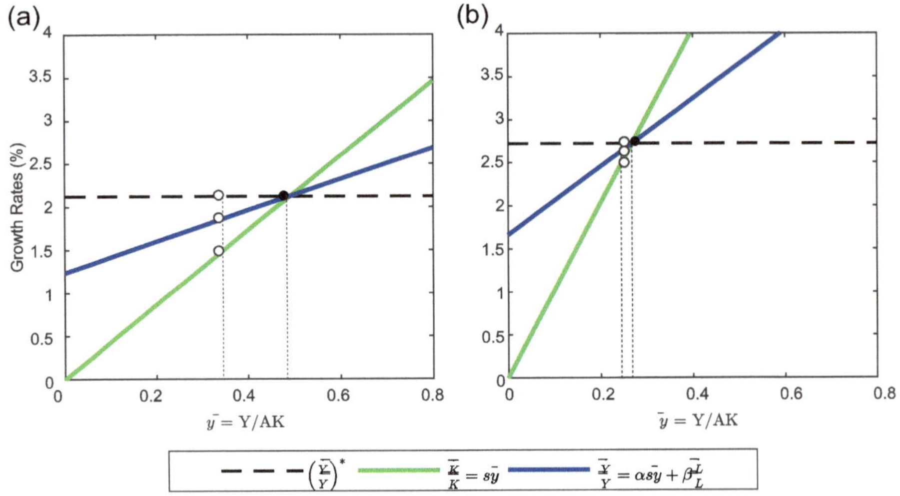

Fig. 6.4 Output-effective capital ratio and stability: **a** Japan, **b** the U.S. *Source* Estimated by authors

rate. As derived in Sect. 6.3.1.5, we have two relationships: $\dot{\bar{Y}}/\bar{Y} = as\bar{y} + \beta \cdot \dot{\bar{L}}/\bar{L}$ and $\dot{\bar{K}}/\bar{K} = s\bar{y}$, where $\bar{y} = \bar{Y}/\bar{K}$ and s is a fraction of output used to create additional effective capital. We illustrate these two equations in Fig. 6.4. The solution of these two equations (the intersection of two lines in each panel) is the combination of $\{\bar{y}^*, G^*\}$.

In Japan, calculated $\bar{y} = 0.367$ is lower than $\bar{y}^* = 0.490$, and $\bar{y} < \bar{y}^*$. This result differs from Sato and Morita (2009); data from 1960 to 2004 revealed that $\bar{y} > \bar{y}^*$. Sato and Morita stated, "Japanese economic growth was still lower than the growth rate of effective capital and had not reached its steady state. We can find here that there was overinvestment that kept the return on investment very low" (p. 426). In the present data, we observed that the problem of overinvestment may be ceased in 2010s and witnessed recovery of capital efficiency in Fig. 6.1. Consequently, without the concerns of overinvestment legacies, Japan has the potential to achieve a steady state if investments are made effectively.

In the U.S., analogous to the result in Sato and Morita, the difference between $\bar{y}$ and $\bar{y}^*$ is minimal ($\bar{y} = 0.245$ and $\bar{y}^* = 0.268$). The growth rates of effective capital and effective labor are balanced, allowing the U.S. to keep steady-state growth rates.

To visualize how the economies follow or are away from steady-state growth, we draw the lines and their slopes on the growth rates on a semilogarithmic plane (Fig. 6.5). The thick line is the actual growth rate of each economy. The dashed line depicts the steady-state growth rates (2.12% for Japan and 2.72% for the U.S.). When the slope of actual output growth is steeper than the dashed line, the economy grows faster than steady-state growth rates; conversely, the flatter the slope, the slower the growth. The green arrow guides periods in which GDP grows equal to, the gray arrow lower than, and the yellow arrow faster than steady-state growth rates.

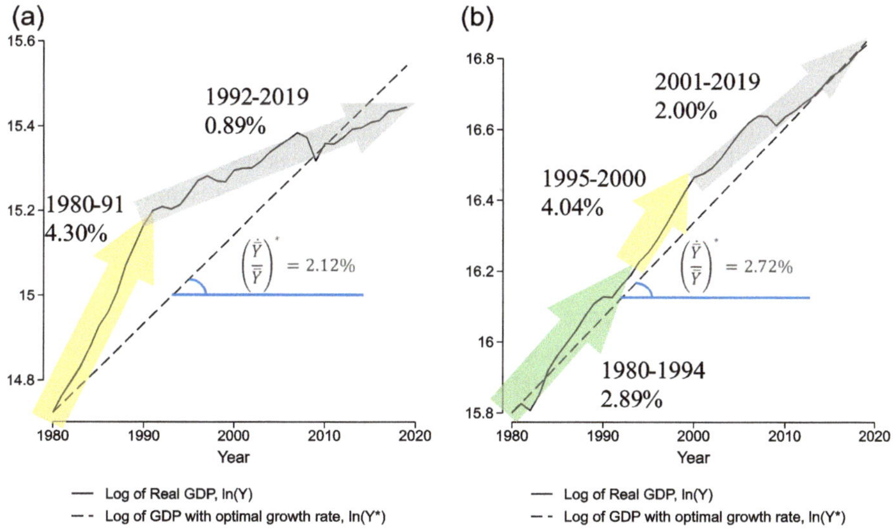

Fig. 6.5 Actual GDP and simulated GDP with the stable growth rate: **a** Japan, **b** the U.S. *Note* The green arrow shows periods in which GDP grows almost equal to, the gray arrow shows lower than, and the yellow arrow shows faster than steady-state growth rates. *Source* Estimated by authors

The 1980s were a period of faster-than-steady-state rates for the Japanese economy, averaging about 4.3% annually, when the bubble economy led to economic expansion. However, this momentum suddenly halted with the bubble's burst[10] at the beginning of the 1990s, resulting in a significant contraction of growth to an annual 0.89% until 2020. The aftermath of the Lehman Shock in 2008 led to an appreciation of the Japanese Yen against the U.S. Dollar. The strong Yen and global recession stalled Japan's exports and stagnated GDP growth.

As for the U.S., it maintained an average growth rate aligned with its steady-state growth from 1980 to 1994. Even during the dot-com bubble of the late 1990s, which peaked in March 2000, the U.S. growth rate was no more than around 4% and irrational exuberance was short-lived. The U.S. economy effectively experienced a soft landing from 2001 to 2019. It is noteworthy that, although the Lehman Shock originated in the U.S., the U.S. recovery was earlier than Japan, primarily due to interventions such as the Troubled Asset Relief Program (TARP)[11] and aggressive quantitative easing (QE) measures. These strategies may have played a crucial role in stabilizing financial markets and maintaining a steady growth rate, contrasting sharply with Japan's prolonged stagnation.

[10] Figures of Japan's asset prices (representative stock price and land prices) are shown in Appendix 8.3.

[11] See U.S. Department of Treasury (2024).

To confirm the differences between Japan and the U.S., we examine the five-year average contribution charts. Recall that Eq. (6.16) explains the relationship as follows: $\frac{\dot{\bar{Y}}}{\bar{Y}} = \alpha\left(\frac{\dot{A}}{A} + \frac{\dot{K}}{K}\right) + \beta\left(\frac{\dot{B}}{B} + \frac{\dot{L}}{L}\right) = \alpha\frac{\dot{\bar{K}}}{\bar{K}} + \beta\frac{\dot{\bar{L}}}{\bar{L}}$.

From Eq. (6.16), the growth rates of an economy can be attributed to the growth rates of $\alpha\bar{K}$ and $\beta\bar{L}$, with α and β being constant at their period averages. Figure 6.6 presents a stacked area graph, with the line with markers representing the growth rate of $\bar{Y}$. The dashed lines indicate the steady-state growth rate $\bar{Y}^*$ for each country.

In Japan, the contribution of $\beta\left(\dot{\bar{L}}/\bar{L}\right)$ was much greater than that of $\alpha\left(\dot{\bar{K}}/\bar{K}\right)$ until 1989. After that, the difference narrowed, and $\beta\left(\dot{\bar{L}}/\bar{L}\right)$ turned negative in the 2005–2009 period. The growth in labor efficiency could not offset the decline in labor, and the growth of effective capital has also been sufficient. The balance between $\alpha\left(\dot{\bar{K}}/\bar{K}\right)$ and $\beta\left(\dot{\bar{L}}/\bar{L}\right)$ fluctuates and remains unstable. We can confirm the lack of balance in Japan's economic growth.

Conversely, the U.S. economy has benefited from a relatively balanced contribution from $\alpha\left(\dot{\bar{K}}/\bar{K}\right)$ and $\beta\left(\dot{\bar{L}}/\bar{L}\right)$, except for 2005–2009, when the Lehman Shock likely impacted $\alpha\left(\dot{\bar{K}}/\bar{K}\right)$, leading to a slightly negative contribution. This balance between effective capital and effective labor has kept the U.S. economy on a stable growth path, reconfirming its stability.

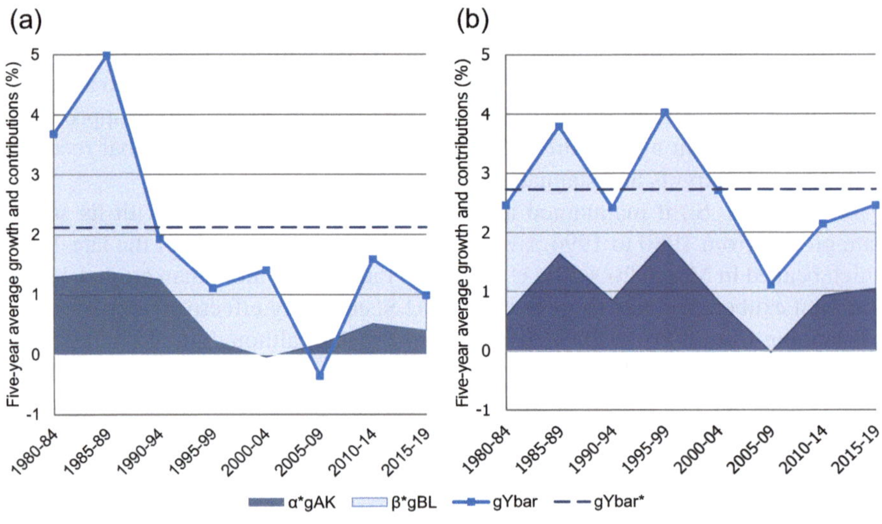

Fig. 6.6 Contributions of the effective capital and labor to the GDP growth rate: **a** Japan, **b** the U.S. *Note* $\alpha^*gAK = \alpha\left(\dot{\bar{K}}/\bar{K}\right)$; $\beta^*gBL = \beta\left(\dot{\bar{L}}/\bar{L}\right)$; $gY\text{bar}^* = \left(\dot{\bar{Y}}/\bar{Y}\right)^*$; $gY\text{bar} = \dot{\bar{Y}}/\bar{Y}$. *Source* Estimated by authors

6.6 Summary and Concluding Remarks

This study examines the drivers and stabilities of economic growth of Japan and the U.S. in the context of biased technical change. To maintain consistency with the authors' previous study, which analyzed the period 1960–2004, the discussion begins with the issues of data discontinuity and the comparison of two datasets.

The primary focus of this study is on the period from 1980 to 2020, which is characterized by significant structural changes such as globalization, technological advancements, and demographic shifts. The findings indicate that: (1) Japan needs to enhance capital efficiency, in addition to improving labor efficiency, in response to a declining population; and (2) the U.S. economy has shown stability.

Using the PWT data from 1980 to 2019, it is evident that Japan has not yet recovered from the bubble burst. Over the entire period analyzed, Japan's GDP growth was 1.91% annually, supported by capital growth—despite negative capital efficiency growth—and a decline in labor, although labor efficiency growth outpaced the decline.

Examining efficiencies by decade reveals that the high labor efficiency growth experienced in the 1980s has diminished significantly. Capital efficiency turned positive in 2010, indicating the potential for a long-awaited recovery from overinvestment and the associated negative growth in capital efficiency. However, the balance of contributions from effective capital and effective labor fluctuates and remains unstable, suggesting that Japan is still far from achieving a steady-state growth path.

In Japan, improving labor efficiency is crucial as the working population decreases due to a declining birthrate and an aging population. Furthermore, it is essential to increase not only the value of capital but also "effective" capital.

In contrast, the U.S. experienced stable growth despite facing the dot-com bubble and Lehman shock. Over the period, the U.S. GDP grew 2.64%, uplifted by the increase of all factors—capital, capital efficiency, labor, and labor efficiency. The efficiencies by decades represents stability, when capital efficiency was nonnegative except for 2000s (notably 2008), and labor efficiency being positive with less fluctuation than that of Japan. Effective capital and effective labor contribute equally to economic growth, confirming that the U.S. economy has maintained the stable growth path.

Compared to Sato and Morita's (2009) policy recommendations (see Sect. 6.1.2), we propose the following: (1) This study exposes the importance of investing in education and training to enhance labor efficiency. Japan needs to improve the performance of its education system. The decline in the birth rate has created a situation where the number of university openings exceeds the number of applicants, resulting in increased under-enrollment. Without political support, the quality of higher-education is at risk of decline (followed by the drop in middle- and lower- education quality), which could eventually reduce labor efficiency; (2) As the previous study mentioned, the Japanese government should explore the possibility of allowing immigration for workers who can assist those in need. While increasing immigration may have potential social repercussions, it could help mitigate the effects of the anticipated population and labor efficiency decline; (3) The Japanese government should also explore the possibility of allowing immigration for lower-skilled workers who could assist those in need. While increasing immigration may have potential social repercussions, it could help mitigate the effects of the anticipated population decline and labor efficiency decline; (4) The effect of bursting of the bubble economy that diminished companies' ability to foster technical change seems to be moderating as this study revealed a recent improvement in capital efficiency. To further enhance the efficiency of both capital and labor, the Japanese government should provide incentives to stimulate private investment. This includes advancing information technology, effectively utilizing artificial intelligence (AI), and introducing innovative technologies.

Looking ahead, SNA 2025 was announced in March 2025.[12] ISIC Revision 5, adopted in 2023, introduces substantial updates to reflect structural changes in the global economy. The revision eliminates the distinction between in-store and non-store retail, classifying retail activities by product specialization. It expands the coverage of digital services by introducing distinct categories for cloud computing, data processing, web search portals, and cybersecurity activities. The classification of financial services has been refined to capture emerging fintech activities better. In addition, greater emphasis is placed on environmental services, including waste management and sustainability-related activities. The structural framework has been updated to 22 sections, 87 divisions, 258 groups, and 463 classes, enhancing the classification's relevance for contemporary economic analysis and improving international comparability. The UN plans to make more revisions in 2025 or 2026, affecting all countries' official data. Balance of Payments Manual, Seventh Edition (BPM7), is led by the International Monetary Fund (IMF).

From the revisions onward, we should tackle the problem of balancing the analysis of the current situation with an exploration of historical perspectives. We need to overcome these obstacles and continue monitoring when and how the Japanese economy will achieve its steady-state growth path.

Appendix 6.1: Hicks Neutrality Tests

Tests of Non-Unity for Elasticity of Substitution

Sato (1970, pp. 192–193) introduces the test to identify whether the production function of each country is Cobb–Douglas type. Define $R(y/r)$ as the ratio of $\dot{y}/y$ to $\dot{r}/r$ and $R(x/\omega)$ as the ratio of $\dot{x}/x$ to $\dot{\omega}/\omega$. Then,

$$R\left(\frac{y}{r}\right) = \frac{\sigma}{1 + (\sigma - 1)\frac{\dot{A}/A}{\dot{y}/y}} \tag{6.18}$$

[12] SNA 2025 was officially adopted at the United Nations Statistical Commission during its 56th session, held from 4 to 7 March 2025.

Table 6.11 Test statistics estimated for the non-unity test

	Japan		United States	
	Average	SE	Average	SE
$R(y/r)$	0.361	1.009	2.902	10.893
$R(z/w)$	1.478	5.279	1.180	2.927
$R(x/\omega)$	4.621	19.603	-2.274	14.931

Source Estimated by authors

Also, define $z = Y/L$, $x = L/K$, and $R(z/w)$ to be equal to the ratio of $\dot{z}/z$ to $\dot{w}/w$. Then we get:

$$R\left(\frac{z}{w}\right) = \frac{\sigma}{1 + (\sigma - 1)\frac{\dot{B}/B}{\dot{z}/z}} \tag{6.19}$$

$$R\left(\frac{x}{\omega}\right) = \frac{\sigma}{1 + \frac{(\sigma-1)(\dot{A}/A - \dot{B}/B)}{\dot{x}/x}} \tag{6.20}$$

If $\sigma = 1$, then $R(z/w)$, $R(y/r)$, and $R(x/\omega)$ should be, on average, the same and equal to unity, regardless of whether or not A and B are the same. That is,

$$\bar{R}\left(\frac{y}{r}\right) = \bar{R}\left(\frac{z}{w}\right) = \bar{R}\left(\frac{x}{\omega}\right) = 1 \tag{6.21}$$

where the upper bar indicates the average value of Rs. Therefore, Eq. (6.21) may be used to test the Cobb–Douglas function.

The average values calculated are presented in Table 6.11 and Fig. 6.7.

$\bar{R}(y/r)$ is not equal to one. $\bar{R}(z/w)$ of neither country can reject the null hypothesis that z/w is unity. To reject the null hypothesis, p-value of $\bar{R}(y/r)$ of the U.S. is 0.1381, $\bar{R}(x/\omega)$ of Japan is 0.1249, and U.S. is 0.0867.

Rs are statistically not equal to one. Therefore, we can conclude that Eq. (6.20) does not hold and σ is not unity, which means that the production functions of both countries are not Cobb–Douglas.

Tests of Hicks-Neutrality

When technical change is biased, the following fundamental equations hold.[13]

$$\frac{\dot{w}}{w} = \frac{\dot{B}}{B} - \frac{\alpha}{\sigma}\left(\frac{\dot{B}}{B} - \frac{\dot{A}}{A} - \frac{\dot{k}}{k}\right) \tag{6.22}$$

$$\frac{\dot{r}}{r} = \frac{\dot{A}}{A} + \frac{\beta}{\sigma}\left(\frac{\dot{B}}{B} - \frac{\dot{A}}{A} - \frac{\dot{k}}{k}\right) \tag{6.23}$$

[13] See Sato (1970, p. 183) for discussing these fundamental relations.

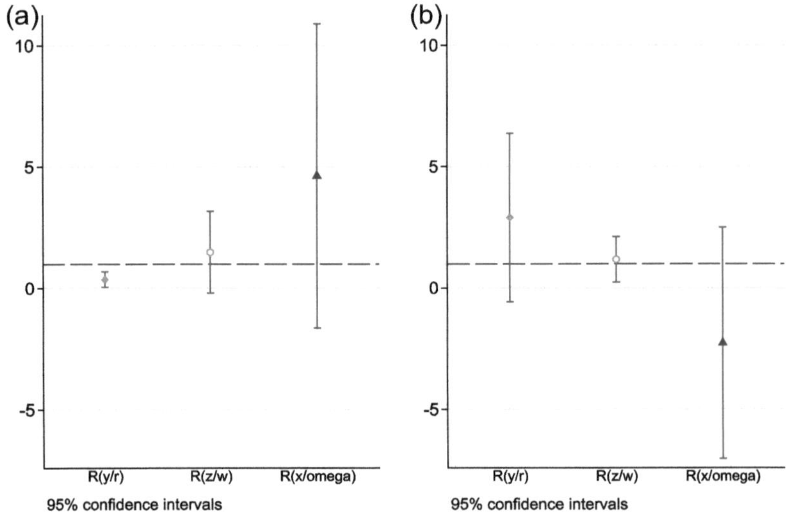

Fig. 6.7 95% confidence intervals of test statistics estimated for the non-unity test. *Note* The left chart is Japan, and the right chart is the United States. *Source* Estimated by authors

where $k = 1/x = K/L$.

When technical change is Hicks-neutral, equations must satisfy the two equations below:

$$\frac{\dot{w}}{w} = \frac{\dot{T}}{T} + \frac{\alpha}{\sigma}\frac{\dot{k}}{k}. \tag{6.22'}$$

$$\frac{\dot{r}}{r} = \frac{\dot{T}}{T} - \frac{\beta}{\sigma}\frac{\dot{k}}{k}, \tag{6.23'}$$

where $\frac{\dot{T}}{T} = \frac{\dot{A}}{A} = \frac{\dot{B}}{B}$. If the technical change is Hicks-neutral, the two regressional estimates $\frac{\dot{T}}{T}$ from Eqs. (6.17′) and (6.16′) should be equal. The results are in Table 6.12.

In all cases, the coefficients of determination are very low, except for Japan's $\dot{w}/w$. Statistically, the variance is substantial and we cannot derive valuable results. The difference between the two estimated $\dot{T}/T$ s is not equal at the significance level of 31.47% for Japan and 66.90% for the U.S., which means we cannot say they are different in both countries. The U.S. case rather suggests Hicks neutrality.

Table 6.12 Tests of Hicks neutrality results

	Japan				United States			
	$\dot{w}/w$		$\dot{r}/r$		$\dot{w}/w$		$\dot{r}/r$	
OLS estimations								
Coefficient of $\dot{k}/k$ ①	0.455	***	−0.662	**	0.128		−0.574	**
	(0.087)		(0.233)		(0.118)		(0.183)	
Constant ②	0.006	*	0.015	*	0.0134	***	0.0130	**
	(0.003)		(0.007)		(0.002)		(0.004)	
N	40		40		40		40	
Adjusted R2	0.406		0.154		0.004		0.185	
Test statistics								
Average *T* (Observed from data)	0.0096				0.0113			
Average *T* (Constants of OLS, ②)	0.0060		0.0150		0.0134		0.0130	
Average α or β (Actual)③	0.4184		0.5816		0.3910		0.6090	
σ (Observed from data)	0.4532				0.4595			
σ (calculated from OLS, ③/①)	0.9192		−0.6846		3.0635		−0.8005	

Notes 1. Standard errors are in the second row for the OLS estimation results in the upper section.
2. + $p < 0.10$, * $p < 0.05$, ** $p < 0.01$, *** $p < 0.001$
Source Estimated by authors

Appendix 6.2: Estimated GDP with Various Elasticity of Substitution Values

Elasticity of substitution, σ, plays an important role in estimating the CES production function of biased technical change (Eq. 6.9 in Sect. 6.3.1.4). We simulated when σ equals 0.2, 0.3, 0.4, 0.5, and 0.6 for Hicks neutral technical change and biased technical change. In the case of Japan, where the economy is not on a stable growth path, the difference in σ brings significant differences to the results.

Japan

See Fig. 6.8

The United States

See Fig. 6.9.

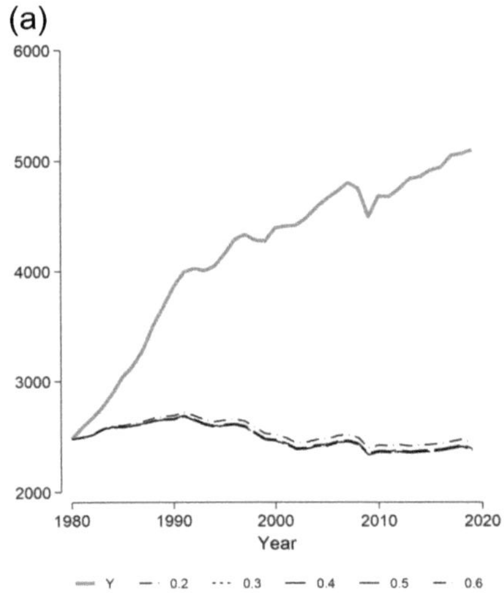

Fig. 6.8 Simulation with various elasticity of substitution—Japan: **a** Hicks Neutral Technical Change and **b** Biased technical change. *Source* Estimated by authors

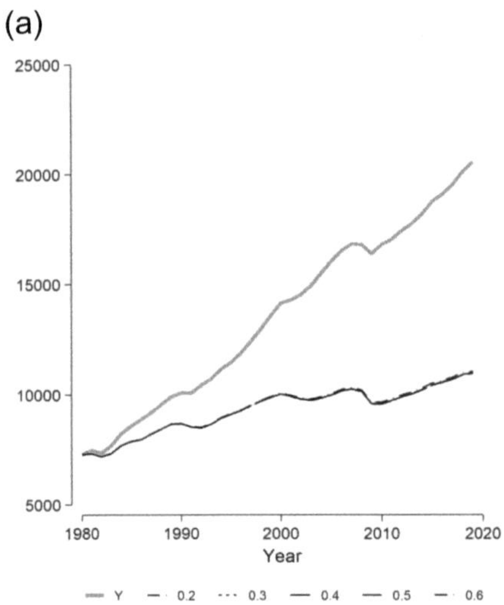

Fig. 6.9 Simulation with various elasticity of substitution—the U.S.: **a** Hicks Neutral Technical Change and **b** Biased technical change. *Source* Estimated by authors

References

Acemoglu, D. (2002). Directed technical change. *Review of Economic Studies, 69*(4), 781–809.

Acemoglu, D. (2003). Labor- and capital- augmenting technical change. *Journal of European Economic Association, 1*(1), 1–37.

Cabinet Office. (2004, November 8). Application of the chain-linking method to the compilation of Japan's SNA. The announcement of the Department of National Accounts, Economic and Social Research Institute, Cabinet Office, Japan. https://www.esri.cao.go.jp/en/sna/sankou/contents/egizisokuho.html

Commission of the European Communities, International Monetary Fund, Organisation for Economic Co-operation and Development, United Nations & World Bank. (1993). *System of national accounts 1993*. https://unstats.un.org/unsd/nationalaccount/sna1993.asp

Cui, X., Elahi, E., Xu, B., Xing, J., Shuaib, M., & Khalid, Z. (2024). Quantifying biased technical progress in China: Heterogeneous human capital and labor force dynamics. *Heliyon, 10*(13). https://doi.org/10.1016/j.heliyon.2024.e33540

Diamond, P., McFadden, D., & Rodriguez, M. (1978). Measurement of the elasticity of factor substitution and bias of technical change. In M. Fuss & D. McFadden (Eds.), *Production Economics* (Vol. 2, pp. 125–147). North-Holland.

Doraszelski, U., & Jaumandreu, J. (2018). Measuring the bias of technological change. *Journal of Political Economy, 126*(3), 1027–1084.

European Communities, International Monetary Fund, Organisation for Economic Co-operation and Development, United Nations, & World Bank. (2009). *System of national accounts 2008*. ISBN 978-92-1-161522-7.

Feenstra, R. C., Inklaar, R., & Timmer, M. P. (2015). The next generation of the Penn world table. *American Economic Review, 105*(10), 3150–3182. https://doi.org/10.1257/aer.20130954

Harrod, R. F. (1948). *Towards a dynamic economics: Some recent developments of economic theory and their application to policy*. Macmillan.

Herrendorf, B., Rogerson, R., & Valentinyi, Á. (2014). Growth and structural transformation. Chapter 6 in *Handbook of Economic Growth* (Vol. 2B, pp. 855–941).

Hicks, J. (1932/1963). *The theory of wages* (2nd ed.). Macmillan.

International Monetary Fund. (2004). *Revision of the balance of payments manual* (5th ed.) (Annotated outline).

International Monetary Fund. (2009). *Revision of the balance of payments manual* (6th ed.) (BPM6). ISBN 978-1-58906-812-4

Japan Institute for Labour Policy and Training. (2024, March 11). *2023-nendo ban rōdōryoku jukyū no suikei (sokuho), [Labor demand and supply estimates, 2023 fiscal year edition (preliminary estimates)]* [PDF]. https://www.jil.go.jp/press/documents/20240311.pdf (in Japanese).

Jin, H., & Jorgenson, D. W. (2010). Econometric modeling of technical change. *Journal of Econometrics, 157*(2), 205–219. https://doi.org/10.1016/j.jeconom.2009.12.002

Jorgenson, D. W., & Schreyer, P. (2013). Industry-level productivity measurement and the 2008 system of national accounts. *Review of Income and Wealth, 59*(2), 185–211. https://doi.org/10.1111/j.1475-4991.2012.00516.x

Kennedy, C. (1964). Induced bias in innovation and the theory of distribution. *Economic Journal, 74*(295), 541–547. https://doi.org/10.2307/2228295

León-Ledesma, M. A., McAdam, P., & Willman, A. (2010). Identifying the elasticity of substitution with biased technical change. *American Economic Review, 100*(4), 1330–1357. https://doi.org/10.1257/aer.100.4.1330

Ngai, L. R., & Pissarides, C. A. (2007). Structural change in a multisector model of growth. *American Economic Review, 97*(1), 429–443. https://doi.org/10.1257/aer.97.1.429

Oberfield, E., & Raval, D. (2021). Micro data and macro technology. *Econometrica, 89*, 703–732. https://doi.org/10.3982/ECTA12807

Rose, H. (1968). The condition for factor-augmenting technical change. *The Economic Journal, 78*(312), 966–971.

Samuelson, P. A. (1965). A theory of induced innovation along Kennedy-Weizsäcker lines. *Review of Economics and Statistics, 47*(4), 343–356. https://doi.org/10.2307/1927763

Sato, R. (1970). The estimation of biased technical progress and the production function. *International Economic Review, 11*, 179–208. Reprinted in R. Sato, *Growth theory and technical change, the selected essays of Ryuzo Sato*, Vol. 1, Economists of the Twentieth Century Series, Edward Elgar Publishing, 1996, Ch. 12.

Sato, R., & Beckmann, M. J. (1968). Neutral inventions and production functions. *The Review of Economic Studies, 35*(1), 57–66. Reprinted in Sato, R. (1996). *Growth theory and technical change, the selected essays of Ryuzo Sato*, Vol. 1, Economists of the Twentieth Century Series, Edward Elgar Publishing, Ch. 11.

Sato, R., & Morita T. (2009). Quantity or quality: The impact of labour saving innovation on US and Japanese growth rates, 1960–2004. *The Japanese Economic Review, 60*, 407–434. https://doi.org/10.1111/j.1468-5876.2008.00467.x. Revised in R. Sato & R. V. Ramachandran (2014). *Symmetry and Economic Invariance. Advances in Japanese Business and Economics*, vol 1, Ch. 10, 177–208. Springer. https://doi.org/10.1007/978-4-431-54430-2

Sato, R., & Ramachandran, R. (1987). Factor price variation and the Hicksian hypothesis: A microeconomic model. *Oxford Economic Papers, 39*(2), 343–356. https://doi.org/10.1093/oxfordjournals.oep.a041791

Solow, R. M. (1956). A contribution to the theory of economic growth. *Quarterly Journal of Economics, 70*(1), 65–94. https://doi.org/10.2307/1884513

Solow, R. M. (1957). Technical change and the aggregate production function. *Review of Economics and Statistics, 39*(3), 312–320. https://doi.org/10.2307/1926047

Solow, R. M. (1962). Technical progress, capital formation, and economic growth. *American Economic Review, 52*(2), 76–86.

United Nations. (1990). International standard industrial classification of all economic activities, third revision. Statistical papers, Series M, No. 4, Rev.3, New York.

United Nations. (2008). International standard industrial classification of all economic activities, third revision. Statistical papers, Series M, No. 4, Rev. 4.

United Nations. (1996). *Handbook of national accounting: Use of the system of national accounts in economies in transition*, Studies in Methods, Series F, No. 66. http://unstats.un.org/unsd/nationalaccount/pubsDB.asp

United Nations, Commission of the European Communities, International Monetary Fund, Organisation for Economic Co-operation and Development, and World Bank. (1993). *System of National Accounts 1993.*

U.S. Bureau of Economic Analysis. (1996). Comprehensive revision of the national income and product accounts: New estimates of chain-type quantity and price indexes. *Survey of Current Business, 76*(1), 1–31. https://apps.bea.gov/scb/pdf/national/nipa/1996/0196niparev.pdf

U.S. Department of Treasury. (2024). Troubled Asset Relief Program (TARP). https://home.treasury.gov/data/troubled-asset-relief-program

Uzawa, H. (1961). On a Two-Sector Model of Economic Growth. *The Review of Economic Studies, 29*(1), 40–47. https://doi.org/10.2307/2296180

Wicksell, K. (1934). *Lectures on political economy. Volume I: General theory* (E. Classen, Trans.). Routledge (original work published 1901 in Swedish as *Föreläsningar i nationalekonomi* and 1922 in German as *Vorlesungen über Nationalökonomie*).

Zhang, S., Li, X., Zhang, C., Luo, J., Cheng, C., & Ge, W. (2023). Measurement of factor mismatch in industrial enterprises with labor skills heterogeneity. *Journal of Business Research, 158*. https://doi.org/10.1016/j.jbusres.2023.113643

Chapter 7
A Two-Sector Model of Differential Productivity Growth with Quesnay-Baumol Effects: Japan-U.S. Comparisons, 1980–2020 (From the Post-oil Crisis to the Pre-COVID-19 Years)

Ryuzo Sato, Takayuki Yamashita, and Tamaki Morita

Abstract This study examined how differentiated technical growth has affected overall growth in Japan and the U.S. A new feature of this work is introducing a structural aspect of the economy by dividing the economy into two sectors. We incorporated ideas developed first by Quesnay and later by Baumol into the two-sector analysis as "Quesnay-Baumol effects." According to Quesnay's insight, a sector with high technical progress will lead to high value-added growth. Baumol insists that the unit cost per output is stable in a progressive sector but rises in a nonprogressive sector. First, we theoretically constructed a new two-factor, two-sector neoclassical growth model that explains the Quesnay-Baumol effects. Although the equilibrium path for the system in general does not exist, we proved the existence of the equilibrium paths when assuming two types of special cases, such as Hicks-neutral and Harrod-neutral. Second, the Quesnay-Baumol effects were empirically tested using a total productivity analysis and other methods. We found the effects apparent in the

---

We dedicate this chapter to the Late Professor William Baumol. Sato received much academic inspiration and benefit from him as a colleague at New York University for nearly 30 years. Sato feels as if he has finally fulfilled one of the promises with Professor Baumol. The promise was to build a model linking the Baumol effect with the Quesnay effect and to apply an econometric analysis to the model. We hope he would have approved of the main propositions of this paper.

R. Sato
C.V. Starr Professor Emeritus of Economics, New York University, New York, USA

T. Yamashita (✉)
School of Global Studies and Collaboration, Aoyama Gakuin University, Sagamihara City, Kanagawa, Japan
e-mail: yamashita.takayuki@gsc.aoyama.ac.jp

T. Morita
Faculty of Aviation Management, J. F. Oberlin University, Tama City, Tokyo, Japan
e-mail: morita_t01@obirin.ac.jp

T. Yamashita and T. Morita (eds.), *On the Structural Transformation of the Japanese Economy 1985-2023*, Advances in Japanese Business and Economics 38,
https://doi.org/10.1007/978-981-95-7230-4_7

U.S., but during Japan's Lost Decades, the Quesnay effects were insignificant, which explains why Japan's economy had serious problems.

Keywords Baumol disease · François Quesnay · Japan's lost decades · Total factor productivity analysis · Two-sector growth model · Technical change

7.1 Introduction

7.1.1 Motivation and Objectives

French economist François Quesnay is known as an economist who made a major contribution to the authorship of *Le Tableau Économique* (Quesnay, 1758). However, it is not well known that he was also the first economist to emphasize differential productivity growth.[1] He found that the economy has several different sectors with differential productivity growth, and the driving force of overall economic development depended on the productive sector. He represented the physiocracy because agriculture was the most productive sector of his time, but he is the founder of two-sector growth analysis.

As technical progress occurred, the Industrial Revolution turned agriculture into a nonproductive sector, and the growth driver shifted from the agricultural sector to the industrial sector, first to heavy industry and then to the technology industry. However, Quesnay's contribution has not been valued as much as it should be. The two-sector economic growth model was not appreciated until William J. Baumol's contribution.[2]

Baumol's two-sector model, however, does not analyze the long-term effects on economic growth. Baumol was interested in price effects, and his approach is a considered short-run type. In addition, he did not include capital and used only labor as a factor of production.

Both Quesnay and Baumol assumed differential productivity sectors, but Quesnay emphasized the growth effect of the productive sector on overall economic growth, while Baumol emphasized the price effect on wage rates and relative price levels. Combining these effects, we coin the term "Quesnay-Baumol effects."

We further develop the Baumol model and construct a new theory that can express the impact on economic growth pointed out by Quesnay and the impact on price levels and wage rates pointed out by Baumol. This chapter considers two-factor, two-sector neoclassical growth models with differential productivity due to differential technical change in two sectors. Our model is designed to apply empirical analyses to the

---

[1] Professor Hiroshi Yoshikawa of Tokyo University suggested referring to the articles by Dr. Irizawa (1936), who was a medical doctor and introduced Quesnay as a medical doctor to a Japanese medical society. Irizawa noted that Quesnay became a physician-turned-economist.

[2] Theoretical two-sector growth models had been advanced by Uzawa and others, but they have not been applied to empirical analysis.

Japanese and U.S. economies. Two-factor, two-sector neoclassical growth models with differential productivity in two sectors have not been used in the literature. Furthermore, our empirical analysis may clarify whether the Quesnay-Baumol effects are observed in Japan and the U.S.

The impact of the productivity discrepancy among sectors on Japan's macro economy is analyzed. Japan has been suffering from the symptom of the "Lost Decades"[3] since the 1990s.

Among the multiple possible reasons for such a long economic stagnancy, we focus on the discrepancy in technical growth among sectors. We conjecture that the hollowing out of the productive sector (manufacturing sector) curbed economic growth in Japan.

The unbalanced growth between the service and manufacturing sectors had negative effects in Japan, whereas it had positive effects in the U.S. The two economies differ in that the U.S. economy has overcome several economic crises, while the Japanese economy has not thrived in crises and has been stagnant for more than thirty years. No productive industry could ever replace the shrinking manufacturing industry.

7.1.2 *Quesnay-Baumol Effects and a Brief Literature Survey*

Quesnay indirectly mentioned the differential rate of productivity growth among industries in the eighteenth century (Quesnay, 1758). He represented the physiocracy, but his significant contribution was recognizing the productive class that consisted of all agricultural laborers (husbandmen). The sterile class comprised other industries; artisans, manufacturers, and merchants were nonproductive classes.[4] He emphasized the importance of the agricultural sector for developing nations' wealth and considered other sectors less productive than agriculture and worth less for economic growth.

Over time, the Industrial Revolution changed the productive center of economics from agriculture to light manufacturing, heavy manufacturing, and then to high-technology sectors. The leading role of productivity shifted.

Quesnay's contribution to economic growth has not been valued much. Only some recognize that, for example, "Quesnay was among the first to analyze economic growth theory as a function of capital accumulation" (Schachter, 1991, n.p.). Schachter, referring to Brewer (1987), Vaggi (1985), and Eltis (1975), explains Quesnay's findings that the entire process of development is based on capital accumulation and that since the net product originates with farmers, farmers have become

[3] Japan's Lost Decade is often cited as occurring from 1992 to 2002, but the continuous stagnation made economists consider it was prolonged for two or three decades. Therefore, we do not define the period precisely and call the 1990s and after until the 2010s the "Lost Decades."

[4] Quesnay also stated that the proprietary class consisted of only landowners (landlords), but it only received land rents and consumed the products of both productive and nonproductive classes.

rich. It is conditional for the Tableau to have a stationary state equilibrium. Not following the path induces economic decline. Eltis (1975, p. 335) notes that "Quesnay was far from alone in believing that consumption of the 'correct' goods produced growth, for it was a central argument in the *Wealth of Nations* (Smith, 1776) that the rate of growth depended partly on the ratio of 'productive' to 'unproductive' consumption." Eltis says that Quesnay finds that a nation's expenditure on the sterile sector rather than the productive sector would continuously lead to a decline in the nation's revenue.

Baumol argued for a differential rate of technical change. The effect is first mentioned in his study with Bowen on the arts sector's performance (Baumol & Bowen, 1965, 1966). In their words, the art sector's productivity is stagnant relative to that of other sectors that can be nurtured by technical progress. "The output per man-hour of the violinist playing a Schubert quartet in a standard concert hall is relatively fixed. It is fairly difficult to reduce the number of actors necessary for a performance of Henry IV, Part II. In order to attract the best musicians, wages in the music industry needed to increase as well—even if the musicians are playing the same melody." Therefore, Baumol and Bowen insisted on increasing support for the performing arts to maintain and cultivate the cultural life of countries because the cost of relatively low productivity rises higher than average labor costs.

Baumol (1967) formally modeled Baumol and Bowen's concern as unbalanced economic growth in two sectors: a nonprogressive or stagnant[5] sector in which labor productivity is fixed and a progressive sector in which labor productivity rises at a fixed compounded rate. His analysis insists that the unit cost of the nonprogressive sector will rise without limit, while that of the progressive sector will remain constant. The outputs of the nonprogressive sector whose demands are not highly inelastic tend to decline and may ultimately vanish. If the output ratio of the two sectors is held constant, the labor force must be transferred to the nonprogressive sector. An attempt to achieve balanced growth must lead to a declining rate of growth relative to the labor force growth rate. If productivity in one sector and the total labor force remain constant, the economy's growth rate will asymptotically approach zero.

These propositions were highly controversial at the time, and Vandermeulen (1968) called these phenomena "Baumol's disease," which Baumol seemed to dislike at the time (Baumol, 1968). Baumol and other followers' models do not discuss long-term growth. Since Baumol's primary concern is the input price rather than the growth path, we call his findings on price and input cost the Baumol effect.

The Baumol effect has been discussed mainly based on empirical explanations rather than theoretical explanations (Abbing, 2002; Akdede et al., 2021; Baumol et al., 1985; Hartwig, 2011, 2019; Nishi, 2019; Nordhaus, 2002, 2008; Thompson, 2021).

Baumol himself emphasized the need to subsidize the arts sector (Baumol, 1991), and the book *The Cost Disease* edited by Baumol (Baumol & De Ferranti, 2012) collects articles discussing the problems caused by uneven cost changes: from rising

[5] The adjective "stagnant" was used in Baumol's later writings.

costs in stagnant sectors such as hospitals, education, and business services to falling costs in progressive sectors that stimulate terrorism and climate change.

In Sect. 7.2, we introduce models of Quesnay-Baumol differential productivity. Assuming two sectors with differential productivity growth, we explain Quesnay's growth effect and Baumol's price effect, which sums up to what we call Quesnay-Baumol effects. In Sect. 7.3, we empirically test whether Quesnay-Baumol effects are observed. In Sect. 7.4, we present a summary and suggestions for future study.

7.2 A Model of Quesnay-Baumol Differential Productivity

7.2.1 Baumol Model

We begin with a summary of the Baumol (1967) model. Assume that the economy is divided into two sectors, Sector *A* and Sector *B*. In Sector *A*, output per man-hour grows cumulatively at a constant compound rate *a* due to technical progress, while in Sector *B*, it is constant because there is no technical progress. The production functions with "unbalanced productivity growth" are as follows:

$$
\begin{aligned}
Y_A &= c_A L_A e^{at} \\
Y_B &= c_B L_B
\end{aligned}
\tag{7.1}
$$

It is assumed that Y_A and Y_B are the values of outputs, L_A and L_B are the labor employed in the two sectors, and c_A and c_B are constants. $L_A + L_B$ is the total labor force and is assumed to be constant.

Suppose that wages W_t are equal in the two sectors because of competition. Thus,

$$W(t) = We^{at} \quad (W = \text{constant}).$$

Then, with Baumol, we can derive the following proposition.

Proposition The cost per unit of output of Sector*A* will remain constant, while the unit cost of Sector *B* will rise without limit, i.e.,

$$
\begin{aligned}
C_A &= W(t) \cdot \frac{L_A}{Y_A} = \frac{W}{c_A} = \text{constant} \\
C_B &= W(t) \cdot \frac{L_B}{Y_B} = \frac{We^{at}}{c_B}.
\end{aligned}
$$

The Baumol model has two basic problems: first, production is determined by labor alone, and second, the model is static. In this chapter, we aim to use traditional two-sector neoclassical growth models with capital and labor.

7.2.2 *Quesnay-Baumol Model*

We now present the traditional neoclassical growth model with exogenous technical change. The economy has two sectors: Sector *A*, the productive sector, and Sector *B*, the stagnant sector.[6] We will see how the conclusions of Baumol may be modified in general and in two special cases.

Since the essential features of traditional two-sector growth models are well known, we present our model without elaborate explanations (see Sato et al., 1997; Sato, 1969).

7.2.2.1 Outline of the Model

(1) Production Functions

The production functions are defined as follows:

$$Y_A(t) = F_A[K_A(t),\ L_A(t),\ A(t)] \tag{7.3}$$

$$Y_B(t) = F_B[K_B(t),\ L_B(t),\ B(t)], \tag{7.4}$$

where Y_A and Y_B are the outputs of each sector and K_A, K_B,L_A, and L_B are the capital and labor inputs in each sector. F_A and F_B represent neoclassical constant returns to scale technology and satisfy the Inada derivative conditions. Y_A may represent capital goods production and Y_B consumer goods production. We assume that the technical change factor $A(t)$ is more productive than $B(t)$,

$$A(t) > B(t), \tag{7.5}$$

We interchangeably use the capital goods sector as the manufacturing sector and the consumer sector as the non-manufacturing (or service) sector.

(2) Full Employment and Perfect Competition

Using $k_A = \frac{K_A}{L_A}$, $k_B = \frac{K_B}{L_B}$, $y_A = \frac{Y_A}{L_A}$, and $y_B = \frac{Y_B}{L_B}$, we have the following:

$$y_A = f_A[k_A, A(t)] \tag{7.6a}$$

$$y_B = f_B[k_B, B(t)]. \tag{7.6b}$$

[6] The theoretical two-sector growth model has been developed by Uzawa (1961), Takayama (1965), Sato (1969), Chang (1970), and other economists, but the model has not been applied to empirical analysis, especially with technical progress. A three-sector model was advanced by Inada et al. (1992): it was a model for developing economies and consists of the subsistence sector (the *S*-sector), light industry sector (the *X*-sector) and the heavy and chemical industries sector (the *Z*-sector). The model was applied to the Japanese economy and showed that Japan took off in the mid or late 1920s.

Hence,

$$r = P_A \frac{\partial f_A}{\partial k_A} = P_B \frac{\partial f_B}{\partial k_B}$$
$$w = P_A\left(f_A - k_A \frac{\partial f_A}{\partial k_A}\right) = P_B\left(f_B - k_B \frac{\partial f_B}{\partial k_B}\right), \tag{7.7}$$

where $r =$ return to capital, $w =$ the wage rate, and $P_{.A.}$ and $P_{.B.}$ are the price level in each sector.

With the full employment assumption of K and L,

$$K = K_A + K_B \tag{7.8a}$$

$$L = L_A + L_B \tag{7.8b}$$

where $L(t) = L(0)e^{nt}$, $n \geq 0$, and n is the growth rate of the total labor force.

The wage-rental ratio R (the marginal rate of substitution) is written as follows:

$$R = \frac{w}{r} = \frac{f_A - k_A \frac{\partial f_A}{\partial k_A}}{\frac{\partial f_A}{\partial k_A}} = \frac{f_B - k_B \frac{\partial f_B}{\partial k_B}}{\frac{\partial f_B}{\partial k_B}} \tag{7.9}$$

Define $k = \frac{K}{L} = \frac{K_A + K_B}{L_A + L_B}$ and

$$\dot{K} = \frac{dK}{dt} = Y_A - \mu K \tag{7.10}$$

where μ is the depreciation rate of capital.

Additionally, define ρ_A and ρ_B as $\rho_A = \frac{L_A}{L}$ and $\rho_B = \frac{L_B}{L}$. Thus, $\rho_A + \rho_B = 1$, and we have the following:

$$k = \rho_A k_A + \rho_B k_B \tag{7.11}$$

(3) Saving-Investment Behavior

We now close the system by introducing the saving-investment behavior of the classical type[7]: that is, savings, S, are done by capitalists, i.e., $S = srK$, where s is the proportion of capitalists' income saved and $0 < s \leq 1$. In equilibrium, savings, S, are equal to investments, I, and I is equal to $P_A Y_A$. Thus, using $P_A Y_A = srK = sP_A \frac{\partial f_A}{\partial k_A} K$ and $P_A = 1$, we have the following:

$$\frac{Y_A}{L_A} = y_A = f_A = \frac{srK}{L_A} = s\frac{\partial f_A}{\partial k_A}\frac{K}{L_A} = s\frac{\partial f_A}{\partial k_A}\frac{k}{\rho_A}$$

---

[7] In this work, we take up the classical saving case, but the stability condition will be almost identical to the general case. See Sato (1969).

$$\therefore \quad f_A = s\frac{\partial f_A}{\partial k_A}\cdot\frac{k}{\rho_A} \tag{7.12}$$

We can now summarize the dynamic system as follows:

$$y_A = f_A[k_A, A(t)] \tag{7.6a}$$

$$y_B = f_B[k_B, B(t)] \tag{7.6b}$$

$$R = \frac{f_A - k_A\frac{\partial f_A}{\partial k_A}}{\frac{\partial f_A}{\partial k_A}} = \frac{f_B - k_B\frac{\partial f_B}{\partial k_B}}{\frac{\partial f_B}{\partial k_B}} \tag{7.9}$$

$$k = \rho_A k_A + \rho_B k_B \tag{7.11}$$

$$f_A = s\frac{\partial f_A}{\partial k_A}\cdot\frac{k}{\rho_A} \tag{7.12}$$

From Eq. (7.10), we have the following:

$$\frac{\dot{k}}{k} = \frac{\rho_A f_A(k_A,\ A(t))}{k} - n - \mu \tag{7.13}$$

(4) Fundamental Differential Equation

Given $f_A'' = \frac{\partial^2 f_A}{\partial k_A^2} < 0, f_B'' = \frac{\partial^2 f_B}{\partial k_B^2} < 0$, and

$$\frac{\partial R}{\partial k_A} = \frac{-f_A f_A''}{f_A'^2} > 0$$

$$\frac{\partial R}{\partial k_B} = \frac{-f_B f_B''}{f_B'^2} > 0,$$

we can determine k_A and k_B as follows:

$$k_A = \Phi_A(R,\ A(t)),\ \ \Phi_A' > 0$$

$$k_B = \Phi_B(R,\ B(t)),\ \ \Phi_B' > 0.$$

Additionally, ρ_A and ρ_B can be expressed as follows:

$$\rho_A = \frac{sk}{R + \Phi_A}$$

$$\rho_B = 1 - \frac{sk}{R + \Phi_A}$$

Thus, using Eq. (7.11), we can write the following:

$$k(R,\ A(t),\ B(t)) = k(R,\ t) = \frac{[R + \Phi_A] \cdot \Phi_B}{R + (1 - s)\Phi_A + s\Phi_B}$$

.

Substituting f_A in Eq. (7.13) for Eq. (7.12), we obtain[8] the following:

$$\frac{\dot{k}}{k} = s\frac{\partial f_A[\Phi_A(R,\ t)]}{\partial k} - n - \mu \tag{7.14}$$

Equation (7.14) is the fundamental differential equation that determines the path of K/L, i.e., the path of the Quesnay-Baumol dynamic system. This system is different from the standard two-sector growth model because of $A(t)$ and $B(t)$, which is expressed as follows:

$$\Phi_A(R,\ t),\quad \frac{\partial \Phi}{\partial t} \neq 0 \tag{7.15}$$

In general, there is no stable solution such that $\frac{\dot{k}}{k} = 0$ for all t. Thus, **we conclude that, in general, there exists no equilibrium path for this system**.

7.2.2.2 Special Cases that Solve the Problem

We show two special cases that allow the system to achieve equilibrium solutions. One is the case of Hicks-neutral technical change in Sector B. The other is the case where both sectors have Harrod-neutral technical change.

Let us see why these two cases solve the problem. Looking at Eq. (7.14), we notice that the marginal product of capital in the more productive sector, Sector A, should not be affected by technical change. The simplest change is the form of the Hicksian type. Under the Hicksian type, the wage-rental ratios, or the marginal rates of substitution in both sectors are not affected. Hence, the economy's total income, or GDP, should be written as follows:

$$Y = P_A \cdot Y_A + P_B \cdot B \cdot Y_B,$$

, where

[8] Compare the result with Sato (1969), Eq. (8).

$$Y_A = F_A[K_A,\ L_A].$$

and

$$Y_B = F_B[K_B,\ L_B].$$

Here, $B(t)$ is the Hicksian type of technical change, and Y_A and Y_B have no explicit technical improvement factors, i.e., $\frac{\partial Y_A}{\partial t} = \frac{\partial Y_B}{\partial t} = 0$.

Under the second case, Eq. (7.14) is affected by the technical change of the Harrod type. Since Sector B's technical change does not affect Eq. (7.14), we also assume that Sector B's technical change is of the Harrod-neutral type,

$$Y = P_A \cdot Y_A + P_B \cdot Y_B, Y_A = F_A[K_A,\ A \cdot L_A]$$

and

$$Y_B = F_B[K_B,\ B \cdot L_B]$$

where $A(t) = A(0)e^{at}$ and $B(t) = B(0)e^{bt}$. By defining $\overline{k}_A = \frac{K_A}{\overline{L}_A} = \frac{K_A}{A(t)L_A}$, and $\overline{k}_B = \frac{K_B}{B(t)L_B}$, we can study the stability condition of the equilibrium solutions.

Case 1: Hicks-Neutral Technical Change

Note that to have stable solutions, a dynamic Eq. (7.14) should not contain the technical progress factors, $A(t)$ and $B(t)$.

Consider that technical change is "Hicks-neutral" in both sectors:

$$Y_A(t) = A(t)F_A[K_A(t),\ L_A(t)]$$

$$Y_B(t) = B(t)F_B[K_B(t),\ L_B(t)]$$

and with Baumol, $A(t) > B(t) = 1$, and we normalize the system as follows:

$$Y_A(t) = F_A[K_A(t),\ L_A(t)] \tag{7.16a}$$

$$Y_B(t) = \frac{B(t)}{A(t)}F_B[K_B(t),\ L_B(t)] = \frac{1}{A(t)}F_B[K_B(t),\ L_B(t)] \tag{7.16b}$$

Let us assume that $A(t) = A(0)e^{at}$, at $A(0) = 1$, and $B(t) = B(0) = 1$. Thus, Eqs. (7.16a) and (7.16b) imply that in this Q-B economy, the technical chance of stagnant Sector B is "deteriorating" compared with Sector A.

Thus, we have the following:

$$Y_A(t) = F_A[K_A(t),\ L_A(t)] \tag{7.17a}$$

$$Y_B(t) = e^{-at} F_B[K_B(t),\ L_B(t)]. \tag{7.17b}$$

In Eqs. (7.17a) and (7.17b), the wage-rental ratios (the marginal rate of substitution) in both sectors are not affected by technical change. The differential Eq. (7.14) is reduced to the case where there is no technical change:

$$\frac{\dot{k}}{k} = s\frac{df_A[\Phi_A(R)]}{dk} - n - \mu. \tag{7.18}$$

The steady-state solution is obtained as follows:

$$s\frac{df_A}{dk} = n + \mu = \lambda \tag{7.19}$$

i.e., the equilibrium value of $k = K/L =$ constant.

By introducing Hicks-neutral technical change in Sector B, we have the following:

$$P_A \cdot f_A' = P_B \cdot e^{-at} f_B'$$

.

In equilibrium, k is constant, and k_A and k_B are also constant, which implies that $f_A\prime$ and $f_B\prime$ are also constant. Thus, we have the following:

$$\frac{\dot{P}_A}{P_A} = \frac{\dot{P}_B}{P_B} - a \text{ or } \frac{\dot{P}_B}{P_B} = \frac{\dot{P}_A}{P_A} + a. \tag{7.20}$$

The price level of Sector B must increase faster than that of Sector A by a % a year.

Consider the following Cobb–Douglas example:

$$Y_A = K_A^{\alpha_A} L_A^{1-\alpha_A}$$

$$Y_B = e^{-at} K_B^{\alpha_B} L_B^{1-\alpha_B}$$

where $\alpha_B > \alpha_A$ and thus $k_B > k_A$. We can show that the equilibrium capital-labor ratio of the economy is $k^* = \frac{\alpha_B}{1-\alpha_A} \cdot R^*$, and the equilibrium labor allocation to Sector A is $\rho_A^* = \alpha_B$.

In other words, $P_{B.}$, the price level of Sector B, must increase by the same amount as Ce^{at}. In short, by introducing Hicks-neutral technical progress in Sector B, we can modify the original two-sector model's features with minimal modification.

Case 2: Harrod-Neutral Technical Change

By introducing Harrod-neutral technical change, as defined in Eq. (7.16a, b),

$$\overline{k}(t) = \frac{K(t)}{A(t) \cdot L(t)} = \frac{K(t)}{\overline{L}(t)} \tag{7.21}$$

and Eq. (7.18) can be used to write the following:

$$\frac{\dot{\overline{k}}}{\overline{k}} = s\frac{df_A[\Phi_A(R)]}{d\overline{k}_A} - (n + \mu + a), \tag{7.22}$$

where $\overline{k}_A = \frac{K_A}{\overline{L}_A} = \frac{K_A}{A(t)L_A}$ and $\overline{k}_B = \frac{K_B}{B(t)L_B}$; $A(t) = A(0)e^{at}$, $a > 0$, and $B(t) = B(0)e^{bt}$, $b \geq 0$.

Incidentally, we assume $s = 1$ and $A(t) > B(t) = B(0)e^{bt}$, which means that under $A(0) = B(0)$, $a > b \geq 0$. Without loss of generality, again, we can set $b = 0$ or $B(t) =$ constant, and we have the following:

$$\frac{Y_A}{AL_A} = f_A\left(\overline{k}_A\right)$$

$$\frac{Y_B}{L_B} = f_B(k_B)$$

, where

$$k_B = \frac{K_B}{L_B}$$

.

In equilibrium, $\frac{\dot{\overline{k}}}{\overline{k}} = 0$, and under the usual stability conditions, capital K and "effective labor" $\overline{L}$ increase at the same rate. However, $\frac{K}{L} = k(t)$ increases faster than $\overline{k}(t)$ based on the technical progress factor in Sector A.

From $P_A \cdot f_A'\left(\overline{k}_A\right) = P_B \cdot f_B'\left(\overline{k}_B\right) = r$, in equilibrium, we can show that $P_A \cdot f_A'\left(\overline{k}_A\right)$ = constant and.

$$\frac{\dot{P}_B}{P_B} = \frac{\dot{P}_A}{P_A} - \frac{\frac{d(f_B')}{dt}}{f_B'}$$

where

$$\frac{\frac{d(f_B')}{dt}}{f_B'} < 0$$

.

We have successfully constructed models that take into account Quesnay-Baumol effects.[9]

Let us summarize the two theoretical cases discussed thus far. The neoclassical two-sector growth model shows both the Quesnay growth effect and the Baumol price effect in an explicit way. We begin with the case of the Harrod-neutral type.

Given $Y_A = F_A[K_A, A \cdot L_A]$ and $Y_B = F_B[K_B, B \cdot L_B]$, we have Y (GDP) as $Y = P_A \cdot Y_A + P_B \cdot Y_B$. The growth rate of Y can be expressed as the sum of the Quesnay growth effect and the Baumol price effect, i.e.,

$$\frac{\dot{Y}}{Y} = \beta_A\left(\frac{\dot{P}_A}{P_A} + \frac{\dot{Y}_A}{Y_A}\right) + \beta_B\left(\frac{\dot{P}_B}{P_B} + \frac{\dot{Y}_B}{Y_B}\right) \tag{7.23}$$

where $\beta_A = \frac{P_A Y_A}{Y}$, $\beta_B = \frac{P_B Y_B}{Y}$, and $\beta_A + \beta_B = 1$.

For any given $\frac{\dot{Y}}{Y}$ and β_A, we have the following:

$$\frac{\dot{P}_A}{P_A} \overset{>}{<} \frac{\dot{P}_B}{P_B} \text{ depending upon } \frac{\dot{Y}_A}{Y_A} \overset{<}{>} \frac{\dot{Y}_B}{Y_B}. \tag{7.24}$$

The Quesnay effect is closely related to the Baumol effect.

To see the effects of Harrod-neutral technical change on$P_{.A.}$ and$P_{.B.}$, Eq. (7.23) can be decomposed into the following:

$$\begin{aligned}\frac{\dot{Y}}{Y} &= \beta_A\left[\frac{\dot{P}_A}{P_A} + \gamma_A\frac{\dot{K}_A}{K_A} + (1-\gamma_A)\left(\frac{\dot{L}_A}{L_A} + a\right)\right] \\ &\quad + (1-\beta_A)\left[\frac{\dot{P}_B}{P_B} + \gamma_B\frac{\dot{K}_B}{K_B} + (1-\gamma_B)\left(\frac{\dot{L}_B}{L_B} + b\right)\right]\end{aligned}$$

where $a = \frac{\dot{A}}{A}$, $b = \frac{\dot{B}}{B}$, $a > b \geq 0$, and γ_A and γ_B are the income shares of capital in Sector A and Sector B.

In equilibrium, K/AL is constant, which also implies $\frac{\dot{K}_A}{K_A} = \frac{\dot{K}_B}{K_B} = n+a$. By setting $\left[\frac{\dot{P}_A}{P_A} + \gamma_A\frac{\dot{K}_A}{K_A} + (1-\gamma_A)(n+a)\right] = \left[\frac{\dot{P}_B}{P_B} + \gamma_B\frac{\dot{K}_B}{K_B} + (1-\gamma_B)(n+b)\right]$, we obtain the following:

$$\frac{\dot{P}_B}{P_B} = \frac{\dot{P}_A}{P_A} + (1-\gamma_B)(a-b) \tag{7.25}$$

Finally, to show the effect of Hicks-neutral technical progress in Sector B, we simply modify Eq. (7.23) as follows:

[9] Takayama (1965) and others discussed technical changes in two-sector growth models, but their conditions (α conditions) for stable solutions are too complicated. The economic meaning is not easy to interpret.

$$\frac{\dot{Y}}{Y} = \beta_A\left(\frac{\dot{P}_A}{P_A} + \frac{\dot{Y}_A}{Y_A}\right) + \beta_B\left(\frac{\dot{P}_B}{P_B} + \frac{\dot{Y}_B}{Y_B} + b\right) \tag{7.26}$$

In our model, since we assume that Sector B is more inefficient (or stagnant) in technical change, we assume Eq. (7.17b) as $b = -a$.

We can add another useful identity, $Y = rK + wL$, from which we can express the following:

$$\frac{\dot{Y}}{Y} = \textit{Income share of capital} \times \left(\frac{\dot{r}}{r} + \frac{\dot{K}}{K}\right) + \textit{Income share of labor} \times \left(\frac{\dot{w}}{w} + \frac{\dot{L}}{L}\right)$$

where $\frac{\dot{K}}{K} = \frac{\dot{L}}{L}$ and $\frac{\dot{r}}{r} = \frac{\dot{w}}{w}$. However, when $\frac{\dot{K}}{K} > \frac{\dot{L}}{L}$ because of Harrod-neutral technical change, the wage rate will increase faster than $\frac{\dot{r}}{r}$. In a steady state, $\frac{K(t)}{A(t)L(t)}$ = constant, the marginal product of capital in Sector A is constant and equal to $n + \mu + a$ (Eq. 7.22).

7.3 Empirical Application and Testing

We have theoretically proven that an economic sector with a higher rate of technical progress creates more product than a sector with a lower rate of technical progress. This is in line with Quesnay's *Tableau Ēconomique*, which showed that a circular flow of expenditure on the productive sector promoted economic growth (the Quesnay effect). The price of products in a nonprogressive sector will rise faster than that of products in a progressive sector through sectoral interdependencies in the market mechanism (the Baumol effect).

In this section, we empirically investigate how the two sectors (supposedly productive and nonproductive sectors) performed in Japan and the U.S. during the 1980–2020 period.

Before the sector-wise analysis, we offer a bird's-eye view of the macroeconomic trends of the Japanese and U.S. economies in Subsect. 7.3.1. First, a few remarks are made concerning GDP growth, output per labor, and the output-capital ratio in each country. Then, we verify the existence of the Quesnay growth effect in Subsect. 7.3.2 and the Baumol price effect in Subsect. 7.3.3.

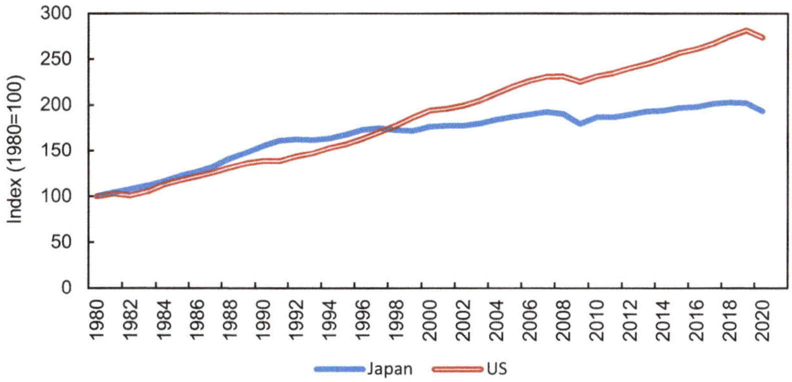

Fig. 7.1 Real GDP in Japan and the U.S. *Source* See Data Source Appendix A1

7.3.1 Japan-U.S. Macroeconomic Comparison

7.3.1.1 Growth Rates

Figure 7.1 shows the indexed data on real GDP (1980 = 100) in Japan and the U.S. Japan's indexed GDP exceeded that of the U.S. from 1980 to 1997. There was an economic bubble in Japan from 1986 to 1991 in which real estate and stock market prices rapidly escalated. The economic bubble accelerated Japanese growth. However, after the bubble economy burst, the Japanese economy stagnated. The prolonged low growth rates represent Japan's Lost Decades.

In contrast to the Japanese economy, the U.S. economy grew steadily without experiencing long-term stagnation. As a result, in 2019, the index reached 281.4, far above Japan's value of 202.3.

7.3.1.2 Productivity

Sustained economic growth requires a continuous improvement in productivity. Figure 7.2 shows the simple labor productivity calculated as real GDP per labor hours (Y/L) in Japan and the U.S.

Japan had a higher growth rate in labor productivity than the U.S. from 1980 to 1991. The compound annual growth rate was 3.36% for Japan and 1.48% for the U.S. Even in the Lost Decades, after the 1990s, Japan's labor productivity showed stagnation but did not decline much compared to the U.S. From 2009 until 2017, the economies had a similar growth rate.

Another indicator of productivity is capital productivity or the output-capital ratio (Y/K). It declined from 1980 to 1993 in Japan and stagnated, while capital productivity in the U.S. was stable with a hill-like ridge from 1995 to 2006 (Fig. 7.3).

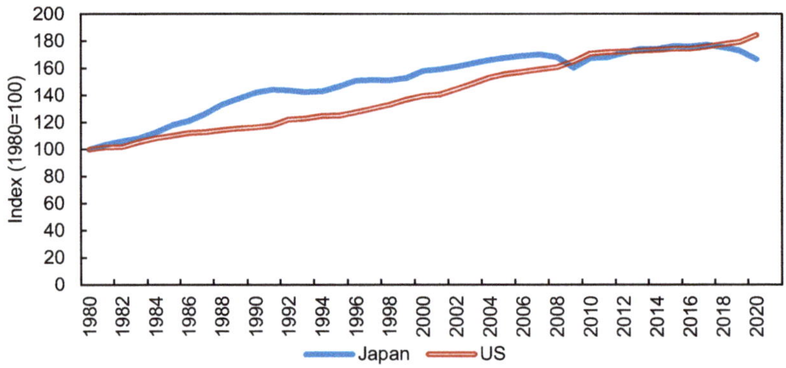

Fig. 7.2 Labor productivity in Japan and the U.S. *Source* See Data Source Appendix A1

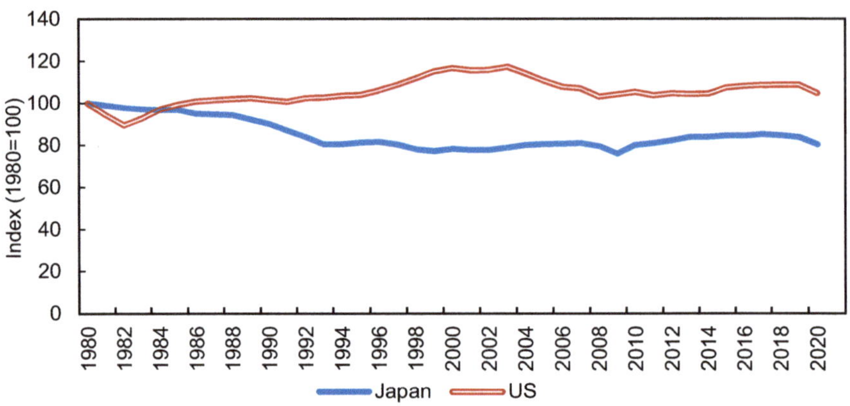

Fig. 7.3 Capital productivity in Japan and the U.S. *Source* See Data Source Appendix A1

A comparison of Figs. 7.2 and 7.3 suggests that the labor-intensive sector led the Japanese bubble boom.

7.3.2 Quesnay Growth Effect

At this point, we divide each economy into two categories: the productive sector represented by the manufacturing industry (Sector A) and the nonproductive sector represented by the non-manufacturing industry (Sector B).

We compare sector productivities in three types of estimations: total factor productivity (TFP),[10] the productivity of the Cobb–Douglas function estimated by

[10] Recently Fukao et al. (2020) conducted a two-sector TFP estimation (the primary sector and the non-primary sector) for Japan in 1885–1970, and the period does not overlap with ours.

Table 7.1 Growth accounting: Japan and the U.S

		Manufacturing		Non-manufacturing	
		Value added (%)	TFP (%)	Value added (%)	TFP (%)
		$\dot{Y}/Y$	$\dot{T}/T$	$\dot{Y}/Y$	$\dot{T}/T$
Japan	1980s	4.692	1.372	4.111	−0.055
	1990s	0.525	0.410	1.605	−0.885
	2000s	−0.389	-0.013	0.217	−0.131
	2010s	1.075	0.640	0.305	−0.243
The U.S	1980s	4.363	3.479	3.955	0.894
	1990s	4.875	4.610	3.724	1.599
	2000s	1.050	1.791	1.880	0.155
	2010s	1.903	0.093	2.819	0.678

Source See Data Source Appendix A1 and A2

regression, and the Baumol-type production function using the generalized reduced gradient method (GRGM). See Lasdon et al. (1974) for the GRGM. The first two models assume the Cobb–Douglas production function in each sector in each country.

7.3.2.1 Total Factor Productivity

In an economy with two inputs, we explain economic growth with the Cobb–Douglas production function of each sector, $F(\cdot)$, as $Y_i = T_i \cdot F(K_i, L_i)$, where Y_i is value added, T_i is total factor productivity, K_i is the capital input, and L_i is the labor input. Taking the log of Y_i and differentiating it with time t, we obtain the following:

$$\frac{\dot{Y}_i}{Y_i} = \frac{\dot{T}_i}{T_i} + \alpha_i \frac{\dot{K}_i}{K_i} + (1 - \alpha_i)\frac{\dot{L}_i}{L_i} \tag{7.27}$$

where α_i is the share of capital, $1 - \alpha_i$ is the share of labor, and $i = A, B$.

The estimation results are shown in Table 7.1.

According to Quesnay's insight, higher TFP growth ($\frac{\dot{T}}{T}$) will lead to high value-added growth ($\frac{\dot{Y}}{Y}$). Growth in the U.S. economy confirms this insight. In the 1980s and 1990s, the manufacturing sector enjoyed a high growth rate of value added in the U.S. This is because the manufacturing sector had a higher TFP growth rate than the non-manufacturing sector. In the 2010s, the nonmanufacturing sector enjoyed a high growth rate of value-added owing to the nonmanufacturing sector's higher TFP growth compared to that of the manufacturing sector. The leadership change in economic growth was due to the emergence of Big Tech.[11] These results are

[11] In Japan, Big Tech is often referred to as "GAFAM," i.e., Google, Amazon, Facebook, Apple, and Microsoft.

consistent with the Quesnay effect. The 2000s were an exception because of the impacts of the dot-com bubble crash and the financial crisis in the U.S.

However, setting a two-factor, two-sector TFP model reveals that the Quesnay effect did not occur in Japan. In the 1980s and 2010s, the manufacturing sector enjoyed higher output growth than the non-manufacturing sector as a function of TFP. In the 1990s and 2000s, the TFP growth in the manufacturing sector surpassed that of the non-manufacturing sector, but value-added growth was lower in manufacturing. The TFP growth and value-added growth combinations between the two sectors, where a sector with higher productivity has more output than the other sector, did not satisfy Quesnay's assumption.

From the results, during the Lost Decades, we clearly find that Japan's economic growth has been disturbed by some obstacles. One explanation may be that the Japanese asset price bubble from 1986 to 1991 and the subsequent burst of the bubble, usually considered a purely monetary crisis, had macroeconomic effects. A disconnection between output growth and TFP growth suggests inefficient resource allocation or an imperfection of Japan's product and factor markets. As a result, a productive sector could not lead to economic growth. After the bubble, Japan fell into a recession, and the burst of the bubble could be a reason for Japan's Lost Decades.

7.3.2.2 Cobb–Douglas Regression Model

We assume the Cobb–Douglas production function and take the regression under a time series framework. We add a trend term $e^{\gamma_i t}$ to the production function, setting γ_i as the technical progress rate ($t = 0, 1, 2, \ldots$) in sector i.

$$Y_i = T_{i0} e^{\gamma_i t} K_i^{\alpha_i} L_i^{1-\alpha_i} \tag{7.28}$$

where T_{i0} is the initial total factor productivity, α_i is the share of capital, and $i = A$, B. We divide (7.29) by L_i and write it in logarithmic form as Eq. (7.29):

$$\frac{Y_i}{L_i} = T_{i0} e^{\gamma_i t} \left(\frac{K_i}{L_i} \right)^{\alpha_i}$$

$$\log\left(\frac{Y_i}{L_i}\right) = \log T_{i0} + \gamma_i t + \alpha_i \log\left(\frac{K_i}{L_i}\right) \tag{7.29}$$

The estimation results for the two sectors using data from 1980 to 2020 are shown in Table 7.2.

This model estimates the constant technical progress rate from 1980 to 2020. The modern Japanese and the U.S. economies seem divided into productive and unproductive sectors, in line with Quesnay's observation in the eighteenth century. The productive sector is manufacturing, and the unproductive sector is the nonmanufacturing sector in Japan. On the other hand, in the U.S., the nonmanufacturing sector is the productive sector.

Table 7.2 Estimations of the Cobb–Douglas production function (1980–2020)

	Japan		U.S	
	Mfg.	Non-mfg.	Mfg.	Non-mfg.
γ_i	0.0130 (7.070)	0.0011 (2.608)	0.0078 (1.249)	0.0107 (29.451)
α_i	0.5068 (7.656)	0.4523 (19.795)	0.9368 (5.591)	0.1216 (3.578)
Adjusted R^2	0.9840	0.9746	0.9800	0.9928
RMSPE (%)	4.02	1.89	7.10	1.18

Note 1. *t*-statistics in parentheses

2. RMSPE, root mean square percentage error, is calculated as $\sqrt{\frac{1}{n}\sum_{i=1}^{n}\left(\frac{\hat{Y}-Y}{Y}\right)^2} \times 100$.

Source See Data Source Appendix A1

Assuming constant technical progress for 40 years is unrealistic in the age of accelerating in technical and industrial structure changes. Our results in Sect. 3.2.1, which split the periods appropriately, are more thoroughgoing.

7.3.2.3 Labor Productivity

We tested Baumol's model using the GRGM. We form production functions for each industry as Eq. (7.30):

$$Y_i = T_{i0}e^{\gamma_i t}L_i, \quad i = A,\ B, \tag{7.30}$$

where we assume $i = A$ for the manufacturing sector and $i = B$ for the non-manufacturing sector. Y_i is value added, T_{i0} is the initial technical level, and L_i is the labor force in each sector.

We found that dividing the observed values into two periods was necessary for the best-fitting estimation based on RMSPE. For Japan, Period I is 1980–1991, and Period II is 1992–2020. For the U.S., Period I is 1980–2008, and Period II is 2009–2020 (Table 7.3).

Breakpoints coincide with the years of the historical events. In 1991 the bubble economy burst in Japan when the land prices plummeted following the stock market crash of 1990, and in 2008, Lehman Brothers went bankrupt in the U.S. This result suggests that the structural change occurred in 1991 for Japan and in 2008 for the U.S. because the employment structure was deeply involved in these events.[12]

The two sectors show different performances. Technical progress is higher in the manufacturing sector than in the non-manufacturing sector in both countries. When

[12] The Bai-Perron test of Y_i also confirmed a breakpoint in 1991 for Japan and in 2009 for the U.S.

Table 7.3 Estimation of the two-sector production function

	Manufacturing		Non-manufacturing	
Japan	Period I 1980–1991	Period II 1992–2020	Period I 1980–1991	Period II 1992–2020
γ_i	0.0335	0.0231	0.0285	0.0030
RMSPE	2.09%	6.40%	1.59%	2.53%
U.S	Period I 1980–2008	Period II 2009–2020	Period I 1980–2008	Period II 2009–2020
γ_i	0.0484	0.0080	0.0117	0.0073
RMSPE (%)	6.32	1.88	1.03	0.90

Source See Data Source Appendix A1

we investigate the non-manufacturing sector, the one-input model provides a better estimation from the perspective of the estimation error, yielding a low RMSPE.

Baumol's one-factor setting appears to explain what is known as the Baumol effect. This model captures the essence of the results in Sect. 3.2.1. Nevertheless, his model with only labor input may be oversimplified in explaining the economic growth process in these two countries.

7.3.3 *Baumol Price Effect*

When the Quesnay growth effect is observed, the price rise in the progressive sector should be lower than that in the stagnant sector. We will examine the general price levels and wage rates.

7.3.3.1 General Price Levels

Let us consider the relationship between economic growth and price fluctuation. We use the GDP deflator as an index of market prices because it is compiled from the broadest goods and services price data.

Fig 7.4 shows the deflators for Japan and the U.S. Panel 1 shows the price increase in the nonmanufacturing sector during Japan's economic bubble. In the early 1980s, the nonmanufacturing deflator increased faster than the manufacturing deflator, as shown by the Baumol effect in Eq. (7.20). After the bubble economy, the Japanese economy suffered from long-term deflation. In the manufacturing industry, the price level declined from 1993 to 2012. The price level became stable since 1993 and then fell from 1998 to 2013 in nonmanufacturing industries, although the rate of decline had been small. Since the price level declined in both sectors, general price levels continued to decline, especially in the 2000s, and the Japanese economy deflated for a long period. It was a deflationary spiral: consumers with the expectation of price

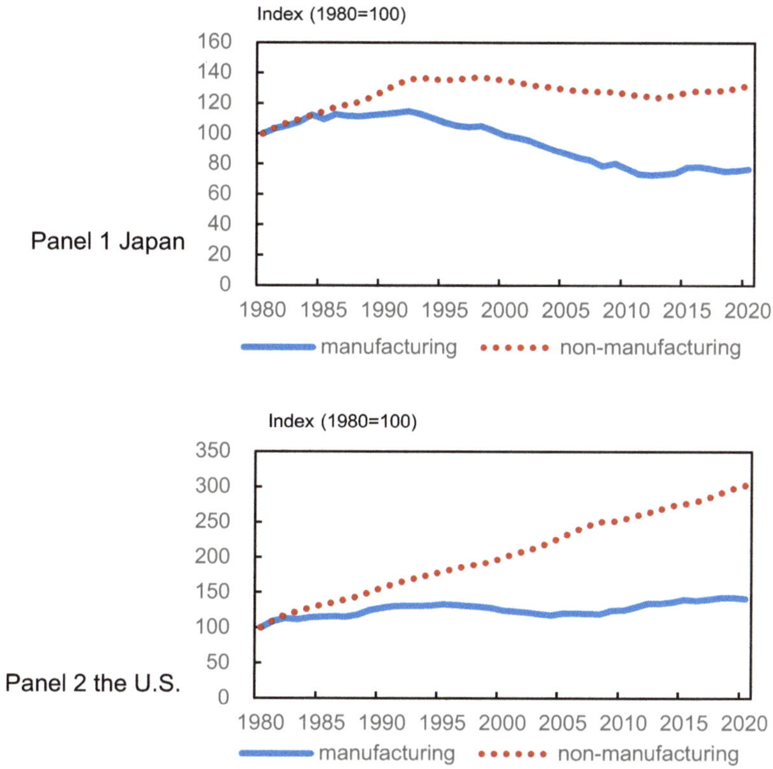

Fig. 7.4 GDP deflators by sectors: Manufacturing and nonmanufacturing. *Source* See Data Source Appendix A3

decline are reluctant to buy goods and services early, and overall demands declines, leading to a further fall in market prices. In addition, deflation means a decline in the value of currency, which increases the burden of repayment for those in debt. This deflationary spiral hindered economic growth and made it difficult for Japan's economy to recover from the Lost Decade.

Panel 2 suggests that the U.S. economy is enjoying healthy economic growth. While prices in manufacturing are stable, those in the non-manufacturing sector are increasing.

7.3.3.2 Wage Rates

Figure 7.5 shows the per capita wages and salaries in both countries, which are the costs behind prices. In Japan (Panel 1), wages and salaries in the nonmanufacturing sector were slightly higher than those in the manufacturing sector from 1991 to 1993. Only this short period is consistent with the Baumol price effect. Wages and salaries

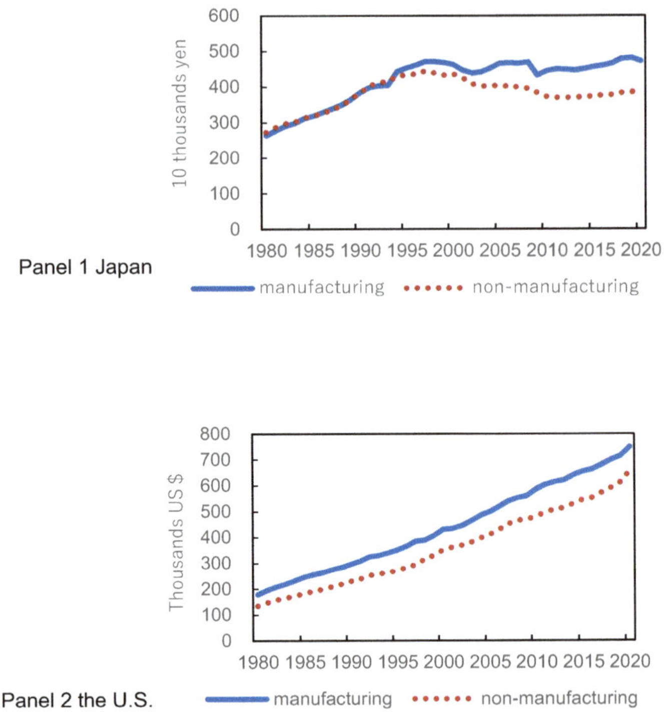

Fig. 7.5 Per capita wages and salaries: Manufacturing and nonmanufacturing. *Source* See Data Source Appendix A4

in the manufacturing sector remained flat over twenty years from 1995 to 2020. However, wages and salaries in the non-manufacturing sector declined from 1998 to 2011, creating a gap with the manufacturing sector. Therefore, there was no Baumol price effect in Japan. There might be an upward rigidity due to a structural change[13] in Japan's wages, which has been a critical issue for over 20 years.

Panel 2 shows the per capita wages and salaries in the U.S. Wages and salaries in the nonmanufacturing sector have been increasing, following wages and salaries in the manufacturing sector, where technical progress is high. This figure convinces us that the U.S. economy experienced the Baumol effect. The two sectors have developed competitively.

---

[13] This issue falls beyond the scope of this chapter. However, we note that the *Amendment of the Act for Securing the Proper Operation of Worker Dispatching Undertakings and Improved Working Conditions for Dispatched Workers* in 2004 (Law number: Act No. 88 of 1985) increased the number of non-regular workers with low wages, which led to the upward rigidity in wage rates.

7.3.4 *Summary of Empirical Testing*

Using national accounts data from Japan and the U.S., we have tested how the Quesnay-Baumol effect has worked. The assumption of forty years of constant technical progress (Sect. 7.3.2.2) did not provide good insights into the sluggish Japanese economy. However, the two-factor, two-sector total productivity approach divided by decades (Sect. 7.3.2.1) revealed that the Quesnay effect did not appear in Japan. Baumol's framework, which solely uses labor as a production factor (Sect. 7.3.2.3), simplifies our results in Sect. 7.3.2.1. The Baumol effect in Japan was unclear because of the prolonged deflation (Sects. 7.3.3.1 and 7.3.3.2).

7.4 Summary and Suggestions for Future Study

This study examined how differential technical growth in the two sectors has affected overall growth processes in Japan and the U.S. It is shown that Japan's Lost Decades are partly due to the existence of the Baumol effect and the absence of the Quesnay effect.

First, we have developed a two-factor, two-sector neoclassical growth model with differential productivity. We proved the non-existence of the equilibrium path for the system in general. However, by assuming two special cases, Hicks-neutral and Harrod-neutral technical changes, we could prove the existence of equilibrium paths under the Quesnay-Baumol conditions.

Next, with the use of the above model, we used econometric analysis to examine whether we can observe the Quesnay-Baumol effects in Japan and the U.S. When we assumed constant technical progress during the 1980–2020 period (Sect. 7.3.2.2), the rate of technical progress in the manufacturing sector was higher than that in the nonmanufacturing sector in Japan. In the U.S., the difference in both sectors was not clear. Focusing on Baumol's settings and dividing the period into two (Sect. 7.3.2.3), we found that the manufacturing sector had higher productivity growth than the nonmanufacturing sector in both countries.'

With our two-factor settings (Sect. 7.3.2.1), we found that Japan's economy has been experiencing structural problems that impeded the Quesnay-Baumol effects. The Quesnay effect was not observed in Japan, while in the U.S. economy, the Quesnay effect has contributed to easing the Baumol effect. These mutual effects are the sources of advances in the U.S. macro economy.

The disconnection between output growth and TFP improvement suggests inefficient resource allocation or imperfection of Japan's product and factor markets. The deflationary spiral after the burst of the bubble economy hindered economic growth. Politically widened non-regular employment caused upward rigidity of the wage rate and distorted the labor market.

For the interested reader, we suggest that our model can be extended to include the monetary sector in the economy (Nagatani, 1970; Tobin, 1965). From the Japanese experience, one might be interested in finding out why expansionary monetary policies undertaken by the Bank of Japan for ten years as a part of Abenomics did not work to overcome stagnant economic conditions in Japan. Also, as Abenomics emphasized the positive effect of the Japanese Yen exchange rate, the model should also include the Yen-Dollar rate in an explicit form. Here, we would like to warn the reader that theoretical models accommodating money and the exchange rate will not be easy to construct. In particular, stability conditions might be entirely different from those in existing models.

We have not covered the effects on the world economy in the period after the COVID-19 pandemic and in the period after Russia invaded Ukraine in 2022. Recent cost-push inflation caused by a rise in energy prices and by the weak Yen can work only to curtail consumption and cannot be a prescription for Japan's deflationary spiral. However, we want to emphasize again that innovation and technical progress can contribute to the growth and prosperity of any economy, even after the COVID-19 disaster and Russian invasions.

Data Source Appendix

(A1) Data from 1994 to 2020 for Japan was taken from the *Annual Report on National Accounts for 2021* (benchmark year = 2015, https://www.esri.cao.go.jp/en/sna/menu.html). We use "Real Gross Domestic Product classified by Economic Activities (Chain-linked)" for Y_i, "Employed Person" for L_i, and "Net Capital Stocks of Fixed Assets classified by Institutional Sectors and Economic Activities: In real term" for K. Data from 1980 to 1993 is estimated from *Annual Report on National Accounts for 2021* (benchmark year = 2000), the *2015 base Simple Retrospective of Expenditure Side GDP Series*, and the *Reference Series for 2015 base Fixed Asset Balance*. Data for the U.S. was taken from the U.S. Bureau of Economic Analysis (https://www.bea.gov/). We use "Real Value Added by Industry" and "Historical SIC Data" for Y and Y_i, "Persons Engaged in Production by Industry" for L and L_i, and "Current-Cost Net Stock of Private Nonresidential Fixed Assets by Industry Group and Legal Form of Organization" for K and K_i. We converted current values to real values (benchmark year = 2012) (accessed July 15, 2023).

(A2) Labor share in Japan is calculated from "Gross Domestic Product and Factor Income classified by Economic Activities" in the *Annual Report on National Accounts for 2021*. We calculated labor share from "Components of Value Added by Industry" in the U.S. Bureau of Economic Analysis (accessed July 15, 2023).

(A3) Japan's 2011 SNA revision, which aligned with the 2008 SNA, adopted the chain-linked method exclusively. As a result, complete chain-linked data is available only through 1994. Therefore, for Japan's manufacturing industry, we connected the chain-linked data for 1990 to 1993 and fixed-base data of "Gross Domestic Product classified by Economic Activities" for 1980 to

1989 in *Annual Report on National Accounts for 2009* to the deflators of "Gross Domestic Product classified by Economic Activities (Deflators: Chain-linked)" in *Annual Report on National Accounts for 2021*. Deflators for Japan's nonmanufacturing sector were calculated from real and nominal value-added. We used "Chain-Type Price Indexes for Value Added by Industry" in the U.S. Bureau of Economic Analysis for the U.S. manufacturing industry. Deflators for the U.S. nonmanufacturing sector were calculated from real and current value-added (accessed August 17, 2023).

(A4) Deflationary spirals lead to reduce wages. Wages and salaries (current prices) in Japan were calculated by subtracting average employers' social contributions from the compensation of employees. Per-capita compensation of employees was calculated using "Gross Domestic Product and Factor Income classified by Economic Activities" and "Employed Persons, Employees and Hours Worked classified by Economic Activities" in the *Annual Report on National Accounts for 2021* and *2009*. We calculated wages and salaries (current) in the U.S. using "Wages and Salaries by Industry" and "Persons Engaged in Production by Industry" in the U.S. Bureau of Economic Analysis (accessed August 17, 2023).

Note: We will provide data upon request.

References

Abbing, H. (2002). The cost disease: Do rising costs in the arts make subsidization necessary? In H. Abbing, *Why are artists poor?: The exceptional economy of the arts* (pp. 152–180). Amsterdam University Press.

Akdede, S. H., Ginsburgh, V., & Uçkaç, A. (2021). Internalizing production costs and changes of tastes: More recent theatre plays feature fewer roles. *The Social Science Journal, 58*(1), 119–125. https://doi.org/10.1016/j.soscij.2019.04.009

Baumol, W. J. (1967). Macroeconomics of unbalanced growth: The anatomy of urban crisis. *The American Economic Review, 57*(3), 415–426.

Baumol, W. J. (1968). Macroeconomics of unbalanced growth: Comment. *The American Economic Review, 58*(4), 896–897.

Baumol, W. J. (1991). Performing arts. In J. Eatwell, M. Milgate, & P. Newman (Eds.), *The world of economics* (pp. 544–548). Palgrave Macmillan.

Baumol, W. J., Blackman, S. A. B., & Wolff, E. (1985). Unbalanced growth revisited: Asymptotic stagnancy and new evidence. *American Economic Review, 75*(4), 806–817.

Baumol, W. J., & De Ferranti, D. (2012). *The cost disease: Why computers get cheaper and health care doesn't*. Yale University Press.

Baumol, W. J., & Bowen, W. G. (1965). On the performing arts: The anatomy of their economic problems. *The American Economic Review, 55*, 495–502.

Baumol, W. J., & Bowen, W. G. (1966). *Performing arts: The economic dilemma*. The Twentieth Century Fund Study.

Brewer, A. (1987). Turgot: Founder of classical economics. *Economica, 54*, 417–428. https://doi.org/10.2307/2554177

Chang, W. W. (1970). A two-sector model of economic growth with induced technical progress. *The Canadian Journal of Economics/Revue canadienne d'economique, 3*(2), 199–212. https://doi.org/10.2307/133672
Eltis, W.A. (1975). François Quesnay: A reinterpretation 1. the tableau economique. *Oxford Economic Papers, 27*(2), 167–200. https://doi.org/10.1093/oxfordjournals.oep.a041311
Fukao, K., Makino, T., & Settsu, T. (2020). Structural change, capital deepening, and TFP growth in Japan: 1885–1970. *Social Science Japan Journal, 23*(2), 185–204. https://doi.org/10.1093/ssjj/jyaa014
Hartwig, J. (2011). Testing the Baumol–Nordhaus model with eu klems data. *Review of Income and Wealth, 57*(3), 471–489. https://doi.org/10.1111/j.1475-4991.2010.00409.x
Hartwig, J. (2019). Further insights into 'Baumol's disease' in Japan. *Economics Bulletin, 39*(4), 2308–2316.
Inada, K., Sekiguchi, S., & Shōda, Y. (1992). *The mechanism of economic development: Growth in the Japanese and East Asian economies.* Oxford University Press.
Irizawa, T. (1936). François Quesnay as a medical doctor. In *Futekishu* (In Japanese) (pp. 279–328). Iwanami Shoten Publishers.
Lasdon, L. S., Fox, R. L., & Ratner, M. W. (1974). Nonlinear optimization using the generalized reduced gradient method. *Revue Française D'automatique, Informatique, Recherche Opérationnelle, 8*(V3), 73–103. https://doi.org/10.1051/ro/197408V300731
Nagatani, K. (1970). A note on professor Tobin's "money and economic growth". *Econometrica: Journal of the Econometric Society, 38*, 171–175. https://doi.org/10.2307/1909249
Nishi, H. (2019). Sources of productivity growth dynamics: Is Japan suffering from Baumol's growth disease? *Review of Income and Wealth, 65*(3), 592–616. https://doi.org/10.1111/roiw.12363
Nordhaus, W. D. (2002). Productivity growth and the New Economy. *Brookings Papers on Economic Activity, Economic Studies Program, the Brookings Institution, 33*(2), 211–265.
Nordhaus, W. D. (2008). Baumol's diseases: A macroeconomic perspective. *The BE Journal of Macroeconomics, 8*(1). https://doi.org/10.2202/1935-1690.1382
Quesnay, F. (1758). *The oeconomical table, an attempt towards ascertaining and exhibiting the source, progress, and employment of riches, with explanations, by the friend of mankind, the celebrated Marquis de Mirabeau.* W. Owen.
Sato, R. (1969). Stability conditions in two-sector models of economic growth. *Journal of Economic Theory, 1*(1), 107–117. https://doi.org/10.1016/0022-0531(69)90017-9
Sato, R., Grivoyannis, E., Byrne, B., & Lian, C. (1997). *Health care systems in Japan and the United States: A simulation study and policy analysis.* Kluwer Academic Publishers.
Schachter, G. (1991). Francois quesnay: Interpreters and critics revisited. *The American Journal of Economics and Sociology, 50*(3), 313–322. https://doi.org/10.1111/j.1536-7150.1991.tb02298.x
Smith, A. (1776). *An inquiry into the nature and causes of the wealth of nations.* W. Strahan and T. Cadell.
Takayama, A. (1965). On a two-sector model of economic growth with technological progress—A comparative statics analysis. *The Review of Economic Studies, 32*(3), 251–259. https://doi.org/10.2307/2295830
Thompson, D. (2021). Stagnant services and the gradual disinflation of advanced economies. *Structural Change and Economic Dynamics, 59*, 128–148. https://doi.org/10.1016/j.strueco.2021.06.013
Tobin, J. (1965). Money and economic growth. *Econometrica: Journal of the Econometric Society, 33*(4), 671–684. https://doi.org/10.2307/1910352
Uzawa, H. (1961). On a two-sector model of economic growth. *The Review of Economic Studies, 29*(1), 40–47. https://doi.org/10.2307/2296180
Vaggi, G. (1985). A physiocratic model of relative prices and income distribution. *The Economic Journal, 95*(380), 928–947. https://doi.org/10.2307/2233257
Vandermeulen, A. (1968). A remission from Baumol's disease: Ways to publish more articles. *Southern Economic Journal, 35*(2), 189–191. https://doi.org/10.2307/1056330

Chapter 8
Long-Run Equilibrium, Adjustment Time, and Economic Conservation Laws

Ryuzo Sato, Takayuki Yamashita, and Tamaki Morita

Abstract This chapter deals with the log-run macroeconomic equilibrium, adjustment time, and economic conservation laws. The original version of this chapter was a lecture (in Japanese) entitled "Dynamic analysis and the role of subjective time" by Sato on June 28, 2014. It was presented at the Sato Workshop, held at the Komaba Campus of the University of Tokyo. The current version is based on the works expanded by Sato, Yamashita, and Morita. The primary purpose is to provide a reasonable justification for the analysis of the trend of the Japanese bubble economy. The concept of "subjective time and subjective discount rate" is a useful device for explaining the time horizon during the period. The concept of the subjective time may be defined as a Lie Group transformation from the objective time. The model starts from the long-run trends of the U.S. and Japanese economies. For the U.S. economy, the usual and traditional "conservation laws" are valuable tools for confirming balanced growth trends. However, for the Japanese economy, subjective time preference is more useful for justifying the long-run trend of the economy.

Keywords Adjustment time · Discount rates · Economic conservation laws · Income-wealth ratio · Optimal growth · Subjective time

R. Sato
C.V. Starr Professor Emeritus of Economics, New York University, New York, USA

T. Yamashita (✉)
School of Global Studies and Collaboration, Aoyama Gakuin University, Sagamihara, Kanagawa, Japan
e-mail: yamashita.takayuki@gsc.aoyama.ac.jp

T. Morita
Faculty of Aviation Management, J. F. Oberlin University, Tama City, Tokyo, Japan
e-mail: morita_t01@obirin.ac.jp

T. Yamashita and T. Morita (eds.), *On the Structural Transformation of the Japanese Economy 1985-2023*, Advances in Japanese Business and Economics 38,
https://doi.org/10.1007/978-981-95-7230-4_8

8.1 From Behavioral Models to Optimal Models

8.1.1 The Long- and Short-Run in Economics

The long-run and short-run issues in modern economics follow the Marshallian equilibrium concept. In Marshallian terms, the short-run equilibrium is the equilibrium obtained by adjusting supply and demand under the condition that production can be increased if prices rise. On the other hand, the long-run equilibrium is the equilibrium obtained by adjusting all input factors. In other words, the short run is the period when fixed factors of production cannot be changed, while the long run is the period when all factors of production can be changed.

John Maynard Keynes wrote, not in his famous book, *The General Theory of Employment, Interest, and Money* (Keynes, 1936), but in his *A Tract on Monetary Reform* (Keynes, 1923) that "The long run is a misleading guide to current affairs. In the long run, we are all dead." This statement was an advocacy of Keynes' awareness of the problems of an adjustment period. For example, the quantity theory of money assumes that doubling the quantity of money would double the price level in the long run. But such an adjustment would take too long. He made his assertion because the basic proposition in his General Theory was based on a short-term problem.[1]

Herman Kahn, a futurist, used to say that "he never makes medium-term predictions because they never come true." He would be right in the short term, and the very long term (say, 100 years) was irrelevant because everyone would die.

There are many economists whose theory is based on long-run adjustments. For example, Wilhelm Georg Friedrich Roscher proposed the roundabout methods of production. His example states that more fish can be caught by investing than by catching fish with bare hands. By investing in production goods, such as boats and nets, he can catch fish. This is a method of "round-about production theory" which is based on long-run assumptions.

As another example, Bohm Bawerk and Wicksell proposed the optimal production period. Since technological progress cannot be achieved soon after investing money, they considered the profile needed to achieve the optimal and best outcome.

8.1.2 Growth Theory in Short-Run and Long-Run

The Harrod-Domar model emphasized unstable growth, characterized by a knife-edge equilibrium. Using Harrod's notations, there are three kinds of growth rates: (1) Actual growth of GDP, G; (2) Natural growth that depends on population growth

[1] Joseph Schumpeter and Niall Ferguson countered Keynes. Schumpeter stated that because Keynes had no children, his philosophy of life was essentially a short-term philosophy; Ferguson professed that because Keynes was gay, he had no children and was only interested in the short term (on May 7, 2013, the grandson of Keynes' aunt defended Keynes in the Telegram: "In the long run, we'll still care about Kaynes," Chivers, 2013).

and technical progress, G_n; (3) Warranted growth rate at which all saving is absorbed into investment, G_w. Warranty is for capitalists' satisfaction, meaning the investment is fully utilized. Then we have,

$$G = \frac{s}{C}, \text{ where } s = \text{savings rate, } C = \text{capital coefficient} = \text{capital income ratios} = K/Y,$$

$$G_n = \text{population growth} + \text{technical progress} = n + \rho, \text{ and,}$$

$$G_w = \frac{s}{C_r}, \text{ where } G_w = \text{warranted rate of growth, } C_r = \text{required capital coefficient.}$$

When $G > G_w$, since $GC = s = G_w C_r$, $C < C_r$, and C rises due to insufficient investment. When $G < G_w$, C decreases. Once they diverge, there is no way to return to a stable equilibrium. Stable growth is possible only when $G = G_w = G_n$.

The Solow-Swan model showed that in the long-run the system can achieve a stable equilibrium. They introduced a neo-classical production function. Assuming capital, K, and labor, L, we consider a simple case of the Cobb-Douglas Production function, i.e., $Y = A \cdot K^{\alpha} L^{1-\alpha} \beta$, $A = A_0 e^{\rho t}$. Then we have,

$$G = \alpha G_w + (1 - \alpha) G_n,$$

where $G_w = \frac{s}{C_r} = s\frac{Y}{K} = s \cdot r$, $\frac{Y}{K} = r = \frac{1}{C}$. In Fig. 8.1, on the intersection, nothing happens because $G = G_w = G_n$ holds. When $G < G_n$ (e.g., point P_A), Y/K increases and moves toward the intersection. When $G > G_n$ (e.g., point P_B), Y/K decreases and moves also toward the intersection. Swan said the Harrod-Domar-type of unstable growth would not be realized in the long run.

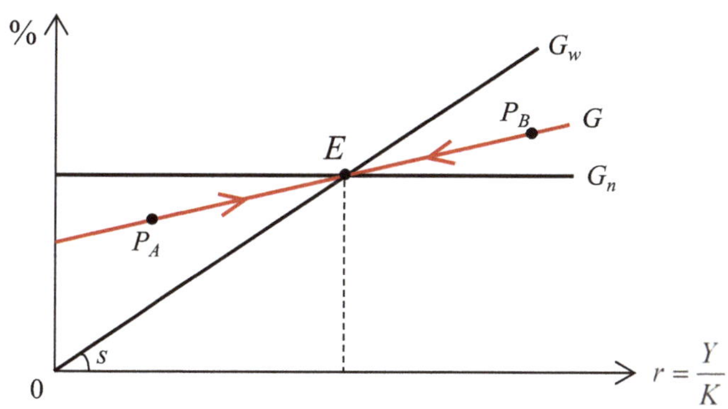

Fig. 8.1 Stable growth model of the Solow-Swan type

8.1.3 Adjustment Time and Long-Run

In Fig. 8.1, suppose the economy is at P_A, then the growth rate of Y is larger than that of K. So $Y/K = r$ must increase, approaching the equilibrium point E. In the same way, when the economy is at P_B, then the system will move toward E. Then the question is "how long does it take to move to the equilibrium?" This question was first answered by Sato (1963, 1964) using the differential equation $\frac{dr}{dt}$, $r = Y/K$. We then have the following differential equation (Sato, 1963, eq. 8).

$$\frac{dr}{dt} = \beta r\left[\left(\frac{\rho}{\beta} + n\right) - \alpha r\right], \; \beta = 1 - \alpha.$$

Since this is a Bernoulli equation by letting $1/r = v = C$, we can obtain the following linear differential equation,

$$\frac{dv}{dt} + (\rho + \beta n)v = \beta s,$$

$$\frac{dv}{dt} + Av = B.$$

The solution is obtained as

$$v = \frac{B}{A} + C_0 e^{-At}$$

as t increases v = approaching to B/A, the equilibrium value at E. Output = equilibrium value + adjustment term (see Fig. 8.2).

We can estimate t by substituting plausible values in A and B. We found that t moves slowly, and it takes more than 90 years to reach equilibrium (30 years to reach 50% and 60 years to reach 75% of the equilibrium). Therefore, we can say the long-term may be defined as 50 to 100 years (see Sato, 1964).

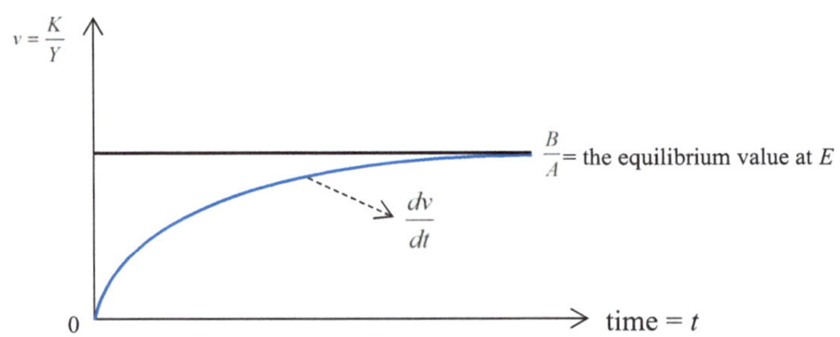

Fig. 8.2 Adjustment time of the dynamics

8.1.4 Economic Conservation Laws

Departing from the short-run and long-run economic issues, we now work on "economic conservation laws." The nomenclature of the "conservation law" comes from the "law of conservation of energy" in Newtonian mechanics. It states that natural forces work to minimize the difference between kinetic energy and potential (gravitational) energy, and the total energy remains constant.

Also in economics, there must be some quantity that remains constant, regardless of whether the periods are in the short run or the long run.

We utilize the concept of transformation groups in group theory, a branch of mathematics. Noether's theorem is most convenient for discussing the economic conservation laws. An example of a transformation group is a rotation group, which is like a clock that moves along time but always remains contained within the dial. Conversion groups are either additive or multiplicative, and have units such as 0, 1, …, etc., and have inverses, all of which are contained within the same system.

Consider a transformation group called the Lie group. Sophus Lie was a Norwegian mathematician at the beginning of the twentieth century, who discovered that differential equation systems consist of the group properties. Emmy Noether was a German mathematician[2] who discovered the methodology to derive conservation laws in Hamiltonian dynamics.

The infinitesimal transformation is written as

$$\begin{cases} \overline{x} = x + \varepsilon\xi(t, x) \\ \overline{t} = t + \varepsilon\tau(t, x) \end{cases}, \tag{8.1}$$

where ε is a parameter. Consider the problem, $\min\int_{t_0}^{t_1}(T(\dot{x}) - U(x))dt$. In Lagrangian mechanics, $T(\dot{x}) = \frac{1}{2}\cdot m\dot{x}^2$ (where m is mass, x is position, and $\dot{x}$ is velocity) is the kinetic energy, and potential energy is a function of position x, $U(x)$.

Let L is equal to $L = T(\dot{x}) - U(x)$

$$\min\int_{t_0}^{t_1} L(\dot{x}, x)dt.$$

Consider the infinitesimal transformation shown above. If $\overline{t} = t + \varepsilon$ then $\tau = 1$. Also, x does not change over time, $\bar{x} = x$ and $\xi = 0$. Then, we can write the energy conservation law using a Hamiltonian function:

$$\begin{aligned} \mathcal{H} &= \dot{x}\frac{\partial L}{\partial \dot{x}} - L = \text{constant} \\ &= \dot{x}\cdot m\dot{x} - \left(1/2\cdot m\dot{x}^2 - U(x)\right) \end{aligned}$$

[2] Hanc et al. (2004, n.p.) summarize that Noether's Theorem states "for each symmetry operation there is a corresponding conservation law. The conservation of momentum is related to the homogeneity of space. Invariance under translation in time means that law of conservation of energy is valid".

$$= 1/2 \cdot m\dot{x}^2 - U(x) = \text{constant}.$$

Dynamic invariance (symmetry) is,

$$\int_{\bar{t}_1}^{\bar{t}_2} L\left(\bar{t}, \bar{x}(\bar{t}), \frac{d\bar{x}(\bar{t})}{d\bar{t}}\right) d\bar{t} - \int_{t_1}^{t_2} L\left(t, x(t), \frac{dx(t)}{dt}\right) dt = O(\varepsilon) + \chi.$$

Noether's theorem then becomes

$$\Omega = -\mathcal{H} \cdot \tau + \frac{\partial L}{\partial \dot{x}} \xi - \Phi = \text{constant}. \tag{8.2}$$

We can show that Ramsey had already discovered economic conservation law without using Noether's theorem. In Ramsey's model, the bliss point is the invariant point—the conservation law.

Set the problem as

$$\max \int_{t_0}^{t_1} (U(C) - V(L)) dt$$

$$\text{s.t.} \dot{K} = f(K, L) - C,$$

where U = utility, V = disutility of labor, K = capital, L = labor, and C = consumption. Obviously $\tau = 1$ and $\xi = 0$. Since time t is not in the Lagrangian, Hamiltonian $\mathcal{H}$ is constant. Then,

$$\mathcal{H} = Bliss = U(C) \cdot \dot{K} + (U(C) - V(L)) = U(C) \cdot \dot{K} - \mathcal{L},$$

where Lagrangian $\mathcal{L} = -(U(C) - V(L))$.

$$\therefore \dot{K} = f(K, L) - C = \frac{B - (U(C) - V(L))}{\frac{dU}{dC}}.$$

This equation is the Ramsey rule, derived from the Ramsey conservation law.

Samuelson found the same conservation law in the von-Neumann dynamic model.

$$\max \int_0^T \dot{K}^1(t) dt$$

$$\text{s.t. } F\left(K^1, K^2, \ldots, K^n\right) = 0.$$

It is the maximization problem $\dot{K}^1$ from time zero to time T. This leads to the conclusion that the ratio of total output to total capital is constant.

Sato (1985) utilized Noether's theorem to derive this relationship, in addition to new conservation laws in Sato and Maeda (1990).

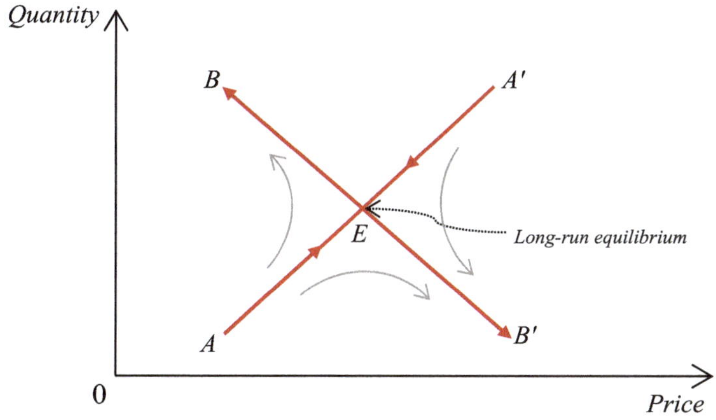

Fig. 8.3 Phase diagram

Consider the standard optimal growth model of Cass (1965)–Koopmans (1965) type.

$$\max \int_0^\infty e^{-\rho t} U(C)dt$$

$$\text{s.t. } \dot{K} = f(K, L) - C$$

$$\dot{L} = nL$$

Sato's (1985) dynamic equations trace the movement online *AA'* in Fig. 8.3. In the equations, quantity and price change with time, but there is also a quantity that does not change (conservation law).

Weitzman (1976) and Sato (1980) found a conservation law of GDP/National Wealth ratio. Using Noether's theorem, by calculating $\tau = 1/\rho$ (inverse of discount rates ρ), $\xi = 0$, Φ, with Eq. (8.1),

$$U(t) - \dot{k}(t)\frac{\partial U(t)}{\partial \dot{k}(t)} = \rho \int_0^\infty e^{-\rho(s-t)} U(s)ds$$

$$\text{Income} = \rho \times \text{Wealth}$$

$$\therefore \text{Income/Wealth} = \rho = \text{discount rates.}$$

8.1.5 Test of the Income/Wealth Conservation Law in Previous Studies

Sato (2006) empirically tested the above relationships among 14 OECD countries prior to 1990 by using GNP data from the national income account and net national wealth data or value of capital goods from the system of national accounts in each country; that is,

$$Y = \rho \times W$$

or

$$\rho = \frac{Y}{W}$$

where $Y =$ national income and $W =$ net national wealth, and ρ is the discount rate.

Sato (2006) verified that the ratio of income to wealth (ρ) in the U.S. has been historically stable from 1896 to 1940 (Fig. 8.3a) and 1947 to 1992 (Fig. 8.4b). World War II may have caused structural changes to the economy, and the postwar period showed business-cyclical tendencies.

Japan's case (Sato, 2006) shows a different pattern. As shown in Fig. 8.5, the discount rate until 1970 has a stable pattern, but after 1970, $\frac{Y}{W}$ ratio declines to 0.12. This pattern shows that the standard conservation law does not hold for Japan's case. It may be due to the bubble phenomeno8.2.3n, which has led Japan's business community to alter its perspectives on the future discount rate. It requires us to develop a new theory of conservation law under a variable discount rate. We will take up this issue later in Subsection.

Among other OECD countries tested by Sato (2006), Australia, Canada, Norway, and Sweden had a constant ratio and satisfied the income/wealth conservation law during the period from 1965 to 1990. Finland, Germany, Greece, and the U.K. had declining ratios during the period.

By using microdata, Sato and Fujii (2006) measured the income-wealth ratio at the industry level and found the same declining trend as shown in Fig. 8.6.

We will analyze how the $\frac{Y}{W}$ ratio remained unchanged or changed in Subsection 8.2.3 and connect Japan's changes to the people's time consciousness and discount rates.

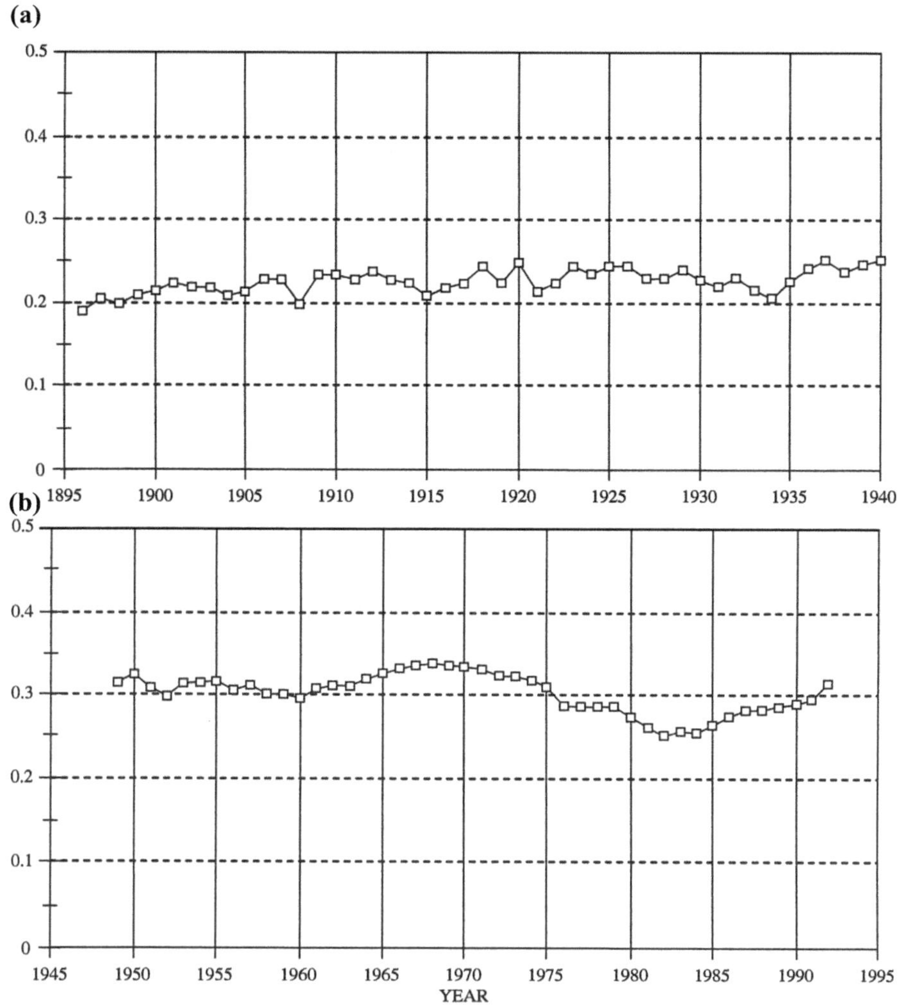

Fig. 8.4 U.S. Income/wealth ratio (a) Prewar, (b) Postwar. *Note* In the original figure, the *X*-axis was displayed up to 0.7. Since it does not affect the depiction of the data, however, the *X*-axis here is set up to 0.5. *Source* Sato (2006, pp. 132–133), (a) Fig. 1, (b) Fig. 2

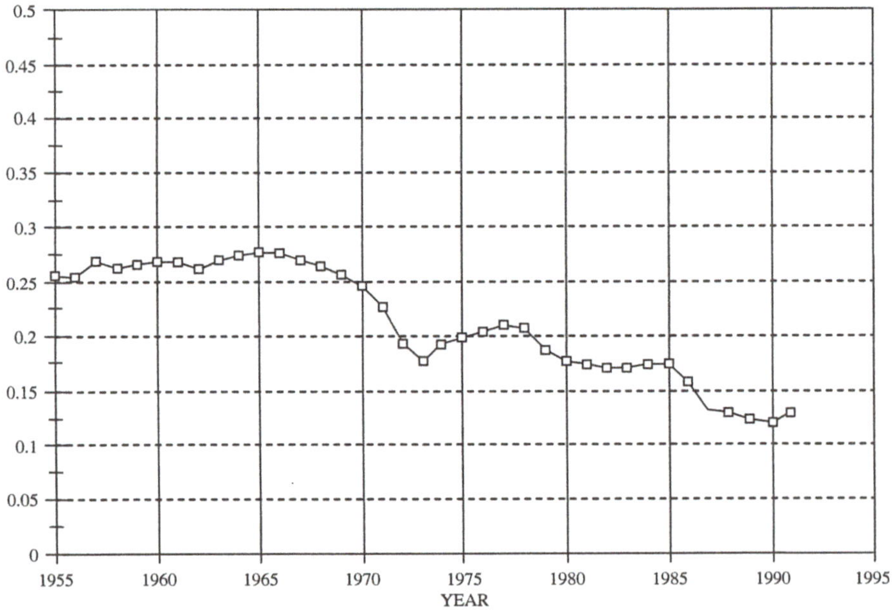

Fig. 8.5 Ratio of GDP/Net wealth in Japan. *Source* Sato (2006, p. 136), Figure 4

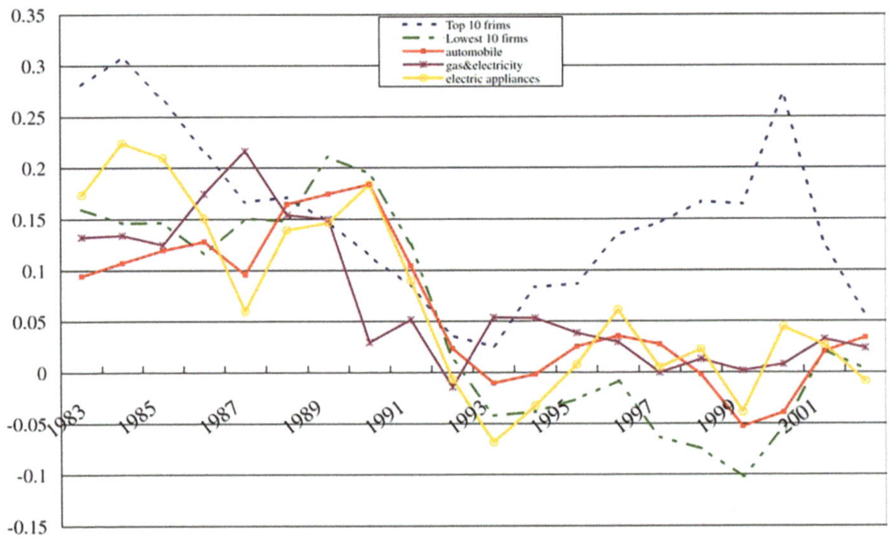

Fig. 8.6 Change of the ratio: Top and lower classes of firms and industrial averages. *Note* (1) The top-10 and lowest-10 firms are selected from the data set that has both 2003 Nikkei performance index and history of financial data. Two dashed lines correspond to these groups: the higher one shows the top-10 average and the lower one shows the lowest-10 average. (2) The bold lines correspond to the average values of the ratio for three industries: automobile, gas and electricity and electric appliances respectively. *Source* Sato and Fujii (2006, p. 165), Fig. 1

8.2 Objective Time Vs. Subjective Time

8.2.1 Concepts

When Japan was in the middle of a bubble period, many people used to say that the time they felt and the actual time were out of sync and different.

This is reflected by an episode in the Japanese movie *Tokyo Monogatari* (A Story of Tokyo), directed by Yasujiro Ozu, introduced in a newspaper (The Asahi Shimbun, 2013). When an old man loses his wife, he murmurs to his neighbor as he walks by, "As I am alone now, my days suddenly get longer." This is a good example of the discrepancy between the objective time and the subjective time.

Many people say that subjective time goes by faster as we grow older. A gorgeous summer day passes in an instant when you get older. This seems to be true in Western culture. In the Opinion section of *The New York Times*, R. A. Friedman wrote, "Ah, the languorous days of endless summer! Who among us doesn't remember those days and wonder wistfully where they've gone? Why does time seem to speed up as we age? Even the summer solstice – the longest, sunniest day of the year – seems to have passed in a flash" (Friedman, 2013, n.p.).

Goethe said man lives perhaps in two kinds of times. One is time that flows on and on and moves onward, or objective time, and another is time that halts, like an old photograph. As Faust told the Moment, "Ah, stay a while! You are so lovely!" (Goethe, 2003, n.p.). So live each day as you did when your whole life began.

There is a psychological phenomenon discovered by Paul Alexandre René Janet and his nephew Pierre Marie Félix Janet that the length of years subjectively recorded is perceived as longer by younger people and shorter by older people. Paul Janet said, "The rate of passage of subjective time is proportional to the age of the person making the judgment" (Wearden, 2021, n.p.).

Alternatively, the French mathematician Évariste Galois, famous for the Galois theory, demonstrated the psychological feelings of human beings. On the night before his fatal duel for a lady in 1832, he wrote to his friends, "I have not time because I have to complete my theory." He felt his time was short because his last day was coming.

In Salvador Dalí's famous drawing "Persistence of Memory" in 1931, a watch is melting. Dalí was focused on the theory of "softness" and "hardness" in time analysis, and the so-called soft watch represents how time bends in the human mind and memory. If objective time is a hard time, then subjective time is a soft time. Next, we formalize the relationship between objective and subjective time by,

$$\bar{t} = f(t), \text{ where } \bar{t} = \text{subjective time and } t = \text{objective time.}$$

Here, $f'(t) > 0$ and $f''(t) > 0$ means "Time Expansion," and $f'(t) > 0$ and $f''(t) < 0$ means "Time Compression." The subjective time may be called psychological time contrasted with the objective or clock time.

In contrast to the objective time, for those who perceive time as longer, time is expanding (Time Expansion), and for those who perceive time as shorter, time is compressing (Time Compression).

In Fig. 8.7, taking the subjective time $\bar{t}$ on the y-axis and objective time t on the x-axis, equality of subjective and objective time ($\bar{t} = t$) can be drawn as a 45-degree line. The line in the upper-left area denotes time expansion, and the line in the lower-right area denotes time compression.

The arrow in Fig. 8.8a shows the time perceptions for those who perceive time as longer when younger and shorter when older. Figure 8.8b shows vice versa.

As people reach their 70 s, many begin to feel pressured to do many things before they die, and they perceive their time to pass quickly.

Fig. 8.7 Objective time and subjective time in $\bar{t}$-t dimension

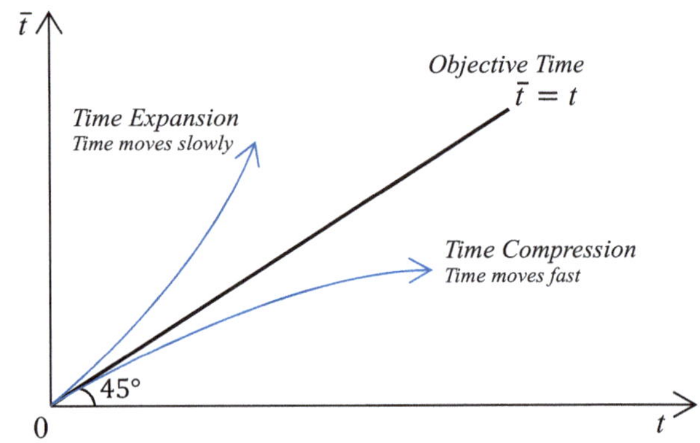

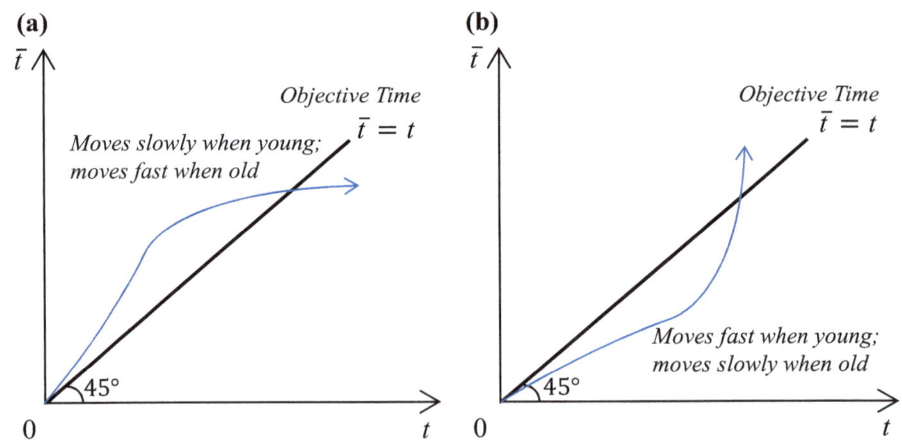

Fig. 8.8 Objective time and subjective time in $\bar{t}$-t dimension (examples): (a) Slow in youth, fast in age, (b) Fast in youth, slow in age.

Consider subjective time $\bar{t}$ as a Lie group function of objective time, t, where there may be various relationships between $\bar{t}$ and t such as:

$$\bar{t} = c \log t,$$

$$\bar{t} = \frac{1}{\alpha} t^{\alpha}$$

where $0 < \alpha < 1$: Time Compression (faster) and $\alpha > 1$: Time Expansion (slower),

$$\bar{t} = b\left(70t - \frac{1}{2}t^2\right)$$

which represents the case of fearing sudden death around the age of 69, like Galois, and

$$\bar{t} = 1 - e^{-t}.$$

In general, the subjective time function ($\bar{t} = f(t)$) depends not only on objective time t but also other variables (income, wealth, and experience, to name a few) as

$$\bar{t} = f(t, x_1, \cdots, x_n).$$

8.2.2 *Application to Macro Dynamics*

We can apply the concept of subjective time as a rational trait in business practices. For example, true or false, there is a common belief that the Japanese are long-sighted while Americans are short-sighted. If this is true, the discount rate may be different for different countries. It may also be true that the discount rate may not be constant for the entire period.

Let $\bar{t}$ be a Lie group transformation group (see Sato, 2004),

$$\bar{t} = f(t, c(t), \cdots),$$

and, more specifically, $\bar{t}$ is a function of discount rates $\rho(t)$:

$$\bar{t} = f(\rho(t)). \tag{8.3}$$

We must note how the income-wealth conservation law should be rewritten when we introduce the subjective time $\bar{t}$.

First, consider the case $\bar{t} = t$, i.e., no time illusion with a constant discount rate[3]:

$$U(t) - \dot{k}\frac{\partial U(t)}{\partial \dot{k}(t)} = \rho \int_t^\infty e^{-\rho(s-t)} U(s)ds. \tag{8.4}$$

Here, $U(t) - \dot{k}\frac{\partial U(t)}{\partial \dot{k}(t)}$ represents national income, Y, and $\int_t^\infty e^{-\rho(s-t)} U(s)ds$ represents national wealth, W. Therefore, $Y = \rho \times W$ holds.

Equation (8.4) is the conservation law under $\bar{t} = f(t) = t + g(\rho = const.) = t + const$. Marginal rate of transformation of $\bar{t} = f(t)$ is same as $\bar{t} = t$. In Eq. (8.4), $\bar{t} = t$ and $\bar{t} = t + const$ are equivalent.

Since $\bar{t} = f(\rho(t))$, we set ρ in Eq. (8.4) as $\rho(t)$. Then Lagrangean becomes

$$\mathcal{L} = e^{-\int_0^t \rho(s)ds} U\big(k(t), \dot{k}(t)\big).$$

If we consider Eq. (8.3) as in the Lie group, and let $\frac{\partial \tau}{\partial k} = 0$,

$$\bar{t} = t + \varepsilon\tau(t, k)$$

$$\bar{k} = k.$$

In a special case that assumes $\tau(t) = 1/\rho'(t)$, where $\rho'(t) = \frac{d\rho(t)}{dt}$ = the rate of the change of discounting function with respect to time, we have the following generalized conservation law:

$$U(t) - \dot{k}\frac{\partial U(t)}{\partial \dot{k}(t)} = \frac{d\rho(t)}{dt} \int_t^\infty \left\{ \exp\left(-\int_t^s \rho(p)dp\right)\left[U - \dot{k}\frac{\partial U}{\partial \dot{k}}\frac{d}{ds}\left(\frac{1}{\rho(s)}\right)\right]\right\} ds \tag{8.5}$$

(see Sato, 1985, p. 381, eq. (7.9) and Appendix 8.2).

The generalized wealth conservation laws now include capital gains and losses depending on if the adjustment term $\dot{k}\frac{\partial U}{\partial \dot{k}}\frac{d}{ds}\left(\frac{1}{\rho(s)}\right)$ is positive or negative.

As an example, assume $\rho(t) = \overline{\rho}t + at^2$, where $\overline{\rho}$ and a are constants. Since $\tau(t) = 1/\rho'(t) = \frac{1}{\overline{\rho}+2at}$, subjective time $\bar{t}$ becomes

$$\bar{t} = t + \varepsilon\tau = t + \varepsilon\frac{1}{\overline{\rho} + 2at},$$

and

$$\frac{d\bar{t}}{dt} = 1 - \varepsilon\frac{2a}{(\overline{\rho} + 2at)^2}.$$

[3] The derivation process is shown in Sato (2006, p. 145), equation (A.11).

Then, we can see the relationship between $\bar{t}$ and t, depending on each setting of a as (assuming $\varepsilon > 0$):

- $a = 0 : \rho(t) = \overline{\rho}t,\ \rho'(t) = \overline{\rho}, \tau(t) = 1/\overline{\rho}, \bar{t} = t + \varepsilon\overline{\rho}^{-1}$ and $d\bar{t}/dt = 1$. Subjective time moves proportionally to objective time.
- $a > 0 : \rho'(t) = \overline{\rho} + 2at$ is increasing in t, $\tau(t)$ is decreasing in t, and $d\bar{t}/dt < 1$. Subjective time moves more slowly than objective time, so people feel like "time moves fast." This is time compression.
- $a < 0$, $\rho'(t)$ is decreasing in t, $\tau(t)$ is increasing in t, and $d\bar{t}/dt > 1$. Subjective time moves faster than objective time, so people feel like "time moves slowly." This is time expansion.

By our assumption $\rho(t) = \overline{\rho}t + at^2$, when $a < 0$, $\rho(t)$ declines.

Figure 8.9 shows how the discount rate $\rho(t)$ varies when the model is extended to include the variable discount rate.

In the next section, we will explore factual cases that involve variable discount rates that decline over time. If we apply the concepts of subjective and objective time, we can explain the following: Under the time expansion, subjective time is perceived as moving slowly, and impatience falls. Time expansion reduces the discounting by subjective time, leads to higher present values, and makes earlier investment optimal. Therefore, when investors perceive time as moving slowly, they may "rationally" choose to invest early, which could collectively lead to a bubble economy.

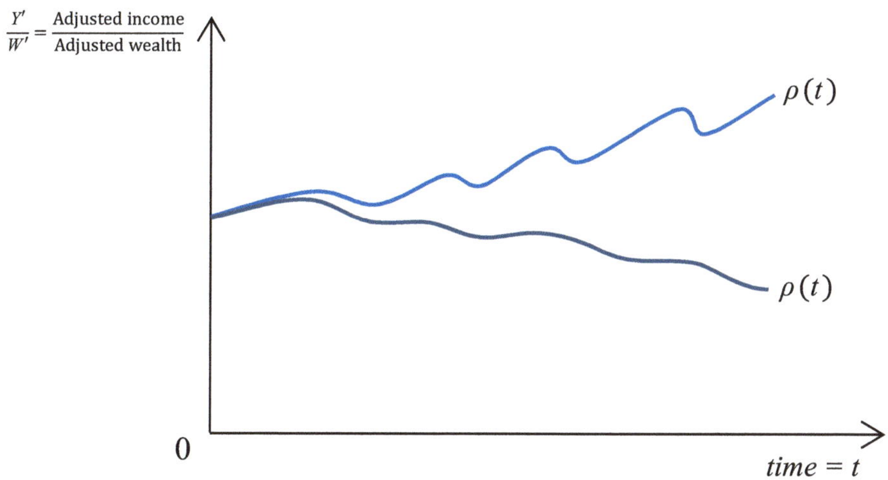

Fig. 8.9 Time and "income-adjusted wealth ratio" when discount rates are functions of time

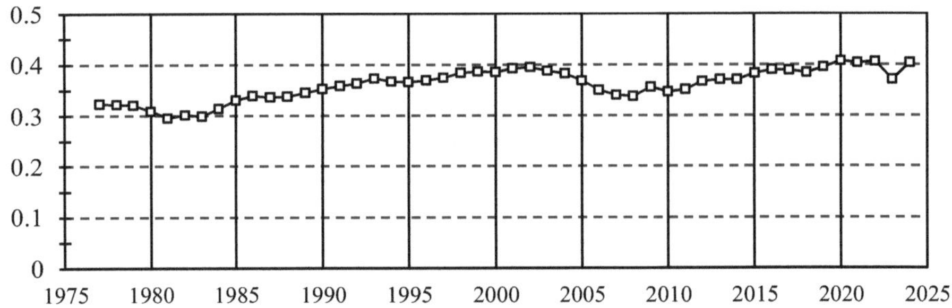

Fig. 8.10 Ratio of GNP/net wealth in the U.S. *Source* Compiled by the author with data from the U.S. Bureau of Economic Analysis

8.2.3 Empirical Applications: Extension to Year 2023 and Cases of Variable Discount Rates

In line with Sato (2006), as introduced in subsection 8.1.5, we use GNP for Y and net national wealth for W. Net national wealth is measured by summing up inventories, tangible fixed assets (reproducible production assets), intangible fixed assets, and then adding net foreign assets.

Figure 8.10 shows the Y/W ratio of the U.S. since 1975. The Y/W ratio looks very high as a discount rate, ρ, (around annual 30% to 40%), but it is due to the limitation of data availability. Because net national wealth is published only for the private sector, each economy has hidden or uncountable national wealth. If we could sum them up in W, the value of Y/W (= estimated discount rates) would be closer to market interest rates, such that they do not surpass 10%. Therefore, we will focus on the trends, rather than the levels of discount rates.

The ratio has been rising since the 1980s. On the one hand, it can be explained by the U.S. net foreign assets turning negative. Against the backdrop of the Federal Reserve Board's low-interest-rate policy and the increase in the use of subprime loans—mortgages for low-income borrowers—housing prices in the United States skyrocketed, causing a housing bubble between 2000 and 2006. This bubble raised national wealth and lowered the GNP/wealth ratio from 2002 to 2007. On the other hand, by adopting variable discount rates in our theory, these bubbles can be explained by the change in people's subjective time. As we discuss later, when the discount rate declines, future cash flows are discounted less.

To see the average value during the period, we conduct the following regression of GNP on net wealth to see the mean discount rate:

$$Y = b \times W + \varepsilon$$

To ensure valid inference in the presence of autocorrelation and heteroskedasticity, we use heteroskedasticity-and autocorrelation-consistent (HAC) standard errors as proposed by the Newey-West method. The result is b= 0.3867 (95%CI [.3694.4040],

SE.0088).[4] In the U.S., business-cyclical movements are still observed, but the ratio is basically stable around 0.3867.

The U.S. $\frac{Y}{W}$ ratio excluding net foreign assets from net wealth (W) is shown in Appendix 8.4.

Looking into the Japanese economy, Japan's result of the following regression of GNP on net wealth during 1970–2023,

$$Y = b \times W + \varepsilon,$$

was $b = 0.1538$ (95%CI [.1495.1581], SE.0022) for Japan. The level was lower than that of the U.S.

Japan's GNP to net wealth ratio has demonstrated contrasting patterns before and after 1990, the critical year when the asset price bubble peaked[5] (Fig. 8.11). It is analogous to what we observed in Subsection 1.5 that the U.S. economy showed contrasting patterns before and after World War II.

After 1990, Japan's ρ has been relatively stable (Fig. 8.11b) (Japan's $\frac{Y}{W}$ ratio excluding net foreign assets from net wealth is shown in Appendix 8.4)

Now, consider the cases of variable discount rates with subjective time.

Figure 8.11a illustrates Japan's GNP/wealth ratio from 1970 to 1990 and Fig. 8.11b from 1990 to 2023. We can compare Fig. 8.11a with Fig. 8.5 (reproduced here as Fig. 8.12), which is taken from the previous study of Sato (2006), because even though the published data has been revised, the trends within the period in both datasets align closely.

The bubble economy, driven by a surge in land prices and an expansion of the value of non-reproducible tangible assets, leads to a decline in the GNP/wealth ratio. The adjusted wealth $W^{'}(t)$ is not easy to estimate, but we can take the ratio of $Y(t)/W(t)$ as an approximation of the (adjusted) income-wealth ratio, i.e.,

$$\frac{Y(t)}{W(t)} \approx \frac{Y(t)}{W'(t)} = \text{(adjusted) income} - \text{wealth ratio.} \tag{8.6}$$

If we look at Fig. 8.12, this ratio may well represent the variable discount rate for this period. If we use subjective time as a basis for a variable discount rate, then we will be able to justify the variable (declining) discount rate during the bubble period. We illustrated hypothetical $\rho^{'}(t) = Y(t)/W^{'}(t)$ (thick straight trend lines) on Fig. 8.12.

---

4 Specifically, we employ the ivreg2 command in the statistical software Stata ver. 18.0, which supports a general class of kernel-based estimators of the variance-covariance matrix. The maximum lag length of autocorrelation accounted for is 32 for the US (28 for Japan). We applied the kernel weighting scheme to downweight higher-order autocorrelations. The estimator corresponds to the Newey and West (1987) HAC estimator.

5 One of the key indices in the Japanese stock market, the Nikkei 225, reached its peak on December 30, 1989, achieving 38,915.87 Yen—this record remained unbroken until 2024. Similarly, the Tokyo Stock Price Index (TOPIX) attained its highest point on December 18, 1989, at 2884.80, also standing as a historical high until 2024. As for land prices, they peaked in 1990 before entering a prolonged period of decline. Trends on the TOPIX and the Land Price Index are illustrated in Appendix 8.3.

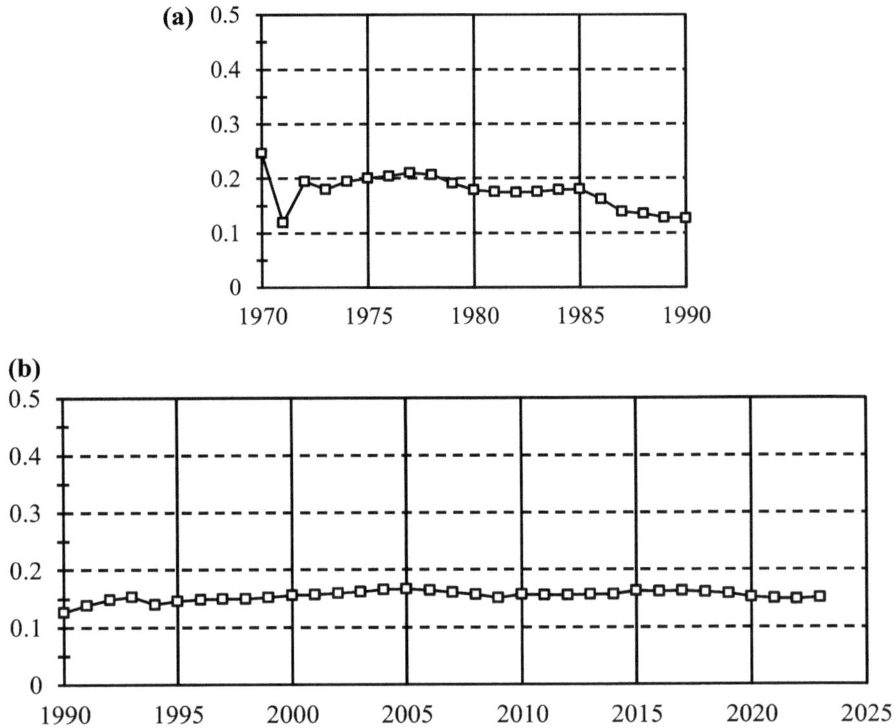

Fig. 8.11 Ratio of GNP/net wealth in Japan: (a) 1970–1990, (b) 1990–2023. *Source* Compiled by the author with data from the Cabinet Office, Annual Report on National Accounts

In both the U.S. and Japan, the asset price bubble is affected by the change in ρ. Koopmans (1960) emphasized that intertemporal preferences depend on how agents perceive the passage of time and insisted on the importance of impatience, noting that people strictly prefer earlier utility to later. Impatience, represented by a higher discount rate and influenced by subjective time, reduces the fundamental value of assets (since future dividends are discounted more heavily) and accelerates the growth of bubble paths. This explosive growth makes bubbles less sustainable. By contrast, greater patience (a lower discount rate) raises fundamental values and slows bubble growth, which makes it easier for bubbles to persist.[6]

It is reasonable to view the bubble era as a time when people feel that "time moves slowly" (Time Expansion). In this period, future payoffs seem closer, diminishing the effect of discounting. Fundamentals appear stronger, which supports the persistence of bubble components, while the optimism fueled by accommodative monetary policies allows bubbles to inflate gradually. At the peak, however, expectations break,

[6] This possibility disappears if the no-bubble transversality condition, $\lim_{t\to\infty} e^{-\rho t}\, U_k(t)\, k(t) = 0$, is imposed.

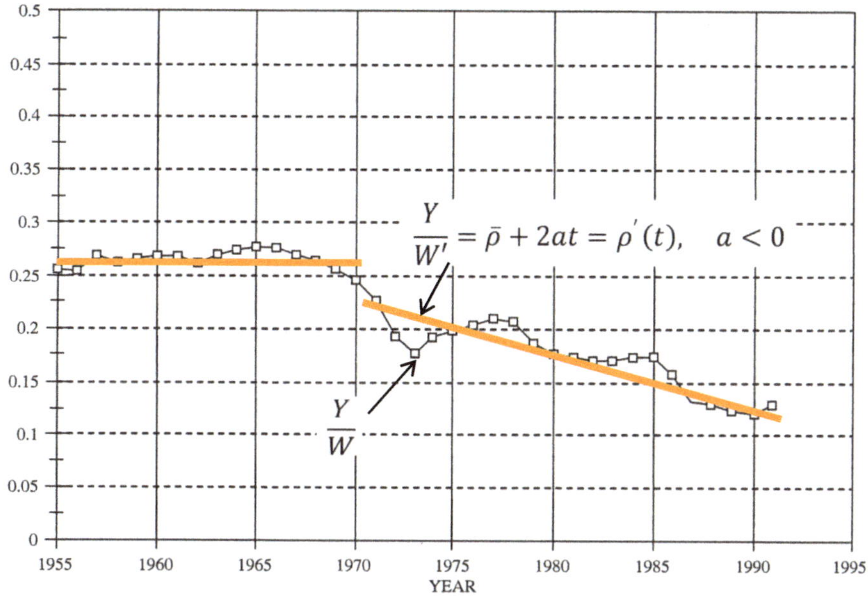

Fig. 8.12 Ratio of GDP/net wealth in Japan: Fig. 8.5 with trend lines. *Note* The trend lines are "adjusted discount rate with subjective time". *Source* Sato (2006, p. 136), Fig. 8.4 and authors

and subjective time perception shifts toward stationarity or even compression. As discounting stabilizes or rises, the bubble collapses back to fundamentals.

The discount rate ρ can differ among countries due to the economic backgrounds and individuals. We have used the concept of subjective time and studied its changes over time. Incidentally, the measurement of the individual's subjective time is conducted through experiments in other fields, for instance, studies by Kim and Zauberman (2009) and Zauberman et al. (2009) may be good examples. We hope our theoretical results will be connected to the psychological foundation of subjective time, thereby informing the reinterpretation of the macroeconomic behavior in countries.

8.3 Concluding Remarks

A Chinese philosopher, Xunzi (Hsün *Tzu*), left us the phrase, "Nature's ways are invariant." Nature's deeds have constants, things that always remain the same. The opposite phrase, "All things are impermanent," is from the Nirvana Sutra, meaning that human deeds continuously change and are not constant. The conservation law actually states that "Nature's ways are invariant." Many laws governing human economic behavior do not change over time like nature's ways, and searching for them is to search for economic laws without considering the long-run and short-run issues in modern economics.

Appendix 1 Conservation Laws when the Objective Function Is the Maximization of the per-Capita Consumption

Conservation laws vary with the type of the objective function depicted. In this Appendix, we present the case when the objective function is the maximization of the per-capita consumption, by summarizing Sato (2006, Section 2, pp. 125−129).

Let consumption of the economy depend on output, which in turn depends on a vector of capital goods, a vector of investment and labor input, so that,

$$C = C\big[Y\big(K; \dot{K}; L; \dot{L}\big)\big], \tag{8.7}$$

where Y = output, which depends on $K = (K_1, \ldots, K_n) = n$ capital goods, $\dot{K} = \big(\dot{K}_1, \ldots, \dot{K}_n\big) = dK/dt$ = investment, and, L = labor input, exogenously given by $\dot{L} = \lambda L$ (see Liviatan & Samuelson, 1969).

Let Y be a homogeneous function of the first degree with respect to its arguments $K,\ \dot{K},\ L, and\ \dot{L}$, together with $\partial Y/\partial K_i > 0$, $\partial Y/\partial L > 0$, $\partial Y/\partial \dot{K}_i \leq 0$, $\partial Y/\partial \dot{L}_i \leq 0\ (i = 1, \ldots, n)$. Also assume that $dC/dY > 0$ and Y is concave with respect to its argument. A special function of eq. (8.5) is a separable case with $dC/dY = 1$:

$$C = Y(K, L) - G\big(\dot{K}, \dot{L}; K, L\big) \tag{8.8}$$

or simply

$$C = Y(K, L) - G\big(\dot{K}, \dot{L}\big) \tag{8.9}$$

The simplest case of (7) is the standard model of "saving = investment"; that is,

$$C = Y(K, L) - \dot{K}\ (i = 1). \tag{8.7a}$$

Another example of (7) may be a well-known form (Caton & Shell, 1971; Sato, 1981; Samuelson, 1990):

$$C = \prod_{i=1}^{n} K_i^{\alpha_i} L^{1-\Sigma\alpha_i}\left(\frac{1}{2}\sum_{i=1}^{n} \dot{K}_i^2 + \frac{1}{2}\dot{L}^2\right)^{\frac{1}{2}} \tag{8.10}$$

with $1 > \alpha_i > 0$, $i = 1, \ldots, n$, and $\sum_{i=1}^{n}\alpha_i < 1$.

Without loss of generality, we can assume that $dC/dY = 1$ and Eq. (8.5) can be rewritten as

$$C = F(K; \dot{K}; L; \dot{L}). \tag{8.5'}$$

One of the distinct features of this model is that $\partial^2 F/\partial \dot{K}_i \dot{K}_j \neq 0$. That is, the investment function is nonlinear, as shown by the example (Eq. (8.8)).

Consumption per capita is given by

$$\begin{aligned} c = C/L &= F\left(\frac{K_1}{L}, \ldots, \frac{K_n}{L}; \frac{\dot{K}_1}{L}, \ldots, \frac{\dot{K}_n}{L}; 1; \frac{\dot{L}}{L}\right) \\ &= F\left(k_1, \ldots k_n; \dot{k}_1 + \lambda k_1, \ldots, \dot{k}_n + \lambda k_n; 1; \lambda\right), \end{aligned}$$

where

$$k_i = \frac{K_i}{L} \; and \; \dot{k}_i = \left(\frac{\dot{K}_i}{K_i} - \lambda\right) k_i, \; i = 1, \ldots, n.$$

Thus, we have

$$c = f\left(k_1, \ldots k_n; \dot{k}_1 + \lambda k_1, \ldots, \dot{k}_n + \lambda k_n; \lambda\right) = f\left(k; \dot{k} + \lambda k; \lambda\right) \tag{8.11}$$

The society's objective is to maximize the discounted future value of consumption per capita, $c(t) = f(t)$, as

$$J = \int_0^\infty e^{-\rho t} f\left(k; \dot{k} + \lambda k; \lambda\right) dt \rightarrow \max \tag{8.12}$$

The necessary condition for the optimal solution is that the Euler-Lagrange equations vanish:

$$\begin{aligned} E_i &= \frac{\partial}{\partial k_i}\left(e^{-\rho t} f\right) - \frac{d}{dt}\left(\frac{\partial}{\partial \dot{k}_i}\left(e^{-\rho t} f\right)\right) \\ &= e^{-\rho t}\left[\frac{\partial f}{\partial k_i} + \rho \frac{\partial f}{\partial \dot{k}_i} - \frac{d}{dt}\left(\frac{\partial f}{\partial \dot{k}_i}\right)\right] = 0, \; i = 1, \ldots, n. \end{aligned}$$

If we define the supply price of the ith capital per labor input as

$$P_i = -\frac{\partial f}{\partial \dot{k}_i}, \tag{8.13}$$

then the time derivative of the supply price of capital is:

$$\dot{P}_i = -\frac{\partial f}{\partial k_i} + \rho P_i. \tag{8.11a}$$

It is very convenient to use the so-called Noether theorem (see Noether, 1971 The citation “Noether, 1918/1971” has been changed to “Noether 1971” to match the author name/date in the reference list. Please check if the change is fine in this occurrence and modify the subsequent occurrences, if necessary.; Nôno, 1968; Nôno & Mimura, 1975, 1976, 1977, 1978) to uncover both hidden and unhidden quantities working along the trajectory of the optimally controlled economy—known as the conservation law (Sato, 1981, 1985; Sato et al. 1984; Sato & Maeda, 1990). Using the Noether theorem and its invariance principle, the general expression for the conservation law is

$$\Omega = \left(e^{-\rho t} f - e^{-\rho t} \sum_{i=1}^{n} \frac{\partial f}{\partial \dot{k}_i} \dot{k}_i \right) \tau + e^{-\rho t} \sum_{i=1}^{n} \frac{\partial f}{\partial \dot{k}_i} \xi^i - \Phi = \text{constant} \tag{8.14}$$

where τ and ξ^i are the so-called infinitesimal transformations of t and k_i, respectively.

In a special case of (12) in which $\tau = 1$, $\xi^i = 0$, $i = 1, \ldots, n$, $d\Phi/dt = -\rho e^{-\rho t} f$, we obtain the well-known conservation law of the income/wealth ratio as

$$f(k) - \sum_{i=1}^{n} \frac{\partial f}{\partial \dot{k}_i} \dot{k}_i = \rho \int_t^{\infty} \mathrm{e}^{-\rho(s-t)} f(s) ds$$

$$c(t) + \sum_{i=1}^{n} P_i \dot{k}_i = \rho \int_t^{\infty} \mathrm{e}^{-\rho(s-t)} f(s) ds \tag{8.15}$$

or

Consumption + Value of investment per capita
= $\rho \times$ (Wealth measured in terms of per-capita future consumption)

or

Income per capita = $\rho \times$ Wealth per capita

or

$$\rho = \frac{\text{Income per capita}}{\text{Wealth per capita}} \tag{8.16}$$

We call the preceding the “Per Capita Income/Wealth Conservation Law.”

Note that eq. (8.14) is not equal to [income per capita/capital per capita]. Equation (8.14) is always constant for all, $0 \le t \le \infty$, while the [income (per capita)/capital (per capita)] ratio varies for $0 \le t \le \infty$ and is constant only at $t = \infty$, or in the steady state in the long run (see Samuelson, 1970; Sato, 1981).

Because we are interested in the time path of the aggregate economy, the above conservation law must be converted to the Aggregate Income/Aggregate Wealth Law.

It is not simply derived by multiplying both sides of (13) by L, because aggregate income must be defined by $C + \sum_{i=1}^{n} P_i \dot{K}_i$, which is not equal to $L\left(c + \sum_{i=1}^{n} P_i \dot{k}_i\right)$. In fact, $L\left(c + \sum_{i=1}^{n} P_i \dot{k}_i\right)$ can be expanded as

$$L \cdot c + \sum_{i=1}^{n} P_i L\dot{k} = C + \sum_{i=1}^{n} P_i\left(\dot{K}_i - \lambda K_i\right) \tag{8.17}$$

where

$$P_\mathrm{i} = -\frac{\partial C}{\partial \dot{K}} = -\frac{\partial c}{\partial \dot{k}}$$

and

$$L\dot{k}_i = L\frac{d}{dt}\left(\frac{\dot{K}_i}{L}\right) = L\left[\frac{\left(\dot{K}_i L - \dot{L}K_i\right)}{L^2}\right] = \dot{K}_i - \lambda K_i$$

However, because $\dot{K}_i - \lambda K_i$ is the adjusted net capital formation ($\dot{K}_i + \delta K_i$ being gross investment with $\delta =$ depreciation rate > 0, we call this an adjustment), we get the aggregate (adjusted) income/wealth conservation law as

$$C + \sum_{i=1}^{n} P_i\left(\dot{K}_i - \lambda K_i\right) = \rho e^{\lambda t}\int_t^{\infty} e^{-\rho(s-t)} f(s)ds \tag{8.18}$$

or

(Adjusted) National Income $= \rho \times$ National Wealth.

If we assume that "Labor" is also endogenous $K_{n+1} = L$ and the society's goal is to maximize the "aggregate" consumption, or if $\lambda = 0$, then eq. (8.16) will reduce to the well-known result by Weitzman (1976) and Sato (1981, 1985).

When a factor such as labor is exogenously given to the system, maximization of consumption per labor input gives different conservation laws compared with the case of aggregate consumption maximization. In the case when a specific technical change exists, another type of conservation law can be observed. For instance, if the aggregate consumption function is under Harrod-Neutral Technical Change, the consumption function can be modified to

$$C = F\left[K;\, \dot{K};\, BL;\, (\dot{BL})\right], \tag{8.19}$$

where $BL =$ effective labor input with $B = B_0 e^{\beta t}$, $B_0 = 1$ and $\beta \geq 0$, or Harrod neutral technical change, and per-capita consumption is then written as

$$c\frac{C}{L} = BF\left[\frac{K}{BL}; \frac{\dot{K}}{BL}; 1; \frac{(\dot{BL})}{BL}\right] \tag{8.20}$$

$$c = e^{\beta t} f\left(\bar{k};\ \dot{\bar{k}} + (\lambda + \beta)\bar{k};\ \lambda + \beta\right)$$

where $\overline{k} = \left(\overline{k}_1, \ldots \overline{k}_n\right), \dot{\overline{k}} = \left(\dot{\overline{k}}_1, \ldots, \dot{\overline{k}}_n\right)$ and $\overline{k}_i = \frac{K_i}{BL}, \dot{\overline{k}}_i = \frac{d\overline{k}_i}{dt}, i = 1, \ldots, n$.

The society's objective is to maximize

$$J = \int_0^\infty e^{-\rho t} c dt = \int_0^\infty e^{-(\rho-\beta)t} f\left[\bar{k}; \dot{\bar{k}} + (\lambda + \beta)\bar{k}; \lambda + \beta\right] dt \tag{8.21}$$

where $\rho > \beta \geq 0$. Eq. (8.19) is identical to eq. (8.10) with ρ replaced by $(\rho - \beta)$, λ by $(\lambda + \beta)$ and k by $\overline{k}$. Since the supply price of the ith capital

$$P_i = -\frac{\partial F}{\partial \dot{K}_i} = -\frac{\partial f}{\partial \dot{\bar{k}}_i}, \ (i = 1, \ldots, n),$$

we obtain

$$c + \frac{1}{L}\sum_{i=1}^{n} P_i\left[\dot{K}_i - (\beta + \lambda)K_i\right] = (\rho - \beta)\int_t^\infty e^{-\rho(s-t)+\beta s} f(s) ds. \tag{8.22}$$

Again, by multiplying both sides of eq. (8.22) by L, we get an aggregate expression for the conservation law:

$$C + \sum_{i=1}^{n} P_i\left[\dot{K}_i - (\beta + \lambda)K_i\right] = (\rho - \beta)e^{\lambda t}\int_t^\infty e^{-\rho(s-t)+\beta s} f(s) ds \tag{8.23}$$

(Adjusted) National Income $= (\rho - \beta) \times$ National Wealth.

This relationship is the modified conservation law; ρ is replaced by $(\rho - \beta)$ and the term expressing national wealth now contains $e^{\beta s} = B(s)$, as labor becomes more efficient due to Harrod-neutral technical progress. However, the conservation laws expressed by eqs. (8.16) and (8.21) are essentially equivalent, which will be used for empirical applications.

Appendix 2 Generalized Income-Wealth Conservation Laws (Sato, 1985, pp. 378–381)

The utility measure of generalized income is

$$W - \dot{k}\frac{\partial W}{\partial \dot{k}}, \tag{8.24}$$

and the utility measure of generalized wealth is

$$-\int_t^\infty \frac{\partial W}{\partial t}\, ds \tag{8.25}$$

where

$$W = e^{-\rho(t)} U\left[k(t), \dot{k}(t)\right] \tag{8.26}$$

and then we have

$$-\int_t^\infty \frac{\partial W}{\partial t}\, ds = \int_t^\infty \rho'(s) e^{-\rho(s)} U\left[k(s), \dot{k}(s)\right] ds \tag{8.27}$$

where $\rho'(t) = d\rho(t)/dt$.

When $\rho(t)$ is a linear function, $\rho(t) = \rho t$, we get the standard $\rho =$ Income/wealth ratio:

$$-\int_t^\infty \frac{\partial W}{\partial t}\, ds = \rho \int_t^\infty e^{-\rho s} U\left[k(s), \dot{k}(s)\right] ds.$$

When time transformation (subjective time) is $\bar{t} = t + \varepsilon\tau(t)$ and $\tau(t) = 1/\rho'(t)$, then we have

$$U(t) - \dot{k}\frac{\partial U(t)}{\partial \dot{k}(t)} = \rho' \int_t^\infty \left\{ \exp\left(-\int_t^s \rho(p)dp \right) \left[U - \dot{k}\frac{\partial U}{\partial \dot{k}} \frac{d}{ds}\left(\frac{1}{\rho(s)} \right) \right] \right\} ds \tag{8.28}$$

Income = The rate of change of discounting function w.r.t. time × Generalized wealth.

Appendix 3 Japan's Asset Prices

Japan's stock market price and land price, as shown in Figs. 8.13 and 8.14, both peaked around the year 1990. The *y*-axis (representing the value of the asset price index) in each chart is displayed on a logarithmic scale, allowing for a linear depiction of exponential growth. The slope of each line signifies the percentage change in the price index; thus, a steeper slope indicates a more rapid change in the price index.

Before 1990, each slope exhibits a pronounced upward trajectory, indicating a robust price rise. In contrast, the trends after 1990 display a more gradual downward slope, except for the commercial land prices in Fig. 8.14.

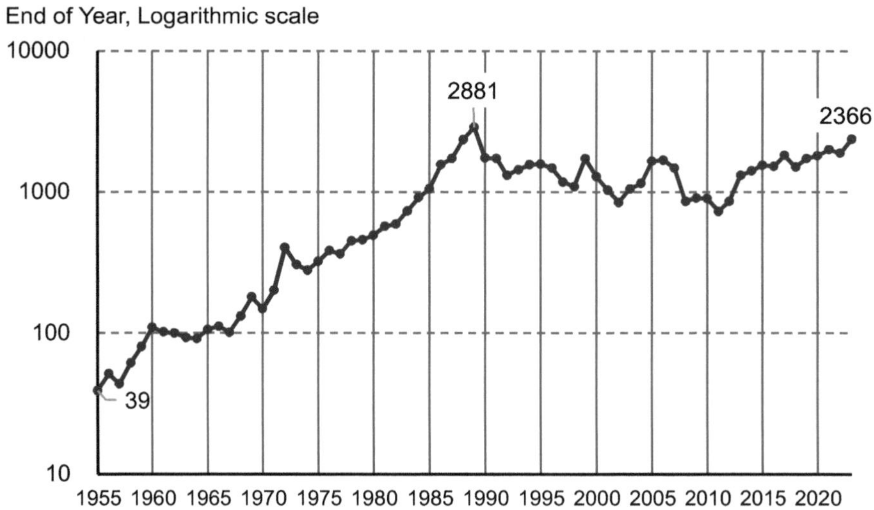

Fig. 8.13 Japan's stock price, 1955–2023 (TOPIX, logarithmic scale). *Source* JPX Market Innovation & Research, Inc.

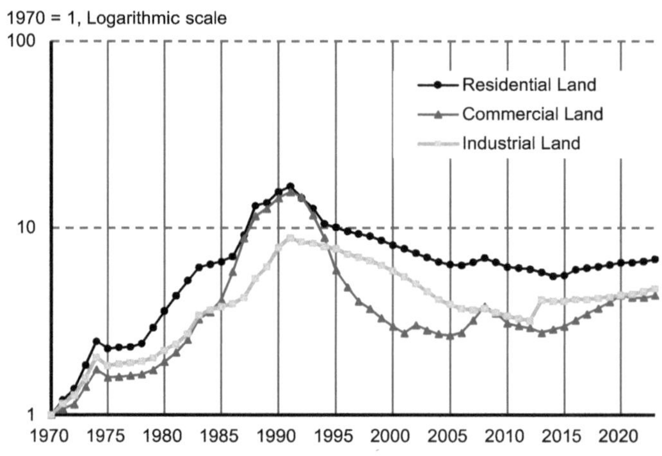

Fig. 8.14 Japan's land price, 1970–2023. *Source* Ministry of Land, Infrastructure, Transport and Tourism, "Land Market Value Publication"

Appendix 4 Wealth Excluding Foreign Assets

As presented in the first paragraph of Subsection 8.2.3, we used GNP and net national wealth for Y and W. W consisted of inventories, tangible fixed assets, intangible fixed assets, and net foreign assets.

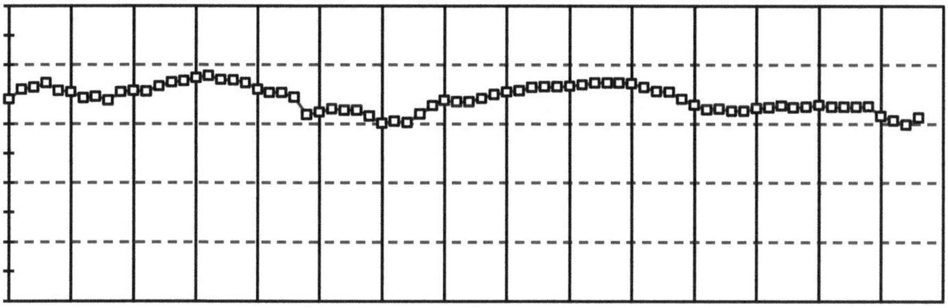

Fig. 8.15 U.S GDP/Wealth ratio when excluding foreign assets from wealth (postwar)

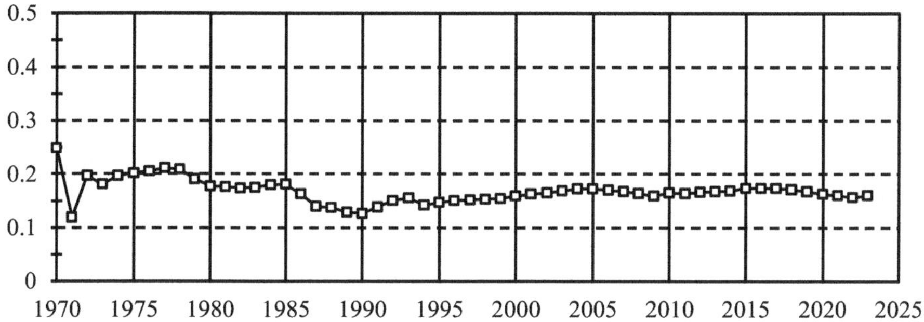

Fig. 8.16 Japan GDP/Wealth ratio when excluding foreign assets from wealth (postwar)

The U.S. net foreign assets turned to a deficit in the latter half of the 1980s; subsequently, the volume of the deficit has been expanding. If we consider only domestic assets (and Gross Domestic Product for income), Y/W after World War II becomes more stable as shown in Fig. 8.15.

In contrast to the United States, Japan's GDP/Wealth ratio has been declining as its net foreign assets continue to increase. However, excluding net foreign assets, the ratio has remained stable as Fig. 8.16.

References

Cass, D. (1965). Optimum growth in an aggregative model of capital accumulation. *The Review of Economic Studies, 32*(3), 233. https://doi.org/10.2307/2295827

Caton, C., & Shell, K. (1971). An exercise in the theory of heterogeneous capital accumulation. *The Review of Economic Studies, 38*(1), 13–22. https://doi.org/10.2307/2296618

Chivers, T. (2013). "In the long run, we'll still care about Keynes" from Wednesday's Daily Telegraph: It is not only great-great-nephews who live in the shadow of our most eminent economist, May 7, 2013. *Tom Chivers on Telegraph Blogs,* https://tommychivers.wordpress.com/2013/05/07/in-the-long-run-well-still-care-about-keynes/

Friedman, R. A. (2013). Fast time and the aging mind. Opinion, *New York Times*. July 21, 2013.
Goethe. (2003). *Faust*. trans. A.S. Kline at "Poetry in Translation." https://www.poetryintranslation.com/PITBR/German/FaustIScenesIVtoVI.php
Hanc, J., Tuleja, S., & Hancova, M. (2004). Symmetries and conservation laws: Consequences of Noether's theorem. *American Journal of Physics, 72*(4), 428–435.
Keynes, J. M. (1923). *A tract on monetary reform*. St. Martin's Press for the Royal Economic Society.
Keynes, J. M. (1936). *The general theory of employment, interest, and money*. Macmillan and, ltd.
Kim, B. K., & Zauberman, G. (2009). Perception of anticipatory time in temporal discounting. *Journal of Neuroscience, Psychology, and Economics, 2*(2), 91–101. https://doi.org/10.1037/a0017686
Koopmans, T. C. (1960). Stationary ordinal utility and impatience. *Econometrica, 28*(2), 287–309. https://doi.org/10.2307/1907722
Koopmans, T. C. (1965). On the concept of optimal economic growth. In J. Johansen (Ed.), *The econometric approach to development planning* (pp. 225–287). North-Holland.
Liviatan, N., & Samuelson, P. A. (1969). Notes on turnpikes: Stable and unstable. *Journal of Economic Theory, 1*(4), 454–475. https://doi.org/10.1016/0022-0531(69)90028-3
Newey, W. K., & West, K. D. (1987). A simple, positive semi-definite, heteroskedasticity and autocorrelation consistent covariance matrix. *Econometrica, 55*(3), 703–708. https://doi.org/10.2307/1913610
Noether, E. (1971). Invariant variation problems. *Transport Theory and Statistical Physics*, 1(3), 186–207. https://doi.org/10.1080/00411457108231446.[*Invariante Variationsprobleme*] (trans. M. A. Tavel, original work published in 1918).
Nôno, T. (1968). On the symmetry groups of simple materials: An application of the theory of lie groups. *Journal of Mathematical Analysis and Applications, 24*(1), 110–135. https://doi.org/10.1016/0022-247X(68)90051-6
Nôno, T., & Mimura, F. (1975). Dynamical symmetries I. *Bulletin of the Fukuoka University of Education, Part III, 25*, 9–26.
Nôno, T., & Mimura, F. (1976). Dynamical symmetries III. *Bulletin of the Fukuoka University of Education, Part III, 26*, 45–49.
Nôno, T., & Mimura, F. (1977). Dynamical symmetries IV. *Bulletin of the Fukuoka University of Education, Part III, 27*, 5–14.
Nôno, T., & Mimura, F. (1978). Dynamical symmetries V. *Bulletin of the Fukuoka University of Education, Part III, 28*, 7–16.
Samuelson, P. A. (1970). Law of conservation of the capital-output ratio. *Proceedings of the National Academy of Sciences, 67*(3), 1477–1479. https://doi.org/10.1073/pnas.67.3.1477
Samuelson, P. A. (1990). Two conservation laws in theoretical economics. In R. Sato & R. V. Ramachandran (Eds.), *Conservation laws and symmetry: Applications to economics and finance* (pp. 57–70). Springer. https://doi.org/10.1007/978-94-017-1145-6_3
Sato, R. (1963). Fiscal policy in a neo-classical growth model: An analysis of time required for equilibrating adjustment. *The Review of Economic Studies, 30*(1), 16. https://doi.org/10.2307/2296026
Sato, R. (1964). The Harrod-Domar model vs the neo-classical growth model. *The Economic Journal, 74*(294), 380–387. https://doi.org/10.2307/2228485
Sato, R. (1980). The impact of technical change on the holotheticity of production functions. *The Review of Economic Studies, 47*(4), 767–776. https://doi.org/10.2307/2296942
Sato, R. (1981). *Theory of technical change and economic invariance: Application of lie groups*. Academic.
Sato, R. (1985). The invariance principle and income-wealth conservation laws: Application of lie groups and related transformations. *Journal of Econometrics, 30*(1), 365–389. https://doi.org/10.1016/0304-4076(85)90147-2
Sato, R. (2004). Economic conservation laws as indices of corporate performance. *Japan and the World Economy, 16*(3), 247–267. https://doi.org/10.1016/j.japwor.2003.05.001y

Sato, R. (2006). Optimal economic growth: Test of income/wealth conservation laws in OECD countries. In *Biased technological change and economic conservation Laws* (pp. 123–146). Springer Science + Business Media.

Sato, R., & Fujii, M. (2006). Evaluating corporate performance: Empirical tests of a conservation law. *Japan and the World Economy, 18*(2), 158–168.

Sato, R., & Maeda, S. (1990). Conservation laws in continuous and discrete models. In R. Sato & R. V. Ramachandran (Eds.), *Conservation laws and symmetry: Applications to economics and finance* (pp. 135–174). Springer. https://doi.org/10.1007/978-94-017-1145-6_6

Sato, R., Nôno, T., & Mimura, F. (1984). Hidden symmetries: Lie groups and economic conservation laws. In H. Hauptmann, W. Krelle, & K. C. Mosler (Eds.), *Operations research and economic theory*. Springer. https://doi.org/10.1007/978-3-642-69909-2_4

The Asahi Shimbun. (2013, December 14). *Tensei Jingo.*

Wearden, J. H. (2021). Paul Janet and changes in the apparent speed of passage of time with aging. *Timing & Time Perception, 10*(3), 279–287. https://doi.org/10.1163/22134468-bja10044

Weitzman, M. L. (1976). On the welfare significance of national product in a dynamic economy. *The Quarterly Journal of Economics, 90*(1), 156–162. https://doi.org/10.2307/1886092

Zauberman, G., Kim, B. K., Malkoc, S. A., & Bettman, J. R. (2009). Discounting time and time discounting: Subjective time perception and intertemporal preferences. *Journal of Marketing Research, 46*(4), 543–556.

Index

T. Yamashita and T. Morita (eds.), *On the Structural Transformation of the Japanese Economy 1985-2023*, Advances in Japanese Business and Economics 38,
https://doi.org/10.1007/978-981-95-7230-4

FSC
www.fsc.org
MIX
Papier aus verantwortungsvollen Quellen
Paper from responsible sources
FSC® C105338

If you have any concerns about our products,
you can contact us on
ProductSafety@springernature.com

In case Publisher is established outside the EU,
the EU authorized representative is:
Springer Nature Customer Service Center GmbH
Europaplatz 3, 69115 Heidelberg, Germany

Printed by Libri Plureos GmbH
in Hamburg, Germany